# THE BIBLE COMES ALIVE

BY

SIR CHARLES MARSTON, F.S.A.
AUTHOR OF "NEW BIBLE EVIDENCE," ETC.

NEW YORK

FLEMING H. REVELL COMPANY

London and Edinburgh

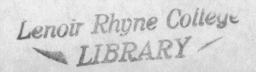

*Made in Great Britain*

OLD JERICHO FROM THE SOUTH

Workmen may be seen above the newly bared Canaanite wall, which lies in the deep cutting on the right front.

# PREFACE

THE Coronation Ceremony of King George VI reminded the English-speaking races throughout the world of the emphasis that had been laid upon the Bible by at least a dozen generations of British ancestors. From the door of Westminster Abbey, to the scene of his enthronement, a Bishop preceded the King carrying a Bible. At the subsequent service the King made his Coronation vows on the Bible. At the conclusion, the Archbishop presented His Majesty with the Bible, and said:

"Our Gracious King; we present you with this Book, the most valuable thing that this world affords. Here is Wisdom; This is the Royal Law; These are the lively oracles of God."

This part of the Coronation Ceremony, and this presentation of the Bible, were instituted nearly four hundred years ago. Have these words any significance to-day?

The attitude of former generations of Americans to the Bible fully endorsed the sentiments enshrined in the Coronation Service. And so the Beliefs there expressed were not confined to the British Isles; far otherwise.—It is a matter of common knowledge that greater emphasis was laid upon the Bible by the original American settlers, and by their descendants, than by any British king and his subjects, with the exception of Queen Victoria.

# PREFACE

Within living memory the Bible has been regarded by many Americans as " the most valuable thing that the world affords" and "the lively oracles of God." But what proportion of the nation really thinks so to-day? That is surely a pertinent question for American civilization which has been founded and developed on a Bible basis. These old Beliefs now need further examination lest they be heedlessly discarded; and they need an examination which is in keeping with present-day ideas of reality and not just to satisfy religious convention.

At first sight the rapid advances of Science during recent years may be thought to have swept away all traditional beliefs. But a closer scrutiny suggests that tradition has suffered far less than the science of fifty years ago. Tradition enshrined the teaching of experience of the remote past. It is not easy to compare the knowledge of those times with the knowledge we possess to-day. But it is easy to compare the knowledge we possess to-day with that of half a century ago. Fifty years ago the scientists supposed that they had found a consistent and comprehensive scheme of interpretation of the physical world with laws which governed all phenomena. They thought that human knowledge was fairly complete, and there was really little left to be known! To-day as we look back and reflect on the discoveries that have since been made, such as those associated with the names of Einstein, or Marconi, or the Curies, and others, we realize how absurd was such an assumption. And yet it was on this basis that the criticism of the Bible was made.

# PREFACE

To-day our search for Truth demands a comparison of present-day knowledge with Bible knowledge. And it must be present-day knowledge based on evidence and no longer on mere conjecture and speculation. Such evidence is being made available through the study of various Sciences. The Science of Archæology in particular is casting a great deal of light on ancient Bible history, and the means whereby that history was recorded and has been transmitted to us. Many detailed results of modern excavations in Bible lands were published in the author's earlier work—*New Bible Evidence.*

But the stream of evidence, long hidden under the soil of Palestine and other Eastern lands, continues to flow so strongly that already another book is needed to describe fresh discoveries and their bearing upon the Old Testament. Here it may be pointed out that although progress has become a feature of the Age in other branches of Learning, yet scholars and teachers still take long to realize that it must be made in their outlook on the Bible. One complains that the trouble of reading the author's previous work is that it renders so many other books obsolete. What has been brought to light by excavation is positive evidence. On the whole it agrees with the Bible; it certainly affects the negative theories and destructive conclusions in vogue at the beginning of this century.

It is true that the discoveries made are quite inadequate to substantiate the whole Bible from Genesis to Revelation. That would be a stupendous task, and may take a long time. For besides archæological

# PREFACE

work, such an investigation would involve a vast increase of knowledge in every branch of Science. And if all were clear, where would remain the need of Faith?

Earlier works have expressed the author's indebtedness and gratitude to those distinguished men who have been instrumental in making and interpreting the discoveries which are now summarized in this book. These authorities are not to be held to assent to all the author's deductions and conclusions. Indeed, some recent archæological works on the Old Testament still seek to reconcile the results with former critical conclusions. This can only be done at the expense of the significance of the finds that have been made; or by wild assumptions—as, for example, that Moses must have come after Joshua!

Archæological evidence is concerned with questions of fact; where statements occur which involve deductions for which archæologists and scholars are responsible, efforts are made in this volume to quote their exact words.

The evidence from the hill of Tell Duweir, in South Palestine, now definitely identified as the site of the Bible city of Lachish, is brought right up to the time of publication. The record of finds made there, occupies a considerable part of this volume. The author is proud that the Expedition which has made discoveries of such magnitude has been one of his promotions.

The leader of this Expedition, James Leslie Starkey, was murdered near Hebron on his way to Jerusalem

on 10th January 1938. Starkey was so popular among
the Arabs that he may have lost his life because he
had just grown a beard which concealed his well-
known features. So the tragedy that has robbed the
world of one of its foremost archæologists was perhaps
due to mistaken identity. None the less the loss is
irreparable. Starkey was only forty-three years of age.
One of his confreres has described him as "the greatest
archæological leader there ever was in Palestine."

Starkey's abilities were of such an order that in
industry or commerce he might have made a fortune.
Instead he gave his talents to the service of mankind.
His name will live in history as the discoverer of the
all-important systems of alphabetical writing used by
the Israelites from the time of Moses. The excellent
staff he had trained, whose names are appended to
this Preface, carried on his work with great fortitude
to the end of the season.

In the first year (1932–3) the Lachish Expedition
was under the auspices of the late Sir Henry Wellcome,
Mr. Harry Dunscombe Colt of New York, and the
writer.

In the years 1933–4–5–6, the Expedition was named
the Wellcome Archæological Research Expedition to
the Near East. Sir Henry Wellcome provided most
of the funds, Sir Robert Mond and the author the
rest.

In consequence of the lamented death of Sir Henry
Wellcome, the 1936–7 and 1937–8 Expeditions have
been financed jointly with his Trustees. It is now
named the Wellcome-Marston Expedition. Sir Robert

# PREFACE

Mond's continued interest and support of the work is greatly appreciated.

Posterity will feel a special debt of gratitude to Sir Henry Wellcome for a generosity which led to the epoch-making discoveries of the Archaic Sinai Hebrew writing, and of the Lachish Letters, written in the later Phœnician-Hebrew script. Our best thanks are due to his Executors and Trustees for so loyally continuing to support the Expedition out of regard for Sir Henry's memory, despite the heavy death-duties on his estate. Also to the officials of the Wellcome Museum for their interest and co-operation in the Exhibitions of the Lachish finds that have been held there. The work of the late Dr. Langdon, Professor of Assyriology at Oxford, is frequently referred to in these pages, and is of supreme importance.

Special thanks are due to other distinguished archæologists whose labours have led to evidence, referred to in these chapters, being brought to light. In particular, to Sir Flinders Petrie and Lady Petrie—where would Bible Archæology be to-day without their invaluable aid? Mention must also be made of the excellent work of Professor Garstang and Mrs. Garstang, who spent a number of winters excavating Jericho under peculiar difficulties, for the site had been disturbed by excavations before the War. It will be noticed how their discoveries have been of the greatest importance.

Gratitude is also due to Sir Leonard Woolley for his wonderful work at Ur of the Chaldees.

Dr. Albright, of the American School of Oriental Research, has contributed to the advancement of

# PREFACE

Palestine Archæology and references are made to some of his discoveries; indeed the credit for the original identification of the ruins on Tell Duweir as being those of Lachish, is due to him.

The French excavations at Ras Shamra, which have brought to light evidence of immense importance to the Old Testament, were conducted by MM. Schaefer and Chenet. Associated with them are M. Charles Virolleaud and M. Rene Dussaud. A deep debt of gratitude is due to them all. Mr. Theodor Gaster has also contributed helpful information on these discoveries.

Professor Torczyner of the Hebrew University, Jerusalem, has accomplished a unique piece of scholarship in the decipherment and elucidation of the Lachish Letters.

For ever ready help, the author's thanks are also due to the Palestine Exploration Fund under the leadership of Sir Charles Close; to the British School of Archæology in Jerusalem; and to the British Museum.

The new Institute of Archæology in Regent's Park, London, under the direction of Sir George Hill, Sir Charles Peers, Sir Frederick Kenyon, and Dr. Mortimer Wheeler, has rendered invaluable assistance in housing the Lachish finds.

| | | |
|---|---|---|
| Starkey, J. L. | | 1932–1938 |
| Harding, Lankester | | 1932–1936 |
| Brown, R. Richmond | | 1932–1937 |
| Inge, C. H. | | 1932–1938 |
| Tufnell, Miss O. | | 1932–1938 |
| Pummell, H. W. | | 1933–1938 |
| Shaw, W. B. K. | | 1932–1935 |
| Brown, Donald | 1932–1933 | 1934–1935 |
| Colt, Mrs. H. Dunscombe | | 1932–1933 |
| McWilliams, H. H. | | 1932–1933 |
| Way, L. Upton | | 1932–1933 |
| Cox, R. M. | | 1933–1934 |
| Dyott, Miss E. | | 1934–1935 |
| Goulden, G. I. | | 1934–1935 |
| Richmond, John | | 1934–1935 |
| Bonney, H. V. | | 1935–1938 |
| Lewis, Alkin | | 1935–1936 |
| Scott, Miss L. McNair | | 1935–1936 |
| Gardner, G. B. | | 1935–1936 |
| Hastings, Mr. and Mrs. E. F. | | 1936–1938 |
| Kirkman, J. S. | | 1936–1937 |
| Parker, Miss B. H. | | 1936–1937 |
| Crowfoot, Miss J. | | 1936–1937 |

# CONTENTS

xiii

# CONTENTS

# CONTENTS

# CONTENTS

# THE PLATES

*at the End of the Book*

xvii

# THE PLATES

xviii

# THE PLATES

## PLANS AND DRAWINGS

# THE BIBLE COMES ALIVE

## I

### THE SCIENCE OF MAN

SOME of the leading scientists in our world of to-day have made an urgent call for the study of the Science of Man. They recognize that our immersion in the study and progress of the sciences of inert matter has become dangerous, because the moral and spiritual sides of human nature have not developed in the same proportion.

But the Bible is our text-book of the Science of Man. It is our authority for moral and spiritual development. Should we have any moral and spiritual development without it? Whether we like it, or whether we do not, on what other authority can we rely? Even if a man assumes his Reason to be his sole authority, nevertheless he has to recognize the Moral Law; and the Moral Law rests on the authority of the Bible. Or one may regard his Church as an authority, but behind its teaching is a background from the Bible. And as for the authority of Science, its present urgent call for the study of the Science of Man is pointing directly to the Bible.

Whichever way we look, therefore, the Bible becomes

again of supreme importance, unless we turn our backs on the realities of life and drift to disaster. Few desire to do that, but many have been taught to regard the Bible as out of date, and they seek some new approach to life. It is here suggested that the way the Bible is presented has become old-fashioned, rather than the Book itself. The discoveries that are now being made by the Sciences remove such objection. They are indeed quite new; and they cast a new light on the Bible; so new that a very considerable time must elapse before they can be absorbed in the orthodox curriculum of knowledge. In themselves they constitute a challenge to resume the study of the Bible, and they supplement the urgent call to do so from other directions. There has been a widespread belief that the Bible has been discredited by Science, and especially the Old Testament. That may be said to have been a deduction of a generation ago, but it is not so now. Science has progressed far in the direction of Truth since those days.

The newest knowledge cannot be said to be drawing us away from the Bible, on the contrary it is bringing us back to it. Our foremost scientists are feeling and finding their way through a vast undergrowth of materialistic facts towards a world horizon much more in harmony with Holy Scripture. And it has further become clear that the leaders of Science a generation ago, both overestimated and overemphasized, the limited knowledge of their time, and neglected to look beyond it. Because education reflects the beliefs of leading minds of the previous generation and not those of the present, so to-day we are suffering from those miscalculations. But in the light of facts not then observed, or whose significance had been overlooked, scientists of the present have ceased to overestimate human knowledge; on the contrary they are emphasizing human ignorance. So-called Miracles are no longer being laughed at, they are being recognized. One distinguished authority declares that the ordinary actions of everyday life partake of the nature of miracles. Others who have studied, the extraordinary, or unusual manifestations in life, are coming to conclusions like those already reached by Lodge, Richet, Crookes, and other distinguished scientists. The realities of psychic phenomena are being recognized. One of the most brilliant French scientists of our time —Dr. Alexis Carrel, of the Rockefeller Institute of New York—has lately testified to the existence of seeming miraculous agencies, such as clairvoyance, telepathy, television, and prediction. Indeed, he has affirmed that the negative attitude towards miracles *can no longer be sustained* in the face of the facts observed by Science during the last fifty years. And this authority in medical research, goes on to accept miracles of healing through prayer, including even organic diseases, such as cancer. The evidences for unusual happenings in human life have always existed, but they are only now at last being recognized, recorded, and vouched for by Science. Since this is being done, it follows that the well informed and unprejudiced, cannot henceforth reject the Bible narrative because it records the occurrence of unusual happenings some thousands of years ago.

A section of our Clergy, who call themselves Modernists, might make themselves familiar with this advance in knowledge if they desire to retain their title; otherwise they have clearly become "Ancient Modernists." Indeed, the whole religious and academic professions need to study the evidence, pouring in from all sides, which is tending to endorse and confirm Scripture. Such work will arouse, and stimulate, and train the imaginations of those who are ordained to lead us through these dangerous days. It is their privileged task, to dissipate the erroneous ideas of those academic specialists, who have been unable to take a comprehensive view of evidence, because their minds were too engrossed in details of preconceived ideas; and to remind the exponents of materialistic research of the moral and spiritual issues that have become of transcendent importance.

This book records but a little of the outside evidence, and that bearing upon the Old Testament, recently supplied by the Science of Archæology. Yet, in order to obtain a true perspective of the whole Bible, it has become necessary to start at the beginning of it. It will be seen that the discoveries tend to vindicate the Sacred Text from the critical doubts that have been cast upon it; just as the evidence for the reality of modern miracles tends to vindicate those recorded in the Bible. But because the archæological evidence in this book refers to the Old Testament, it should not be supposed that similar evidence is lacking for the New Testament. A recent discovery in connection with the latter deserves notice, because it illustrates the uncertainty of the textual criticism that has been applied to that Scripture.

St. John's Gospel has been a principal target for this type of criticism. For a century and more German critics have indulged in wild speculations concerning it. No sort of agreement has been reached in regard to the conclusions of any critics. But there has developed a marked tendency to ascribe the authorship to a later date than Apostolic times. This verdict disagreed with the affirmation that St. John himself wrote it (John xxi. 24). And, having regard to the great importance of this Gospel, painful doubts and perplexities have disturbed the minds of Christian people.

The John Rylands Library in Manchester is now in possession of a fragment of St. John's Gospel found in Egypt, which has been dated to within about a century of the Crucifixion. Since this leaf only represents a copy of the Gospel circulated in a foreign land, and postulates a considerable interval of time for circulation and transmission, the original may well have been written by the Apostle himself, in accordance with the text to which reference has just been made.

In earlier works on the Old Testament, such as *The Bible is True*, and its American edition, *New Bible Evidence*, the writer has set out in considerable detail the reasons for rejecting wholesale the assumptions and the conclusions of the destructive criticism levied against the Old Testament. It is a testimony to the influence abroad of a more realistic attitude towards so-called criticism, that no one has attempted to dispute these reasons. This is written in no spirit of challenge or of boastfulness, but merely to record progress. The objections to the Old Testament criticism have been received in silence because they have become indisputable. There is no longer the need to repeat them in detail. They may be summarized in the statement, that the laws set out in the *Encyclopædia Britannica* for the criticism of the Bible are as yet unworkable, because neither Human Knowledge nor Human Nature have reached a plane where they can be satisfactorily applied. The indisputable fact that Knowledge is always changing is sufficient to demonstrate the truth of this proposition so far as the former is concerned. While those who study highly educated Human Nature, must perceive how genuine evidence of fact is constantly subordinated to preconceived beliefs. The "balanced minds," postulated in the *Encyclopædia Britannica* for the work of Bible criticism, have only been paper products, and have not yet become present realities. So the objections to the whole criticism of the Old Testament are fundamental ones. And if foundations are unsound, what is built upon them is untrustworthy. Two examples will help to illustrate these arguments:

First, in matters of Knowledge—The Old Testa-

ment abounds in prophecies. Critics treated prophecies as incredible, so they based their work on
the assumption that prophecies were written *after* the
events predicted had already occurred. It has already
been pointed out in this chapter that the reality of
prediction is to-day being recognized by Science.

Secondly, in matters of Judgement—The Theory of
Evolution has dominated the critical mind in complete
disregard of historical facts. Whatever may be said for
the evolution of the material Universe, there is little
that can be said for the evolution of Man, as a
dogma. Thus history teaches us that while civilization is progressive it is also retrogressive. When its
moral and spiritual factors decline, civilization destroys
itself. But the evolution conception, being based upon
the idea of steady consistent progress, from barbarism
to the present day, underestimated the knowledge and
culture of Old Testament times, and postulated something far too primitive. Thus, for example, the Israelites
should have been illiterate; but it will now be seen that
they possessed facilities for literary expression, from the
days of Moses onwards, that were actually superior to
those of their contemporaries.

The evidence of many facts of observation that the
Science of Archæology has been instrumental in bringing to light in Bible lands, will be found recorded in the
succeeding chapters. Those who are acquainted with
critical commentaries on the Old Testament will appre-
ciate the extent to which their contents are contradicted by this fresh evidence—such, for example, as the

fact that Monotheism was the original religion, and Polytheism a by-product from it. Or that the Habiru were, after all, the Hebrews and the Israelites under Joshua. Indeed, if at the present time some cynic, or candid friend, sought to make the punishment fit the crime, and proceeded to compile an Encyclopædia of the mistakes that had been made by critics and commentators on the Old Testament, and placed beside each the real facts that have recently come to light, it would surely run into volumes.

It is quite possible that portions of some of the books of the Old Testament are derived from earlier documents. But to suppose that a cut-and-dried method could be found of isolating them, which nevertheless was entirely useless for our contemporary literature, imposed a considerable strain on anyone's credulity. It raised questions as to how, and when, the original books of the Old Testament were written; and above all it raised questions of the literary facilities possessed by the Israelites from the time of Moses onwards. The critical methods met these questions by assuming that the Hebrews were more or less illiterate. The assumption has completely broken down. It will be seen, from the archæological evidence cited in these pages, that the Israelites had, from the time of Moses onwards, at least three alphabetical scripts. First, what is known as the Sinai Hebrew; next, what is known as the Phœnician Hebrew; and lastly, after the captivity in Babylon, what is known as the Assyrian Hebrew. Those facts entirely change the whole literary problem. Oral transmission becomes inadmissible. And the theory of the institution and adoption of the Mosaic ritual many centuries after the time of Moses, becomes grotesque and absurd, in the light of what we now know of his time.

So J, E, and P, the supposed authors of the Penta-teuch, are becoming mere phantom scribes and fetishes of the imagination. They have made Old Testament study unattractive, they have wasted our time, and they have warped and confused our judgements on out-side evidence. It has been assumed that they possessed some sort of prescriptive right and authority superior to the Sacred Text. In the clearer light that Science is casting, these shadows that have dimmed our days of study and devotion are silently stealing away.

Released then from critical shackles concerning Holy Scripture, and reinvigorated by evidence in its favour, constantly supplied by the Science of Archæology, and indeed by several other Sciences as well—the Bible comes alive—to all unprejudiced seekers after Truth. And is it not about time that in the Providence of God this should come to pass?

In October 1936 the Archbishop of Canterbury warned us, "It looked as if civilization were proving incapable of saving itself from destruction."

That statement is emphasized and elaborated in His Grace's broadcast on 27th December 1936: "There is beyond question a drift away from religion. . . . Consider the influence of the new scientific outlook on the Universe, and on man's life within it, which seems

9

to see no place for a personal God. . . . The great gifts of order and freedom will fail to fulfil their purpose unless they are deep rooted in the faith and fear of God."

Beside this warning from a great Ecclesiastic, may be placed others equally recent from a great Scientist— Dr. Alexis Carrel, of the Rockefeller Institute for Medical Research. A few brief sentences taken at random from his book, *Man the Unknown*, suffice:

"We are the victims of the backwardness of the Sciences of Life over those of Matter."

"The Science of Man has become the most necessary of all Sciences."

"There is not the shadow of a doubt that mechanical, physical, and chemical sciences are incapable of giving us intelligence, moral discipline, health, nervous equilibrium, security, or peace." [1]

And so one might fill the pages of this work with similar warnings from other great leaders of thought at the present time. What then is the remedy? It is an accepted historical fact that this dazzling civilization, now in such danger, was originally based upon the Christian Faith and upon the teaching of the Bible. And one may go further and affirm, that the rise of our Race and its expansion throughout the world, synchronize with the translation of the Bible into the English tongue, and its circulation into all lands.

At this distance of time we can look back on ancient

[1] From *Man the Unknown*, by Dr. Alexis Carrel, published in the U.S.A. by Harper Brothers.

civilizations—such as those of Greece and Rome—and realize that they failed because they abandoned ancient ideals and moral standards on which they were reared. Much more then should we consider whether the dangers that threaten our civilization to-day, may not be due to the neglect of our religious privilege and responsibility.

It will enhance the significance of this line of thought, and link it up with the statements of the Archbishop and Dr. Carrel, if we consider a summary of the Bible written more than half a century ago by the late Dr. Grattan Guinness. It runs as follows:

"The Bible is the chart of history. It affords a panoramic view of the whole course of events from the creation and the fall of man, to the final judgement, and the inauguration of the new heaven and the new earth. It gives us, not events only, but their moral character, tracing the motives of the various actors in the drama, as well as the results of their actions. Events are shown in relation to their causes and their effects, and the judgement of God as to their character is revealed. Without the Bible, history would be a spectacle of unknown rivers flowing from unknown sources to unknown seas; but under its guidance we can trace the complex currents to their springs, and see the end from the beginning."

These lines emphasize the fact that the Bible is a text-book of the Science of Man—that Science which Dr. Carrel affirms has become "the most necessary of all Sciences." Still more they make it evident that Holy Scripture contains the antidote to that influence "of the scientific outlook on the Universe which seems to see no place for a personal God" referred to by the Archbishop. On the basis of these assumptions, the conclusion follows—that we have become the victims of the progress of the Sciences of Matter, because there has been no parallel progress in the study and teaching of the Science of Life, as embodied in the Bible.

For a number of years there has either been an acquiescence concerning Bible problems on the part of our Clergy, or an acceptance of destructive critical conclusions. Both lines of thought have led to the neglect of the progressive study and teaching of Holy Scripture, in our Universities, in our Theological and Teachers' Colleges, and in our schools. As a consequence, Christian worship has tended to degenerate into mere formalism, to become self-centred, and self-satisfied, and to lose both its virility and vitality.

A few pages back, reference was made to a distinguished scientist's recognition of the phenomena of prediction in modern life. That in turn links up with ancient prophecy. It is not the purpose of this book to deal with the Bible prophecies; that is a subject as vast, and as important, as the archæological evidence. But let us not forget that the Bible contains a history of the Jewish race from its beginning to its rejection of the Messiah. This history is accompanied by a long succession of prophecies as to the future of this people. The survival of this race, scattered abroad and persecuted throughout the world, and its present prosperity and power, despite these adverse influences, suggest that these prophecies, though obscure to us, are being fulfilled.

And indeed, in proportion as one sets Bible prophecy beside present world happenings, this obscurity becomes less noticeable. A feeling creeps over one that with more study, and rather more data, the veil would disappear.

It would seem that the scenery of the world stage, on which world events are to be enacted, is being set by invisible forces for some great drama; and the various nations, or characters, are moving to their positions; all according to plan—the PLAN outlined in prophecies that are thousands of years old. Even by the time this book is published, and long before it is out of date, its title may be much more justified by present-day fulfilment of prophecy, than by the discoveries it records, that appertain to the remote past.

To-day anything like an unprejudiced student of Holy Scripture, must have lost his imagination and faith, if he fails to recognize how the Jewish race, in its Fortune and in its Misfortune, is a living Witness, unconsciously bearing constant and continual testimony, to the unique character of the Old Testament, as well as to its authenticity and validity.

The doubts cast against the Bible lose their significance when weighed against this tremendous testimony. These doubts, after all, concern details, whose correctness or incorrectness depend on our knowledge or on our ignorance. Thus, as already indicated, people have rejected the Bible because it recorded miracles;

they thought they knew that miracles did not occur, and cannot occur. And now comes the recognition of modern miracles by Science, to prove such criticism unsound, and resting upon ignorance of unusual but existing phenomena. But this Jewish testimony rises far above detail. If there were no Jews to-day, or if they were an insignificant little body that had passed into obscurity in the course of many centuries, like, for example, the descendants of their ancient enemies —the Assyrians—then there would be some reason for regarding the Bible as out of date, even as the Assyrians are out of date.

But since it is impossible to say to-day that the Jews do not count in modern life, it has become equally impossible to say that the Bible is out of date, or that the prophecies, which it contains, are to be treated as dead letters.

But it is urged that the Bible consists of a number of different books, written by different authors, having different values; and one has no right to group them all together in that sweeping verdict in their favour to which reference has just been made. There are, of course, isolated passages in the Old Testament to which exception can be taken. Yet they are useful to-day, in order to contrast them with the ethical values that Christ brought into the world, even among those who do not recognize Him. They also afford evidence for the extreme antiquity of the books in which they occur. And the books in which they occur contain testimony of undoubted value. Reference will be made to some of these books in succeeding pages. Which are we to exclude? Surely all of them record evidence for the study of the Science of Man? It was thought at one time that the Book of Daniel had really succumbed to critical dissection. But it will be noticed in a later chapter of this work that archæological discoveries have already gone far to reverse that verdict.

The emphasis that is laid upon Faith throughout the Bible, may to some extent be due to the fact that the whole phenomena of Life and Matter, are too vast for the comprehension of human intellects. What we know through Science to-day, seems certainly to have been beyond the comprehension of those who lived in remote times. And, judging from the present-day utterances of distinguished scientists, we may even now have only touched the fringe of the garments that enshroud the Great Unknown. The Bible claims to be the Revelation of God to Man throughout the Ages, on subjects which are essential for his material, moral, and spiritual growth. In that case it would be unsafe to reject any book of the Bible as useless to us. The mere fact that all have come down through the Ages in their entirety, suggests that every one of them has a purpose. And it may be, that purpose is to enable us to make a more effective study of the Science of Man.

It has already been pointed out, how progress in the knowledge of material things calls for similar progress in the knowledge of spiritual things. All honour to those who seek such progress in Bible study. It is a pity that in the past it has been sought by dissection of the Sacred Text—and dissection is a process which is destructive of Life. As one approaches universal things, lofty facts may be apprehended but not dissected. The Old Testament is of course a translation from a Hebrew original. Among our Clergy there appears to be a general decline in the study of the Hebrew language. This is said to be due to the discouragements created by the destructive criticism. It is hoped that these have now been removed, and that Hebrew will once more be learned. It is obvious that there are many passages in the Old Testament which need a knowledge of Hebrew to assist in their elucidation. As they stand in our authorized version they are obscure, and do not always make sense. Such difficulties are characteristic of all ancient writings; they testify to their genuineness. Even the works of Shakespeare, less than three and a half centuries old, composed and written in our own language, contain obscure sentences. How much more must we expect such perplexities in the books of the Old Testament, composed from two thousand five hundred to three thousand five hundred years ago, in an archaic form of the Hebrew language, and written down in an archaic script? Even if the one employed was the Phœnician Hebrew referred to in this work in connection with the Lachish Letters, yet that script, after the Captivity, was superseded by a later one—the Assyrian Hebrew. The oldest manuscript of the Hebrew Bible which we possess to-day is written in the latter. There is abundant evidence that, in the transition period, and in course of Ages, some errors have been made in transcription. But it would seem as though these concern minor details, and do not affect the general sense. A comparison with the Septuagint or Greek translation of the Hebrew, made three centuries before Christ, suggest that such mistakes have occurred since then; while before that time, the text on which those translators worked, also contained archaic words whose exact meaning had even then been lost. Such considerations weigh against the assumption of the word for word, and letter for letter, correctness of the whole English Bible. But they are evidences of its authenticity, and the recognition that they exist helps us in difficulties.

We have no right to be discouraged from the study of the Bible because we do not understand it all at once. If the Old Testament is really what it represents itself to be, and the fulfilment of the prophecies concerning the Jews is a guarantee that it is so, then we are reading documents of immense antiquity which enshrine the Divine Wisdom of the Ages.

Our intellectual understanding of parts must always be incomplete; yet as we place it side by side with our experience of life, the whole becomes progressively ours. The study of the Bible is like other studies in life, only more so, for what we gain from it compensates many times for what we put into it. *But we must first put something into it.*

Before direct attention is drawn to the archæological

discoveries in their association with the Old Testament, it is worth our while to pause and reflect upon the wonder that any relics at all of these immensely remote days have survived to tell their story.

We ask ourselves, what will be left of our civilization three thousand years hence? How will the archæologists of that age interpret the jumble of bricks, and the rusty pipes and pieces of iron, that may mark the sites of our houses? Our prolific literature now recorded on paper, and even on parchment, will long since have become dust. Inscriptions cut on stone will be about all that is left of it. Cities that remain will have had their sites cleared a dozen times, and the debris removed to spots where identification will be difficult. Our climate and soil, ruthless agents for corrosion and decay, will have done the rest.

We gain some idea of what our civilization may look like, when we dig up the remains of the Roman occupation of Britain from fifteen to nineteen centuries old. And ours will be much more disturbed. There a few inscriptions carved on stone are all that remain of the Roman period. But in Bible lands, drier climates have preserved more remote relics of the past. Even writing on papyrus, dating back to incredible antiquity, has been preserved in Egypt. It is, perhaps, otherwise in Palestine, where the climate is more humid. The reason why so much more is found in these Bible lands, than we can hope to leave behind as records, is that the remains of remote civilizations after their initial overthrow were not usually disturbed. Builders did not clear away the ruins, they smoothed them out, and built anew on the top. And the ancient races made, and used, and broke, quantities and quantities of earthenware or pottery. The fragments were thrown over their city walls, or remained imbedded in the debris of the interior, when a place was wrecked. So the mounds, that mark the sites of the old cities of Palestine, are literally full of bits of pottery down to a great depth. The remarkable advance made in Biblical archæology during the past twelve years, sprung from Sir Flinders Petrie's suggestion that these fragments might be classified and dated. The shapes and sizes, the texture, the construction, and the ornamentation of pottery, in Bible days, changed from time to time. There were in addition infiltrations of pots from outside sources. Then again, the tombs are full of unbroken pots, placed there to contain votive offerings for the deceased. The fragments could be compared with these, and so identified and classified. Approximate dates were obtained when fragments or pots were found associated in some spot with a dated object, such, for example, as the scarab or seal of an Egyptian Pharaoh whose date was known. And since the layers of pottery pieces on a particular site lay one above the other, in chronological order, archæologists are now able to assign a date to each layer, to within a space of time of from five-and-twenty to fifty years. The excavations of Jericho, to which detailed reference will be made, furnish a typical example of pottery dating. With the aid of this system, excavations are yielding such definite results, because the evidence dug up in Bible lands is now dated evidence. We know what is contemporary with Abraham, or what is contemporary with Joshua, or what is contemporary with Ahab, or what with Hezekiah. So it has come about that the various pieces of evidence, like parts of a jigsaw puzzle, can be fitted into the Bible narrative, and they do fit into it. What is more, they help to supplement and explain it. If it is suggested that in some instances elements of conjecture remain, it may be pointed out that they belong to a more certain class of conjectures than those which have found such ready credence among many distinguished scholars. For the latter were based on purely speculative assumptions, while the former enjoy the more substantial foundation of observed facts. To sum up then—the assumption that has dominated many minds, and still dominates some, is that the Sacred Narrative must be mythical, or more or less mythical, because so-called miracles do not happen! The progress of Science has now reached a point where such an assertion can no longer be regarded as valid. So-called miracles do happen, Science is recording them. And the evidence supplied by the Jewish Race, particularly at the present time, certifies that the Bible must be substantially True. That fact is indeed further confirmed by the effect that the circulation of the Bible has exercised on our own civilization. This constitutes the proper basis on which to examine the Bible in the light of our present knowledge.

If allowance is made for our partial knowledge of ancient civilization even at the present time, it will be seen how remarkably archæological evidence testifies in its turn to the authenticity of the Bible. It is true that Bible history is incomplete, but it chronicles history for the one great Purpose for which it has been written and preserved for us.

Science keeps telling us all the time that the foundation of our faith in anything must be laid on a basis of observed facts. Yet popular research often reverses the process; it positively teaches as observed facts, results that are based on theory—the theory of Evolution.

This has come about somewhat as follows:

The idea of Evolution afforded such a plausible explanation of all the phenomena associated with Life and Matter, that we did not pause to modify it. Here was the key to everything! And in that everything, we included all Religion and all History. Whenever it appeared as though the key did not fit the facts, then why not make the facts fit the key? And call it Science! So we spun stories of the evolution of religion from dreams. And of the evolution of the human race from apes. We paid little respect to History, less to the Bible, and none to Tradition. Our flights of fancy spurned such commonplace sources of information. We overlooked previously recognized facts. The real Sciences are now marshalling the evidence of observed facts for our consideration.

It will be seen that the theory of evolution of religion has definitely broken down in the light of evidence from the Sciences of Archæology and Anthropology. So does a crude theory of Evolution of Man break down before the facts of written History, and before the facts brought to light by excavation.

Man's progress has not been one of steady consistent advance, else to-day we should have neither wars nor rumours of war. Instead, human civilization has been marked by progress and decay, repeated over and over and over again. The dominating factor has always been recognized to belong to moral and spiritual forces, even as they are illustrated in the Bible.

History, and its handmaid Archæology, furnish facts which flatly contradict the evolution theory of consistent and unbroken progress of our branch of the human race, or of any other branch of it. All stages of civilization exist to-day throughout the world, and so far as we are aware, always have existed. And where glorious monuments certify to a great past, those who now dwell around them often testify to a great decay.

How does our own civilization stand to-day?

If we define progress in terms of universal suffrage, aeroplanes, motor-cars, radios, cinemas, gramophones, refrigerators, high explosives, machine guns, poisoned gas, and the like, then we are at present on a peak, and a very dangerous one.

If we define progress in terms of a balanced development of Happiness, Contentment, and Peace, we seem to have lost more ground than we have ever made by our many inventions. And it does not seem much use people trying to emphasize moral teaching, or formulating systems that provide for the distribution of other people's wealth, which after all are not moral. What the world needs is power—power other than that of internal combustion engines, or high explosives, power that will put things right. Our forefathers believed that that Power came to them from the Unseen; it is the Power that we learn about in the Bible.

## II

## FROM THE CREATION TO ABRAHAM

IN the last half-century the various branches of
Science have made a number of important discoveries which, when rightly used, benefit mankind. But few yet realize that Archæology and Anthropology have contributed what may prove to be the
most beneficial discovery of all.

In the year 1931 these two Sciences simultaneously
reached the conclusion that the evidence in their
possession pointed to the fact that Monotheism was
the original Religion of Man. Seven years have
elapsed; yet even now the discovery is but little
known, and its immense significance but little appreciated. The intellectual world still struggles on in a
tangle of bewilderment concerning its Belief, because
it has been led to subordinate Revelation to hypotheses
which do not fit observed facts. The earlier chapters
of the Book of Genesis have received an endorsement
from Science, which in course of time will stabilize our
outlook on the whole Bible. Let us briefly glance at
the sources from which these observed facts of archæology are derived.

In the beginning of the Bible, the river Euphrates is
associated with the earliest settlements of civilized man,

It flows through a country anciently known as the land of Shinar, or the land of the Chaldees, or as Babylonia, or Mesopotamia. To-day it is called the kingdom of Irak. It is a land of alluvial plains, or mud flats, through which the Euphrates and the Tigris wend their way to the Persian Gulf. The country is studded with the ruins of ancient cities, and scored with the channels of old irrigation canals. Excavations have revealed the remains of a vast civilization which reaches back some six thousand years before Christ.

Here, then, in the very part of the world where the Book of Genesis placed it, archæologists have been digging up evidence that concerns the history of civilized man—history reaching back to a time that was utterly mythical to the classical writers of anti-quity. The late Dr. Langdon, Professor of Assyriology at Oxford, played a leading part in this work: both as the excavator of Kish, near Babylon; as a scholar in deciphering the quantities of cuneiform tablets which he found; and as an author in transmitting to the world the conclusions derived from them. His great book, entitled *Semitic Mythology*, published by the Archæological Institute of America (Marshall Jones Co., Boston), formed Volume V of the series, " The Mythology of all Races." The following extracts which confirm the foregoing statements about Mono-theism, are quoted by permission. There Dr. Langdon writes:

"I may fail to carry conviction in concluding that, both in Sumerian and Semitic religions, monotheism preceded polytheism and belief in good and evil spirits. The evidence and reasons for this conclusion, so contrary to accepted and current views, have been set down with care and with the perception of adverse criticism. It is, I trust, the conclusion of knowledge and not of audacious preconception."

And again:

"In my opinion, the history of the oldest religion of man is a rapid decline from monotheism to extreme polytheism and widespread belief in evil spirits. It is in a very true sense the history of the fall of man."

Dr. Langdon has since amplified this statement as follows:

"Monotheism in the Old Testament, and Islamic monotheism, were not the results of direct evolution from polytheism. It was a false conception of the history of religion to suppose that polytheism was necessarily connected with low types of culture. In fact polytheism was characteristic of the greatest cultures of antiquity, but it grew out of monotheism, and was only a theological interpretation of primitive monotheism.

"The history of Sumerian religion, which was the most powerful religious and cultural influence in the ancient world, could be traced by means of pictographic inscriptions back almost to the earliest religious concepts of man. The evidence pointed unmistakably to an original monotheism. The inscriptions and literary remains of the oldest Semitic peoples, also indicated a primitive monotheism, and the totemistic origin of Hebrew and other Semitic religions was now entirely discredited.

"The evidence of anthropological studies among most primitive Races still extant, also proves that the first concept of deity was that of a supreme Being, sometimes associated with the sky. This agreed with all modern results of philologists and decipherers of the most ancient Sumerian, Semitic and Indo-Germanic religions." (*The Scotsman*, 18th November 1936.)

And yet again:

"It seems to be admitted that the nature myth gods of India, Greece, and Italy, and all Indo-Germanic religions, started with a Sky-God, Zeus, Zeus-pater. Dyauspitar, Jupiter, 'God the father,' all derived from the root *div*, to 'shine,' whence the word *deus*, 'god'."
(*Evangelical Quarterly*, April 1937.)

It is hard to name a modern book about the Old Testament, or about ancient history, or about archæology in Bible lands, which is unaffected by these pregnant conclusions.

If Dr. Einstein's Theory of Relativity is true, it renders all previous books on Physics obsolete. In like manner Dr. Langdon's archæological discovery that Monotheism was the original Religion of civilized man, affects modern books that write about ancient beliefs. Since these lines were written, the world has to mourn the loss of this great scholar. His last article on the subject of Monotheism, is reprinted in the appendix of this book, by permission of the *Evangelical Quarterly*, the Review in which it was published in April 1937. Dr. Langdon refers there to the fact that the Science of Anthropology, or the study of the Primitive

Races, confirms the conclusions of archæology. Professor Schmidt of Vienna has announced that discovery on behalf of Anthropology in his book, *The Origin and Growth of Religion—Facts and Theories*. It was published in the same year as *Semitic Mythology*. Thus the evidence of observed facts postulates Monotheism, or the worship of one God, as the original religion of both the civilized, and the primitive, Races of mankind.

Another subject on which Evolution theories have led many astray, is that of early beliefs in a future life. The two Sciences, to which reference has just been made, are finding evidence that testifies to the existence of such belief. On behalf of Anthropology, Professor Schmidt writes:

"All primitive people, without exception, believe in a future life." (*Origin and Growth of Religion*, p. 275.)

And on behalf of ancient civilization Dr. Langdon wrote:

"The theological view running through Babylonia before 2000 B.C. was of a Heaven for the righteous, whom the Gods might choose to receive into Paradise, where is the Bread and Water of Eternal Life."

The statements of Jesus Christ on the subject of the Bread and Water of Life, as quoted in St. John's Gospel, are of startling significance in this connection. For HE claimed to have brought these gifts, down from the righteous, the select few, in Heaven, and made them accessible to sinners on Earth. There is therefore a profound relationship, not with the Old

Testament alone, but with the oldest religious beliefs of Babylonia, in existence long before any book of the Bible was written. And beside this theological link, it will be pointed out in the next chapter how the evidences left behind by civilizations which flourished before Abraham, had moral standards, and moral maxims, which link them with the original Monotheism on the one hand, and with Jesus Christ on the other.

Let us next notice the Creation Stories—they too have the testimony of Archæology in their favour. They are of great importance, because they affirm the fundamental principle of a Personal God as the Creator of Nature and its Laws. In so far as they are being ignored in our schools, and an evolutionary account substituted for them, we must expect to find that lack of Belief in a Personal God to which the Archbishop of Canterbury has drawn attention. In this connection Dr. Langdon pointed out:

"Darwinian evolution applied to the origin and progress of religion can have only one result: it must destroy the faith of mankind that there is any reality in religion at all."

The discovery by the Sciences that Monotheism was the original Religion will change our attitude to these Creation Stories. For example, since Monotheism, or the Belief in one God, antedates Polytheism or the belief in many, then it is reasonable to regard the Creation, and other stories in Genesis, as representing the original version; and the polytheistic ones as corruptions of it. The mere fact of Archæology having only found polytheistic accounts, no longer entitles us to assume that the monotheistic ones are derived from them.

Again, the progress of other Sciences dwarfs the evolutionary account of Creation. The subject has become too vast to be treated as though we possessed exact knowledge. As a recent writer in *The London Times* has pointed out, "The further science prosecutes her inquiries into the secrets of the physical universe, the more secrets await her." So we need to take to heart the reminder the Deity gave to Job:

"Where wast *thou* when I laid the foundation of the World?"

The incredulity with which some regard Bible statements, is in painful contrast to the credulity with which they accept so-called "scientific" speculations. For example, one well-known divine has stated that it was perfectly well known that our world was created between four and five thousand million light years ago! The consideration of how much we need to know of what happened four or five thousand years ago, makes us wonder at a strange superstition which causes people to talk glibly about four or five thousand million! The discovery of Relativity might serve as a warning against such over-confidence. Further discoveries are likely to change completely our ideas of Time. If our conception of Time depends upon the uniformity of Nature, what if Nature has not always been uniform? Are we quite sure that it is uniform now? Some of the latest definite discoveries of Science appear to cast doubts on this assumption. Our world would seem to have been created when Time did not even exist; certainly before Man had any means of measuring Time. So the Days of the Creation were Days of God. And on this basis the first chapter of Genesis cannot be swept aside as a myth; does it not rather look like a correct summary of what really did happen, so far as human knowledge can take us to-day?

The infinitely wider outlook on the Universe which is now being revealed to Science, makes us feel ashamed of the hair-splitting dissection to which the Grand Masterpiece of Revelation—the Creation Narrative—has been subjected. The humbler attitude of present-day knowledge makes us feel inadequate to even discuss its details.

It is true that we have, for instance, the telescope, the microscope, the spectroscope, and the photographic camera. Such instruments of observation, so far as we are aware, were unknown to the Old Testament civilization. Yet, perhaps, we approach the Creation narrative with too great a sense of superior knowledge. We forget that we read English translations of archaic Hebrew documents which were made by scholars who lacked our knowledge of the Universe. This fact was bound to have affected their rendering of the original Hebrew. What if the original words contain a far wider meaning than is conveyed to us in our English text?

It has indeed been contended that when translated in the light of to-day's knowledge, the Hebrew text conveys expressions in accordance with modern scientific phraseology. We have further to take account of the fact that despite our knowledge to-day, there may have been, and there is ample evidence that there were, Revelations from the Unseen which we no longer directly receive. So from the standpoint of our knowledge, even as it is to-day, there has come down from early civilization through the Bible a clear philosophy, and sufficient evidence to enable us to formulate that Science of Man for which requisition is now being made.

As one goes over the ancient cuneiform writings, some before Abraham, and the engraved seals and stone carvings from Babylonia, Assyria, and other early civilizations, a remarkable trend of evidence is revealed to us. Even from the comparatively small proportion of these relics of a remote past that come to our notice, we derive the impression that the stories of the Creation, the Temptation and Fall of Man, and the death of Abel, as described in Genesis, were then matters of current knowledge. And that perhaps under a polytheistic setting, they were taught in the schools of Ur of the Chaldees when Abraham dwelt there.

It is the lofty aim of Science to seek the real Truth. That truth is reached through the study of observed facts. It is not long since Sir James Jeans told the British Association that the Science of Physics had come to grief because it had built on conjecture and speculation. It is suggested that other fruits of conjecture and speculation, misnamed science, have been accorded more credence than the Bible. And because these fruits were unsound, they have proved bitter fruits for Man's most important asset—his Religion. The Science of Archæology is accumulating evidence that tends to restore our knowledge of the Truth to a setting more in harmony with Holy Scripture.

Archæological evidence, as will soon be seen, has established the reality of the Flood. Let us, therefore, briefly examine the course of events described in the book of Genesis as taking place before it. These occupy little more than two chapters, although they purport to cover a period in the case of the Hebrew Bible of 1656 years, or in the case of the Septuagint 2262 years. The larger figures more nearly coincide with those of the Jewish historian Josephus, who makes the period to be 2256 years. Berosus, the Chaldean, says that there were ten kings before the Flood, which agrees with the ten patriarchs of Genesis. He has also quoted figures which have been worked out to the equivalent of 2261 years. It must, however, be remembered that the antediluvians may have had very inadequate means of recording Time. A book has recently been published by the New York University Press, entitled *Time and its Mysteries*. The late Dr. Henry Breasted there states that the civil calendar of Egypt was introduced in 4236 B.C. But as yet archæology has no means of telling whether the Flood occurred before this date, or after it.

The names of the ten patriarchs before the Flood, as given in Genesis, are obviously related to those derived from other ancient sources. The cuneiform clay prism in the Ashmolean Museum, Oxford, written during the lifetime of Abraham, 2050 B.C., has the names of eight of them. As already stated, Berosus (250 B.C.) mentions them. So does Sanchounyathan (1000 B.C.), so do the Greek, the Sumerian, and the Indian legends. This widespread confirmation of the Old Testament statement implies a historical background. The Sumerian records of 2300 B.C. refer to five cities before the Flood—Eridu, Badtibira, Larak, Sippar, and Shuruppak, and one list includes a sixth—Ellasar. The cuneiform tablets found in both Babylonia and Assyria frequently refer to the time before the Deluge. On one tablet a king praises himself because he loved to read "the writings of the Age before the Flood."

Dr. Langdon wrote that:

"the Babylonians and Assyrians believed that all revealed knowledge, the mysteries of the expiation rituals, and all true rules of conduct, had been preserved for them directly from the hands of the sages who lived before the Flood."

In proportion as we become used to the fact that Monotheism was the original Religion, so this Truth helps to explain the continuity of religious beliefs, of the rituals, of the moral standards, and of the types and symbols. Though they degenerated through the influences of polytheism, yet they were not entirely obliterated. In the next chapter it will be pointed out that they were restated for the Israelites under Moses. It may well be that all ancient religious beliefs originated from this primeval revelation.

That Noah's flood must have been a historical event, has long been recognized by the few scholars who were familiar with the constant allusions to it in the cuneiform writings. As long ago as 1872, George Smith read his translation of the Chaldean account to a London audience. Great interest was aroused at the time, but its full significance, as well as later discoveries, were denied to the public, and relegated to the region of myth and legend. Since Sir Leonard Woolley discovered the Flood deposits at Ur of the Chaldees in the winter of 1928-9, it is no longer possible to treat the incident as a myth. Indeed, Father Burrows has pointed out that a version of the story has been discovered in which the name NAHMOLEL, corresponding in Hebrew to Noah, is recorded. The date of the Flood, and the extent of the Flood, remain uncertain. As regards the former, according to the Hebrew Bible, the Flood occurred 292 years before Abraham, but according to the Septuagint there was an interval of 1072 years. Evidence will shortly be brought forward that fixes the date of Abraham's birth at 2160 B.C. Then, according to the Bible, the Flood should have occurred in 2452 B.C., or, according to the Septuagint, in 3232 B.C. The archæological evidence seems to favour the latter date, and even earlier. Sir Leonard Woolley says that the grave of Queen Shubad, which he found at Ur of the Chaldees, was made above the Flood deposits, although it cuts into them. And Sir Leonard places the date of this queen at 3200 B.C. Then again, the 1st Dynasty of the Babylonian city of Kish is fixed at about 5500 B.C., and Kish was not one of the cities that existed before the Flood. But the extent of the Flood may also have some bearing upon its date. Sir Leonard, and other authorities, appear to regard the Flood as though it were a local inundation, confined to the Euphrates delta. In that case how do they account for the Dispersion? Legends of a Great Flood appear to exist all over the world. Like much evidence that agrees with the Old Testament, efforts are made to explain them away. Nevertheless they are not without significance. But how can one explain away the Dispersion? All civilization seems to centre back to the neighbourhood of the Caucasus, where Mount Ararat, on which the Ark is said to have grounded, is situated. In the case of Egyptian civilization, Sir Flinders Petrie declares that the geography of the Book of the Dead is certainly to be located in the Caucasus. He writes:

"In the Book of the Dead, the sun is said to rise over the Mountains of Bakhau, and the modern Baku is at the eastern extremity of the Caucasus. The sun is said to set in Tamanu, and the Taman peninsula is at the western end of the Caucasus. . . . In the

Caucasus region the natural fires of petroleum springs both in the west at Batoum, in Colchis, and in the east at Baku on the Caspian, are claimed as the original idea of the lakes of fire in the Book of the Dead."

Herodotus also insists on the close resemblance between the Colchians and the Egyptians, both in looks, customs, and products. The late Professor Fessenden drew extensively on Greek Mythology to prove that its civilization also came from the Caucasus.

Again, Sir Flinders identifies the Badarian or pre-historic civilization of Egypt which he discovered, with the Solutrean culture of Europe. He contends that it must have travelled down from the Caucasus. The Badarian civilization is pre-dynastic; and Sir Flinders dates Mena, the first Pharaoh of the first dynasty, as reigning in 4300 B.C. So the Badarian civilization must have come down from the Caucasus at a very early date. Was it before or after the Flood? If we assume that the Flood was a local event, it emphasizes the evidence for a subsequent Dispersion. And then again, how account for the Ark grounding on Mount Ararat? It must have been something more than a local deluge which caused Noah's Ark to drift northward instead of towards the Persian Gulf, and to ground itself on such high ground.

The evidence as a whole makes one feel inclined to place the Flood before 3200 B.C.; and to regard it as a far wider catastrophe than present-day authorities are yet in a frame of mind to accept.

The evidence that Monotheism was the original Religion applies again to all the polytheistic narratives of Noah's Flood. It stamps the monotheistic narrative of Genesis as the original, and the polytheistic as corrupt copies of it. Again let us remark, it is surely unsound reasoning to assume, that because we have as yet only found the corrupt copies, that therefore they must be the originals!

Much has already been written in the preceding paragraph to testify to the reality of the Dispersion:

"These three (*i.e.* Shem, Ham, and Japheth) were the sons of Noah, *and of these was the whole earth overspread.*" (Gen. ix. 19.)

The spread of the descendants of the survivors of the Flood over the whole earth implies the lapse of a long period of time. In effect the Bible states that from the region of the Caucasus sprung three great Races of Man.

Genesis x. goes on to enumerate the descendants of these sons of Noah, and the various parts of the then known world occupied by them. It has been generally assumed that this chapter concerns geographical connections, rather than ethnological relations; in other words, that it outlines maps and not pedigrees. This suggestion ignores the natural tendency, first for members of the same family, and then for those of the same tribe, to keep together. And when, with our modern knowledge, we endeavour to retrace the civilized races of the world to their origins, there seems to emerge three main divisions that have inhabited the earth for the last six thousand years; and they all appear to come originally from the Caucasus. No more satisfactory name has been found for the Western Races than Japhetic (*i.e.* descendants of Japhet); while the Semites (or descendants of Shem) are not in doubt. The descendants of Ham, of course, include those of Mizraim, the Egyptians to whose connection with the Caucasus reference has already been made.

All excavations, in lands associated with the Old Testament, reveal the advanced civilization of their inhabitants before the days of Abraham. For example, in March 1937, the Director of the American Institute for Persian Art and Archæology, suggested to a New York audience that civilization first emerged in the country of Iran, between 8000–5000 B.C. This may well have been the case after the Flood, for modern Iran includes ancient Elam, and Elam is named as the eldest son of Shem (Gen. x. 22). According to Sir Flinders Petrie, the people who lived in Palestine once derived their culture from Elam. His excavations of ancient Gaza, its southern seaport, have revealed the presence there of a highly civilized race coming from the direction of the Caucasus, whose early remains date back to 3200 B.C. And in the report on the excavations at Lachish, some thirty miles north of Gaza, it will be noticed that Mr. Starkey has provisionally dated its most important occupation to a similar remote period.

Professor Garstang working at Jericho, a city in the

interior by the Dead Sea, at the end of the Jordan Valley, has now dug down far below the levels of the city destroyed by Joshua to even earlier periods than 4000 B.C. Evidences drawn from such remote antiquity raise interesting problems about the Flood, otherwise they little concern the Sacred Narrative which passes on towards the life of Abraham.

About the year 2800 B.C. the Semitic Race, that is to say, the descendants of Noah's son Shem, seem first to have sprung into prominence. A priest in a Sumerian Temple, named Sargon of Accad, ascended the throne of Assyria, conquered Babylon, overran the whole of Western Asia, and perhaps even reached the Mediterranean. His successor, Naram Sin, certainly did so. Here then began a supremacy of the Semitic Race, which resulted in a long line of kings of Semitic origin sitting upon the throne of Babylon and adjacent countries. They absorbed and spread the ancient Sumerian culture, right down through Syria and Palestine, to the very borders of Egypt. Herodotus assigns the founding of Tyre in Syria to the year 2756 B.C., so that was probably one of the earlier results of their conquests. On account of its proximity to Egypt, it would be natural to suppose that the culture of ancient Palestine would be Egyptian, but on the contrary the evidence of this Semitic Babylonian occupation is strongly marked right down to the days of Joshua.

The very tablets on which the petty kings of Palestine sent their appeals for help to the Pharaoh of

Egypt against the Hebrews under Joshua, are written in the Babylonian cuneiform script.

This Semitic Babylonian influence has its bearing upon the Bible, for when we come to examine the descent of Abraham it will be seen how he was related to it.

Attention has already been drawn to the way these earlier chapters of Genesis summarize history. The events of a thousand years are condensed into a single chapter. For the Old Testament's purpose is to illustrate the Science of Man. Thus, there is no direct reference in Genesis to those mysterious Hyksos or Shepherd Kings, who came down through Syria and Palestine before the days of Abraham, and conquered Egypt. We read about them in the Works of Josephus—the Jewish historian who lived soon after Christ—and in Egyptian history.

Sir Flinders Petrie has spent a number of years in excavating the remains of this civilization on the borders of Palestine and Egypt, and indeed in Egypt itself. He more than confirms the statement of Manetho, the Egyptian historian, quoted by Josephus, that these Hyksos ruled Egypt for five hundred and eleven years. Sir Flinders says that they ruled from 2371 B.C. to 1583 B.C. And as they came through Syria and Palestine, they may have ruled those countries for an even longer period of time.

The landmarks that remain of their occupation consist of a particular type of fortification. Instead of perpendicular walls, for defence purposes, the Hyksos made sloping ramparts, or glaces, with ditches. These defences have been found in Syria: and in Palestine, from Hazor in the north to Gaza in the south, as well as at Jericho, Lachish, and other places. These Shepherd Kings were apparently the first to introduce horses for purposes of warfare in the countries they overran. They probably originated the horses and chariots which are mentioned so often in the Old Testament. Such weapons of war may have proved as effective surprises in ancient times as our Tanks did in the Great War. And they perhaps facilitated the Hyksos conquest of Egypt.

Josephus, the Jewish historian, calls these Hyksos or Shepherd Kings "*our ancestors*"—that would be the ancestors of the Israelites.

Josephus himself, as a Jew, was descended from the Israelite Tribe of Judah. And according to the Book of Genesis, these Israelites sprung from a still older branch of the Semitic Race, called the Hebrews. So when Josephus writes of the Hyksos as "our ancestors," he must be referring to the Hebrews, for he refers to a time before the Israelites were in existence.

The whole trend of archæological discovery is to emphasize the trustworthiness of much that was written by ancient authorities. The critical habit of ignoring Josephus is therefore no longer admissible. In another place, Josephus remarks of these Hyksos or Shepherd Kings, "Some say they were Arabs." This would still make them part of the original Hebrew stock. The very word Hyksos means "Royal Bedouin," that is to say, "Royal Arabs." And in support of this identification, the tablets recently discovered at Ras Shamra in Syria refer to the presence of Arabs, speaking Archaic Hebrew, in South Palestine in patriarchal times.

The cataclysmic destruction of Sodom and Gomorrah, and the other cities round the Dead Sea, as recorded in Genesis xix., occurred in 2061 B.C. The occurrence was probably due to volcanic action, and its effects must have been felt over a wide area. According to ancient tradition, the Phœnicians were descended from people who fled from the surrounding country in consequence of this catastrophe, and the Ras Shamra tablets tend to confirm the legend.

When Joseph stood before Pharaoh, he said:

"Indeed I was stolen away *out of the land of the Hebrews*." (Gen. xl. 15.)

How then came the country to receive that designation? When this text is considered in the light of our new information, one reaches the conclusion that there were more Hebrews then in Palestine than Abraham's descendants, and that they were *the predominant race*.

Archæological discoveries have now definitely identified the Hebrews with the Habiru, a warlike race of people who were in Babylonia and Assyria before the time of Abraham. These facts together suggest that the Habiru or Hebrews formed an important part of the Hyksos invaders. There appear to have been two distinct Hyksos periods—Early and Late. And in accordance with Josephus, one is tempted to identify the earlier Hyksos with these Habiru, and the later with their cousins the Arabs, also descendants of Heber, who, according to Genesis x., had originally settled in South Arabia.

A gifted writer in a recent periodical described Abraham as a "herdman." This is not a correct designation; it belongs to a school of thought which misunderstands and misinterprets the sacred narrative. Thus we associate the word "herdman" with a man who lacks education, and lives in the country. Abraham was not a herdman at all, but a great Sheikh. It is quite clear from the narrative (Gen. xiii. 7) that he was *an employer* of herdmen—some hundred or more, in fact (Gen. xiv. 14). Nor was Abraham an Amorite, which others choose to call him; as though they were ignorant of the genealogy in the eleventh chapter of Genesis, which traces his descent from Shem; or, that the Amorites were fellaheen descended from Canaan, the son of Ham. Archæology actually confirms the lower social status of the Amorite. The word was used in Babylonia as synonymous with labourer (*Cambridge Ancient History*, vol. i. p. 420).

Lord Beaconsfield once told a critic in Parliament, who taunted him with his Jewish origin:

"My ancestors were princes before the noble lords had emerged from breech clout."

The school of evolutionary critics have postulated something as primitive as "breech clout" for Abraham's ancestry. Sir Leonard Woolley's excavations at Ur of the Chaldees, where Abraham spent his youth, have proved that he lived in a city which had an advanced culture. The education enjoyed by its inhabitants in the days of Abraham, has been demonstrated by the discoveries of cuneiform clay tablets in the remains of the houses of this period. Some were historical, others were hymn-books, others were treatises on mathematics or arithmetic. Among the latter were forms for extracting both square and cube roots.

Let us glance further into Abraham's ancestry. According to Genesis xi. 26, he was descended from Shem, the eldest son of Noah, through a descendant of the fourth generation named Eber. This Eber must have been an outstanding ancestor, for Shem is referred to in Genesis x. 21 as "the father of all the children of Eber." The Hebrews derived their name from this ancestor Eber; and from Genesis x. 25, we read that Eber had two sons, Peleg and Joktan. Abraham sprang from the Peleg branch, and Joktan's descendants settled in Arabia (Gen. x. 26–30). Some reference has already been made to the probability that these latter were the Arab part of the Hyksos Shepherd King Race mentioned by Josephus. So far as Abraham is concerned, he is called Abram the Hebrew in Genesis xiv. 13.

Now, concerning the Hebrews, Dr. Langdon wrote:

"The Hebrew deity El . . . whose name occurs quite regularly in the plural Elohim . . . is the god of the Habiru, people who appear in various kingdoms and local city dynasties of Babylonia and Assyria from

2200 B.C. . . . I am entering on debatable ground here when I assume that the Habiru and their god Ilani (plural always written ideographically) are identical with the Hebrews and their god Elohim. There seems no doubt at all this was the case. . . . Accepting this thesis the Hebrews had served for six centuries as mercenary soldiers and traders before they entered and occupied Palestine."

(*Vide Semitic Mythology.*)

This identification of the Hebrews with the Habiru is now being generally recognized by scholars.

In the year 1929, the French excavators, MM. Schaeffer and Chenet, began their work on the mounds of Ras Shamra, on the coast of Syria opposite Cyprus. And their discoveries are some of the most important that have ever been made for Biblical archæology. This volume will contain many further references to their work.

In connection with the life of Abraham, a tablet in archaic Hebrew has been found at Ras Shamra and deciphered. It contains an account of some great fight in remote times between Cheret, king of Sidon, and a vast host of enemies commanded by Terach or Terah, the moon god. Here the tribes of Zebulon and Asher, with the Edomites, are mentioned. (A date of between 1400–1350 B.C. has been assigned to the tablet.) And because Abraham was the son of Terah, the French authorities appear to interpret it as referring to Abraham, and his entry into Canaan. It is pointed out that Ur of the Chaldees was a city of moon-god worship, and so was Haran, where the family afterwards dwelt. But according to the Bible

46

the only conflict in which Abraham took part, was with the army of the Babylonian confederation under Chedorlaomer (Gen. xiv. 14–16) when he rescued his nephew, Lot. On the other hand, a work, which purports to be a translation of the Book of Jasher, represents Terah to have been a great soldier and a commander of armies.

Since it is now generally recognized that about 2200 B.C. the Habiru or Hebrews were mercenary soldiers, it is possible that the Ras Shamra tablet is an echo of some great conflict between the Sidonians and Hyksos invaders led by Terah. However that may be, it is becoming evident that when Abraham came into Canaan he came into a land which had been conquered by his Race.

In matters of religion, Terah and his family worshipped the moon god; as Joshua admitted in his address to the Israelites seven centuries later (Joshua xxiv. 2).

But the call of Abraham marks a return to the early Monotheism. The phenomena associated with manifestations and messages from the Unseen, such as are recorded in Abraham's case, are gradually being studied and recognized by Scientists. Materialism can no longer cause us to disregard them. The title of Abraham—Father of the Faithful—was obtained because he believed, accepted, and acted upon, the Divine Revelation accorded him. Most of the places mentioned in the life of Abraham have been identified, and examinations have been made of their ruins. The lower layers of pottery testify to the likelihood that

47

they were all inhabited in Abraham's time. The invasion of Chedorlaomer, to which reference has already been made, commences with the statement that the event occurred in the days of Amraphel, king of Shinar. For a long time this king has been identified with the great Babylonian monarch, Hammurabi. And although this is not universally accepted, yet it is impossible to disregard it. Such a leading authority as Dr. Langdon has declared:

"In my opinion Hammurabi, Ammarabi, etc., is Amraphel, king of Kingin (Kingir, Singir, Heb Shinegar, Shinar, Gen. xiv. 9)."

(*Semitic Mythology*, p. 384.) [1]

The date of Hammurabi has been ascertained both by astronomy and by archæology. It is generally known that ancient Eastern civilizations practised astrology in times that were remote, even when the Wise Men from the East came to visit the New Born Christ.

A certain king of the 1st Dynasty of Babylon, Ammizaduga by name, left behind him cuneiform tablets recording the monthly rising and setting of the Planet Venus over the twenty-one years of his reign. Copies of these tablets have been found at Kish, and elsewhere in Babylonia and Assyria, and they have been deciphered.

---

[1] The Rev. J. W. Jack has drawn attention to the fact that in the State Correspondence of the Assyrian Empire, Hammurabi is twice mentioned as Ammurapi; and as bi = pil (*i.e.* phel) in the cuneiform, it is quite clear that Hammurabi = Amraphel.

The celebrated astronomer, Dr. Fotheringham, who died recently, collaborated with Dr. Langdon in a most erudite work entitled *The Venus Tablets of Ammizaduga*. There, the astronomical date of the King Ammizaduga has been calculated out from the tablets —he reigned from 1921 to 1901 B.C. He was the fourth king of Babylon after Hammurabi, and the names, and the length of reigns, of his predecessors are known from other cuneiform tablets.

Thus, the date of Hammurabi has been definitely ascertained. He reigned from 2067 to 2025 B.C. And the reason for drawing attention to these details, is that this date falls right into the life of Abraham, as calculated from the Fall of Jericho in 1400 B.C. If the intervals of time mentioned in Genesis and Exodus, without any reservation whatever, are added to this date, Abraham was born in 2160 B.C., he came into Canaan in 2085 B.C., and Sodom and Gomorrah were finally destroyed in 2061 B.C., which would be the seventh year of Hammurabi's reign.

The calculations and references for those who desire to compare them with their Bibles, run as follows:

| | |
|---|---|
| According to Professor Garstang's excavations, Joshua destroyed Jericho about . | 1400 B.C. |
| Previous to that the Israelites had wandered in the Wilderness under Moses . . (Deut. ii. 7; Joshua v. 6, etc.) | 40 years |
| So the Exodus occurred in . 1440 B.C. | |
| Previous to that the Israelites had sojourned in Egypt for . . . . . (Exod. xii. 40–41.) | 430 ,, |
| Carry forward . | 1870 years |

# FROM THE CREATION TO ABRAHAM

| | |
|---|---|
| Brought forward . | 1870 years |
| Previous to that Jacob went down to Egypt when he was . . . . . (Gen. xlvii. 9.) | 130 ,, |
| Previous to that when Jacob was born Isaac was . . . . . . (Gen. xxv. 26.) | 60 ,, |
| Previous to that when Isaac was born Abraham was . . . . . (Gen. xxi. 5.) | 100 ,, |
| Abraham was born in . . . . | 2160 B.C. |

*Date of Events in the Life of Abraham that follow from the foregoing as compared with the astronomical date for Hammurabi.*

| | |
|---|---|
| Abraham entered Canaan when 75 (Gen. xii. 4). *i.e.* 2160−75=2085 B.C. | |
| | Hammurabi began to reign ... 2067 B.C. (astronomical date) |
| Kings of Sodom and Gomorrah defeated in reign of Amraphel (Gen. xiv.). | |
| Sodom and Gomorrah destroyed by fire when Abraham was 99 (Gen. xvii. 1). *i.e.* 2160−99=2061 B.C. | |
| Isaac born when Abraham was 100 (Gen. xxi. 5). 2060 B.C. | |
| | Hammurabi died ... 2025 B.C. |
| Abraham died at 175 (Gen. xxv. 7). 1985 B.C. *i.e.* 2160−175=1985 B.C. | |

Thus, Chedorlaomer's raid must have taken place about the first year of Hammurabi or Amraphel's reign. Several books recently published are finding later dates for Abraham, and later Amraphels; but readers may agree that it requires very certain evidence indeed to over-ride this really remarkable confirmation.

The evidence for the Fall of Jericho in 1400 B.C. will be found set forth in Chapter IV; and the whole chronology back to Abraham and down to Rehoboam, at the end of the book. The checks of this chronology are so numerous that its substantial correctness seems assured. So it is obvious that from Abraham onwards, the narrative has assumed a definite historical and chronological sequence.

The reference to the dating of this fourteenth chapter of Genesis naturally leads to some reference to the incidents recorded in it. The battle between the forces of the Babylonian kings, and those of Sodom and Gomorrah, must have been fought close to Jericho. Professor Garstang, with the author's collaboration, made a long series of excavations of this city in the winters from 1928 to 1936. Some evidence discovered bearing upon this narrative deserves notice.

Professor Garstang unearthed a Babylonian wall, to which he assigned a date as early as 2500 B.C., and a Hyksos wall with a sloping glacis of later date. He also discovered ample evidence that Jericho had been a Hyksos store city. This fourteenth chapter of Genesis records the fact that the Kings of the Cities of the Plain (Sodom, Gomorrah, etc.) paid tribute to Chedorlaomer for twelve years, and that it was their rebellion which caused the trouble. It is probable that this tribute was lodged at Jericho, while its earlier wall supplies evidence of Babylonian penetration into the interior of South Palestine down the Jordan valley, at a date which corresponds with a similar occupation of Gaza on the coast.

Genesis xiv. concludes with the meeting between Abraham and Melchizedek, king of Salem—or Jerusalem—outside the walls of the Jebusite city of that name. The excavation of Jebusite Jerusalem, which David captured a thousand years later, was undertaken by Professor Macalister in the winter of 1924, under the auspices of the Palestine Exploration Fund, with the author's co-operation.

The city was situated on the hill of Ophel, outside the south-eastern end of the present walls of Jerusalem. It was on the summit of a narrow ridge of rock, between the deep Tyropean and Kedron valleys. It was found that the ridge had been encircled and enclosed by a great wall, no less than twenty-four feet thick. Underneath, abutting on the Kedron valley, is the celebrated Virgin's Fountain, which discharges its waters at intervals from a natural syphon in the rock. King Hezekiah conveyed this water through the hill of Ophel by means of a tunnel into the pool of Siloam (2 Kings xx. 20). But long before, in the days of Abraham, the water was carried by a rock-cut tunnel along the side of the Kedron valley to the end of the ridge, furthest from Jerusalem. There it watered the king's gardens: It seems probable that this was the Vale of Shaveh, where Abraham met Melchizedek, that mysterious personage referred to in the Psalms and the Epistle to the Hebrews. The problem—who was Melchizedek?—has exercised the minds of Bible students for centuries. Our recent knowledge would suggest that he was a priest king, who still practised the original Monotheism, one of the aristocracy of the Shepherd Kings.

Abraham's visit to Jerusalem would familiarize him with Mount Moriah, the neighbouring height, on which, eleven centuries later, the Temple was erected by Solomon. It was here, in this locality, that Abraham was afterwards going to sacrifice Isaac (Gen. xxii.).

It is interesting to notice that Gaza is never mentioned in connection with Abraham, although if he dwelt at Gerar (Gen. xx.) he was living within about eight miles or so of it. But it is probable that this chapter is a duplicate of Genesis xxvii., and the story really concerns Isaac, his son. Sir Flinders Petrie's excavations of old Gaza have proved that it was the great seaport of South Palestine in these ancient times. Sir Flinders contends that many gold ornaments found at Gaza came from Ireland. And he gives dates which suggest that this incredibly early trade with Ireland began before the days of Abraham. Gaza was the seaport that connected the mainland with Crete; even as Ras Shamra (Ugarit) was the seaport further north that connected the mainland with Cyprus.

It is recorded that Abraham purchased the Cave of

Machpelah at Hebron for a family tomb; and that there, he and his wife Sarah, his son Isaac, and his grandson Jacob, were buried with their wives. The spot has been covered by a Mahometan mosque for many centuries, and the fanatical guardians have suffered no one to examine the cave underneath. But when General Allenby's armies took Jerusalem, one of his officers, Colonel Meinertzhagen, entered the cave and sat on one of the tombs.

Before leaving the life of Abraham, it may not be out of place to refer to the great age at which he died—175 years (Gen. xxv. 7). What is to be said applies also to the 180 years of Isaac (Gen. xxxv. 28), the 147 years of Jacob (Gen. xlvii. 28), and the 120 years of Moses (Deut. xxxiv. 7). So far as our knowledge goes, such great ages are very unusual, but it is too hasty a judgement to declare them to be altogether incredible. For there are examples of people living to such ages within the last few centuries. And the difficulty of checking them may account for the absence of other examples.

Some years ago, attention was drawn to the following remarkable cases of longevity in one family:

1621. IWAN YORATH, buried at Llanmaes, Glamorganshire, Sunday, July 17, 1621. He fought at Bosworth in 1485, and was then 20; died aged 156. (*Register of Llanmaes.*)

1668. ELIZABETH YORATH, wife of Thos. Wilson, Vicar of Llanmaes, Glamorganshire. Buried, February 13th, 1668. Aged 177. (*Ibid.*)

In the cases of Abraham, Isaac, and Jacob, those who doubt their ages must take account of the fact that they were men of unusual stamina and virility. They lived most of their lives in tents under conditions which made for longevity. It is also probable that Palestine was then the healthiest climate in the world.

Llanmaes, where these two representatives of modern longevity lived, is beyond Cardiff, some two miles inland from the sea. The conditions of life in South Wales in the sixteenth and seventeenth centuries Anno Domini, would hardly seem to be as favourable for longevity as were those of three thousand five hundred years earlier in Palestine, when the world was young. So if the longevity of the Yoraths is conceded, the objections to the ages of the Patriarchs lose some of their force.

The astronomical confirmation of the chronology back to Abraham tends, of course, to favour the correctness of the figures given for the length of the patriarchal lives.

## III

## MOSES (1520–1400 B.C.) THE MAN OF GOD

THE evidence that Jericho was captured by Joshua in 1400 B.C. will be set out in the next chapter. Moses died immediately before this event, at the age of one hundred and twenty (Deut. xxxiv. 7). He was therefore born in 1520 B.C.

The Book of Exodus begins with a description of the adverse conditions the children of Israel met after the death of Joseph, and it goes on to describe the early life of Moses. The narrative fits perfectly into the framework of Egyptian history of 1530 B.C. and onwards. Some sixty years before this date, the native dynasties of Egypt, who had been driven up the Nile, succeeded in defeating the Hyksos and expelled them from Egypt. It has already been pointed out how these Hyksos were distantly related to the Israelites; no wonder that the latter, who were left behind, were ill-treated by their new rulers, the earlier Pharaohs of the eighteenth dynasty. The change of attitude is reflected in the words, "There arose a new king over Egypt which knew not Joseph" (Exod. i. 8). Jacob's descendants ceased to be a free pastoral people and became slaves.

About 1537 B.C., or seventeen years before the birth

of Moses, there was born the most remarkable woman in all Egyptian history. Her name was Hatshepsut, the only daughter of Thotmes I. Her mother, Queen Aahmes, offspring of the Pharaoh Amenhetep I, was of royal blood by both parents. Neither Thotmes I, nor his successors, the second and third of that name, enjoyed that privilege. Thus Hatshepsut, because she was Queen Aahmes' daughter, and the descendant of those rulers who had expelled the Hyksos, enjoyed the allegiance of a strong party in Egypt which regarded the blood of her line as alone worthy of royal honours.

Partly on that account, partly because of masterful ability, her father, Thotmes I, associated her with himself in the government about the very time Moses was born. She continued to be the real ruler of Egypt during the reign of Thotmes II, and even for the first sixteen years of Thotmes III, before he became the greatest of the Egyptian conquerors. Thus, what is known of the biography of this extraordinary woman, fits accurately into the Bible references to the daughter of Pharaoh, who found the infant Moses floating in the ark of bulrushes on the Nile. Josephus says her name was Thermuthis. Herein we see an echo of the name Thotmes, which some writers prefer to render as Tahutmes, and others, including Josephus, Tethmosis. Josephus writes quite a long account of Moses' life in Egypt as a young man. He represents him as leading a military expedition up the Nile and capturing Meroe at the junction of the Blue and White Nile. The Egyptian records, on the other hand, tell us that Hatshepsut, instead of turning her attention to Palestine and Syria, like her predecessors and successors, sent fleets of ships up the Nile, and even by sea to Central Africa.

Despite the persecution of the Israelites during Hatshepsut's youth, in her later years when she was associated on the throne with Thotmes III, she rebuilt and adorned the Semitic temple of Serabit, in the middle of the Sinai Peninsula, to which more important references will be made. The Epistle to the Hebrews (xi. 24) affirms that Pharaoh's daughter was ready to recognize Moses as her son. The circumstances surrounding Hatshepsut's life, suggest that she could certainly have done so, and even made him the Pharaoh. The contents of the tomb of Tutankamen, now in the Cairo Museum, give us some idea of what "the treasures of Egypt" (Heb. xi. 26) were like in the days of Moses, although his early life in Egypt was lived a century and a half before this Pharaoh ascended the throne.

"And Moses was instructed in all the wisdom of the Egyptians; and he was mighty in his words and works."                                        (Acts vii. 22.)

The theory of evolution as applied to religion is now being abandoned, but its implications still obscure the archæological evidence. We are unaccustomed to associate "the wisdom of the Egyptians" with anything of a high moral order. We have learned from our modern teachers to recognize the high moral tone of religion as a development that came some six centuries or so after Moses, about the time of the prophet Amos. It takes time to adjust our minds to the fact that this *is all incorrect*; and that many of the sentiments, and some of the language, of the Old Testament Prophets and of the Psalms, were already written down in Egypt when Moses was a young man, and had been written down there for a thousand years and more before he was born. The great American Egyptologist, the late Professor James H. Breasted, has quoted some of these ancient maxims in his book, *The Dawn of Conscience*.[1] They were inscribed upon the walls of the galleries, passages, and chambers of the interior of the pyramids of Sakkara. Those who have been to Cairo will remember the exteriors of these step pyramids. They are almost as old as the better known pyramids of Gizeh, and were placed there by the Pharaohs of the V and VI Dynasties (3360–3235 B.C., Petrie). Despite their great antiquity, the writings inside them convey the moral sentiments that civilization needs to-day. Thus:

"Established is the man whose standard is righteousness, who walketh according to its way."

"Although misfortune may carry away wealth . . . the power of righteousness is that it endures."

"I have made every man like his brother, and I have forbidden that they do evil, (but) it was their hearts which undid that which I have said."

"Speak the truth do the truth, for it is great, it is mighty, it is enduring," etc.

[1] Scribners.

Or again, Moses would have learned the wisdom of Egypt as recorded in the Egyptian Book of the Dead. A perusal of this work proves that the Sins forbidden in at least half of the Ten Commandments were Sins in Egypt when Moses was a young man, and had been Sins from remotest antiquity. Thus we read:

"I did not slay men . . . I did not steal . . . My heart devoured not (coveted not) . . . I did not speak lies . . . I did not commit adultery."

Here, in this confession of the deceased in the Book of the Dead, is a recognition of those moral laws afterwards enacted in the 6th, 7th, 8th, 9th, and 10th Commandments. Other specimens of the wisdom of the Egyptians, which existed in writing in the time of Moses, included sentences and whole passages which are clearly related to the Psalms and Proverbs, and other Books of the Old Testament. All this testifies to primeval morality associated with the primeval Monotheism. So the Christian Church did not "invent" the Moral Laws; they were already in existence before Christ. Moses did not make them; they were already in existence before Moses. Archæology already teaches us that they have come down from the very dawn of civilization. In like manner the Ritual, which was instituted by Moses for the Israelites in the Wilderness, was related to the Ritual used in 1400–1360 B.C. at Ras Shamra in Syria by Arabs speaking Archaic Hebrew. The forebears of these Arabs, according to the testimony of their tablets, were acquainted with the peninsula of Sinai, with Kadesh Barnea, and with

Edom, all places associated with the wanderings of the Israelites in the Wilderness under the leadership of Moses. And again, the Ritual practised at the temple of Serabit, in the centre of Sinai, to which reference has just been made, and which goes back to 1500 B.C., bears definite resemblance to the Ritual which was instituted through Moses. Biographers love to trace the background of the characters they portray. The historical background, the ethical background, the literary background, and the religious background, of the man Moses, have now been revealed by the Science of Archæology.

The Spiritual Revelation came to Moses when he was nearly eighty years old. After the death of his protectress, Hatshepsut, he had fled from Thotmes III to the land of Midian (Exod. ii. 15). There he spent another forty years (Exod. vii. 7; Acts vii. 30), and there he received the Revelation. The country of Midian is remote and inaccessible; it has been but imperfectly explored even up to the present time. The northern end of the Red Sea divides into two Gulfs. The western one—the Gulf of Suez—is familiar because the Suez Canal connects it with the Mediterranean. But the eastern one—the Gulf of Akaba—is little known. It divides the east side of the Peninsula of Sinai from the country of Midian on the mainland of Arabia. About two-thirds of the way down this Gulf is a place called Madyan. A record from crusading times says:

" Near Madyan is the well, and at it a rock which Moses uprooted."

So the tradition of Moses associated with the locality is an old one. The renowned traveller, Sir Richard Burton, wrote of Midian in 1877:

"We who have travelled through a country like Midian finding everywhere extensive works for metallurgy; barrages and aqueducts, cisterns, and tanks; furnaces, fire brick, and scoriae; open mines and huge scatters of spalled quartz; with the remains of some eighteen cities and towns—we cannot but form a different and far higher idea of its mineral capabilities than those who determine them by simple inspection of a few samples."

(*The Land of Midian*, Pref., xxiv.)

Sir Richard was looking for gold, and the metallurgists in Cairo did not find enough of it in his samples. But in the last few years ample evidence has been found of the working of copper mines in the land of Edom immediately north of Midian. And there is no doubt that mining, and ore extraction, were carried on all the way south to the Red Sea, including the Peninsula of Sinai, on the opposite shore of the Gulf. The Temple of Serabit, in Sinai, to which reference has already been made, was worked by miners who observed a similar form of worship to the Israelites. The Midianites themselves, according to Genesis xxv. 2, were actually descendants of Abraham.

Moses was keeping sheep in the interior of this inaccessible country when he witnessed the Vision of the Burning Bush (Exod. iii. 2, 3), and received the Divine Message to go and deliver the Israelites from Egypt in the Name of Jehovah. This Divine Title is written in the Hebrew YHWH or Yahweh; it appears repeatedly in the Lachish Letters, to which reference is made in later chapters. The word signifies "THE BEING." We now know from the Ras Shamra tablets that the earlier form of this word was Y.H. or Jah. The Prayer Book version of the fourth verse of the sixty-eighth Psalm reproduces this ancient original.

Those who believe Christ's Manifestation of Himself to St. Paul in the New Testament (1 Cor. xv. 8; Acts ix. 3, 4), etc., cannot consistently disregard similar Manifestations of the Deity in the Old Testament. And, indeed, Science is now beginning to recognize and study modern manifestations from the Unseen, though not of a Divine order.

Before Moses received his Mission to free Israel from Egypt, the Sacred Narrative opens with the statement:

"It came to pass in the course of those many days that the king of Egypt died."     (Exodus ii. 23.)

Our chronology testifies this to be a record of the death of the greatest of the Pharaohs, Thotmes III, which took place in the year 1447 B.C., probably about thirty-eight years after Moses had fled from Egypt.

Much had happened during those thirty-eight years while he was away. Although Thotmes III ascended the throne of Egypt in 1501 B.C., the throne had to be shared with Queen Hatshepsut till her death, about 1485 B.C. Thereafter he commenced a series of conquests of Palestine and Syria, into which the remnant of the Hyksos had been driven by the earlier kings of his dynasty. He made seventeen expeditions into these countries, captured their cities, and broke down their defences. Accounts of his campaigns, graven in Egyptian hieroglyphics, have been translated and published. They record his great battle at Megiddo in North Palestine (1479 B.C.). There he captured nine hundred chariots and two thousand two hundred horses—legacies of the Hyksos occupation. And many other details of this and his other campaigns are recorded. Did it never occur to Bible critics that if Thotmes III could write such records of his life, then Moses must have been able to do the same? And it has now become evident that Moses possessed greater facilities for literary expression than did the Egyptians, although perhaps not so indestructible. It was during the seven years after the death of Thotmes III that Moses received the Vision of the Burning Bush, and made his return to Egypt. He then appeared before Thotmes' successor, Amenhetep II, and asked that the Israelites be allowed to go three days' journey into the wilderness to sacrifice to the God of the Hebrews (Exod. v. 3). Sir Flinders Petrie has suggested that "the three days' journey into the wilderness" was an expression used to denote the route to the Temple of Serabit in the centre of the Sinai Peninsula, where the then existing ceremonies and ritual of the Hebrews were observed. This sanctuary is at the top of a hill, bare of vegetation; its immense heaps of wood ashes testify to the number of its burnt offerings. They are the more remarkable because the wood must have been carried up a thousand feet.

The fact that Hatshepsut had rebuilt and beautified this temple when Moses was under her protection in Egypt, may have led to pilgrimages there being allowed to Israelites in her lifetime, and perhaps later, when the attention of Thotmes III was concentrated on his campaigns in Palestine and Syria. Amenhetep II seems to have renewed the oppression of the Israelites, but if sacrifices and sacred feasts had been held at Serabit before, it was a precedent for Moses' request that the Israelites might be allowed to go there. The Ten Plagues of Egypt followed the refusal of Pharaoh. These carry us again into the sphere of the so-called supernatural or the miraculous. On the other hand, they may be described as a succession of misfortunes that befell the Egyptians, most of which at any rate may be attributed to natural causes.

It has been the custom in the past for those who disbelieved in miracles to explain the Ten Plagues on these lines. Now that so-called miracles are being recognized by Science, it is no longer necessary to overemphasize natural causes. In doing so, while we are rescuing unusual events from one form of miracle in order to satisfy superficial knowledge, yet on the other hand, we are really consigning them into a region of more profound mystery. What is the nature of natural causes? Why do things happen as they do, and when they do? The Bible, as the text-book of the Science of Man, teaches us that the Deity works through natural causes. And again, according to Scripture, Nature itself and its Laws are God's handiwork, and He is Immanent in them. Too much emphasis has perhaps been laid upon the uniformity of Nature. The weather, for example, is not uniform, life is not uniform, even matter itself seems to be no longer regarded as entirely uniform.

In considering the cause of such incidents as the Plagues of Egypt, it is well to bear in mind that calamities are not uniform. When we come to the incidents associated with the crossing of Jordan by the Israelites under Joshua, and the fall of the Walls of Jericho, it will be seen that earthquakes were the immediate cause of them. The fact that these incidents, like the Ten Plagues of Egypt, happened when they did, constitute the real miracle, and point to the Ultimate Cause. For the rest, the Plagues of Egypt for the most part have occurred in Egypt at other times, except perhaps the last and greatest, the death of the firstborn, including even the death of Pharaoh's eldest son (Exod. xii. 29).

A recent work, entitled *Bible and Spade*, by Stephen L. Caiger, B.D., draws attention to a monument in Egypt which seems to confirm the account of the unexpected death of Pharaoh's eldest son. Amenhetep II, the Pharaoh of the Exodus, was succeeded by his son, Thotmes IV. Some years ago the desert sands, which had been slowly engulfing the Sphinx at Gizeh, were cleared away from its base. The work brought to light an inscription on a red granite slab, which disclosed the fact that Thotmes IV had also cleared the sand, and why he had done so. When a boy he had fallen asleep under the Sphinx, and dreamed she told him that one day he would become king of Egypt, and that he was then to clear the sand from her feet. The inscription makes it evident that when Thotmes had his dream he was not the heir apparent.

The Passover was instituted by Moses under Divine Direction immediately before the Death of the First-born. It is now known that it was based upon a more ancient Rite, which may also go back to early Mono-theism. The Passover became the principal annual feast of the Israelites, and for all time has been asso-ciated with their Deliverance from Egypt.

The length of the sojourn of the children of Israel in Egypt has been the subject of much controversy. As it affects the earlier date for Abraham, a few words about it may be welcomed. Abraham was told that his seed should sojourn four hundred years in a strange land, and be afflicted there; but in the fourth genera-tion they should come to Canaan (Gen. xv. 13–16). Immediately after describing the departure from Egypt the Sacred Narrative says:

"Now the sojourning of the children of Israel, which they sojourned in Egypt, was four hundred and thirty years. And it came to pass at the end of four hundred and thirty years, even the selfsame day it came to pass, that all the hosts of the Lord went out from the land of Egypt."        (Exodus xii. 40, 41.)

Surely a sufficiently definite statement, taken in conjunction with the earlier one which was given to Abraham. The only uncertainty was the allusion to the fourth generation. The Septuagint translation of this passage, however, reads:

"And the sojourning of the children of Israel while they sojourned in the land of Egypt *and the land of Chanaan* was four hundred and thirty years."

On the strength of this statement, some authorities have halved the period of the sojourn in Egypt, and included the days of the Patriarchs, before the children of Israel, the sons of Jacob, were even born! Others have emphasized the affliction referred to in Genesis, as having itself lasted four hundred years, and date the commencement of the period from the expulsion of the Hyksos about 1583 B.C. But the very definite passage in Exodus gives no justification whatever for such an interpretation; it does not isolate the years of affliction from the years the Israelites were not afflicted in Egypt, it groups them all together. If the Septuagint addition of the words "and in Chanaan" means anything, it must refer to a time when Jacob or Israel's children were born, perhaps when Joseph was carried away into Egypt at the age of seventeen (Gen. xxxvii. 2). Since he stood before Pharaoh at the age of thirty (Gen. xli. 46), the addition may be an attempt to account for the odd thirty years of the four hundred and thirty, and bring the remainder into exact agreement with the promise given to Abraham.

On the whole, however, the words added in the Septuagint appear to have been an interpolation. The authority of Josephus is often cited for halving the four hundred and thirty years of the sojourn in Egypt, and representing the other two hundred and fifteen years to date from the arrival of Abraham in Canaan (*Ant.*, II, 15.2). But this statement is contradicted by Josephus himself six chapters earlier (*Ant.*, II, 9.2).

Archæology has not definitely disclosed where the Israelites crossed the Red Sea, or an arm of it, into the Peninsula of Sinai, so it is needless to discuss the subject here. It is a common error to suppose that Pharaoh himself was drowned in the pursuit. References to Exodus xiv. 23 and xv. 4 tell us that it was his horses and chariots.

A more fashionable mistake is to seek another place than the Peninsula of Sinai for the wanderings of the Israelites. However that may be, an authority, who knows the interior of Sinai, declares that its geography satisfies the narrative of the wanderings. And since the whole trend of recent discoveries favours traditional sites, it is unlikely that the Israelites wandered through different wildernesses than those indicated in the Old Testament. Indeed, this scene of their wanderings is beginning to receive some sort of confirmation from evidence inscribed on a Ras Shamra tablet. There the Peninsula of Sinai and Kadesh Barnea are mentioned, associated with mythical happenings, and the birth of a demi-god.

Objections have been advanced, against Moses leading the Israelites into the Sinai Peninsula, on the ground that it was then garrisoned by Egyptians who worked its copper as well as its turquoise mines. These take no account of the fact that the miners were Midianites, the very folk with whom Moses had spent forty years; and if there were any Egyptian soldiers, their numbers would be few in comparison with the Midianite miners. Amenhetep II, about the time of the Exodus, had all he could do to maintain himself elsewhere without depleting his forces by garrisons in Sinai. And the nature of this wilderness, with its rugged mountains and deep wadis, makes it improbable that any permanent Egyptian garrisons were stationed there.

The miraculous incidents attendant upon the march of the Israelites, and the subsequent promulgation of the Law from Mount Sinai, have been attributed to volcanic action, traces of which are believed to exist in the Peninsula. And if earthquakes helped the Israelites under the leadership of Joshua, it is possible that phenomena with which we are familiar to-day, helped the Israelites under the leadership of Moses. But Science is reaching a plane of knowledge where she recognizes that the wonders of the Universe reach beyond her ken, much more do direct Manifestations of the Deity. The Commandments, the Social and Moral Laws, and the Ritual of their Worship, were given by God through Moses after the Israelites had reached Mount Sinai, identified by tradition with a mountain in the south of the Peninsula known to-day as Jebel Musa. Some comparison of the Ten Commandments with the far older writings of Egypt has already been made. It has been shown that the last six, at any rate, belonged to the standard of Morals enjoined in Egypt long before Moses. The Fifth Commandment, "Honour thy Father and Mother," etc., is also clearly implied in the earliest Egyptian Moral Maxims found in the Tombs. These affirm that a man who hearkens to his father *reaches old age.* This actually throws light upon the further part of the Commandment, "that thy days may be long in the land." The first four Commandments which concern (1) Monotheism, (2) Graven Images, (3) taking God's Name in vain, (4) the observance of the Sabbath, alone remain as not definitely included in "the Wisdom of Egypt." But even these are not without their witness. It is true that the Egyptians of Moses' day undoubtedly worshipped more than one God, and that graven images must have been much in evidence. But the more ancient the Egyptian monuments, the more do they testify towards an original Monotheism, and a lack of "graven images," while the prohibition against false swearing was extended in Egypt to a recognition that all Untruths constituted Sins.

There only remains the Institution of the Sabbath. That seems to have been of Babylonian origin. And the word "Remember" with which the Commandment opens, implies that it was already an Institution among the Hebrew Race.

The reference to the Babylonian Sabbath leads on to the consideration of the legislation which was enacted by Moses under Divine guidance. It undoubtedly bears a resemblance to the legislation of Hammurabi, the great Semitic Babylonian king. Reference has already been made to this monarch as a contemporary of Abraham. Traces that his laws were recognized by Abraham are instanced by Sarah giving him Hagar when she herself had no child. They occur again when Rachel and Leah both presented Jacob with their respective handmaids—Bilhah and Zilpah. The code of laws of Hammurabi, engraved on a stele of black diorite eight feet high, was found at Susa in Persia in 1902, and is now in the Louvre Museum. Two figures are carved at the top of this stele; they represent the Deity presenting the laws to Hammurabi. It seems certain that Hammurabi's laws were a codification of the older and existing laws and customs of the Semitic Race—the race that sprung from Noah's son Shem, the race to which the Hebrews belonged.

Brief references have already been made to the relationship that existed between the Sacrifices and Ritual instituted by Moses as recorded in Exodus, Leviticus, Numbers, and Deuteronomy, and earlier Semitic forms of it. Since the tablets found at Ras Shamra in Syria are peculiarly related to the Mosaic Ritual, this seems a suitable place to describe their discovery and their contents in more detail.

The excavation of Ras Shamra, now definitely identified with the ancient Phœnician city of Ugarit, began in May 1929, and has been going on ever since.

The excavators, MM. Schaeffer and Chenet, were so fortunate as to find the contents of a temple library dating back to 1400–1350 B.C. The ruins of a building associated with the finds had been a school or college for scribes. Clay tablets were found there whose surfaces had clearly been used for writing exercises.

Similar discoveries, made in Babylonia and elsewhere, testify to the widespread use of writing in these remote ages. There were tablets at Ras Shamra that had been used for dictionaries or works of reference; there was a register of ships that used the seaport; and there were quantities of other tablets in eight languages and scripts. The most important, for our present purpose, were a series of tablets in cuneiform which employed only twenty-eight different characters, instead of the far larger number used in ordinary cuneiform writing. This suggested that the script was alphabetical. Many of our readers will be familiar with Edgar Allan Poe's story, *The Gold Bug*, which contains an account of how a cryptogram was deciphered. More recently, Conan Doyle included in his series of Sherlock Holmes stories, one called *The Dancing Men*, where similar methods were used. They were also employed in the Great War, to decipher code despatches sent over the wireless.

The alphabetical script of these Ras Shamra tablets constituted a cryptogram, the problem was to identify the language in which it was written. The Hebrew language was tried, and the decipherment was accomplished by the joint efforts of Professor Hans Bauer in

Halle, Professor Charles Virolleaud in Paris, and the Dominican Friar, Emile Dhorme, in Jerusalem. The tablets prove to have been written in archaic Hebrew. Their contents are of a polytheistic character, for some fifty gods and half as many goddesses were associated with Ras Shamra. But they testify that El was the supreme God—the father of the gods. And El, with its plural Elohim, are the Hebrew words translated God, which occur hundreds and hundreds of times in the Old Testament.

The contents of some of the tablets indicate that they record ceremonial rituals or liturgies, and their styles and phrases resemble those of the Old Testament. The ritual tablets refer to a number of sacrifices, and the technical expressions used for them in the archaic Hebrew are precisely the same as those used in the original Hebrew of the Old Testament. Thus there are references to The Trespass Offering, The Peace Offering, The Tribute Offering, The Wave Offering, Whole Burnt Offerings, Offering for the Expiation, New Moon Offerings, Offering of Firstfruits, Offering of Bread of the God, Burnt Offerings.

There is a ritual for offerings on the housetops, to the sun, moon, and stars, a practice which is forbidden in the Old Testament. There is also a ceremony of boiling a kid in its mother's milk—for a milk charm—which is expressly forbidden in Exodus xxiii. 19 and Deut. xiv. 21. A further relationship to the Mosaic ritual is established by reference to objects which relate to the Tabernacle and its contents. Thus:

74

The Courtyard of the Tent, The Holy Place of the Holy Places—c.f. The Holy of Holies (Exod. xxvi. 33), The Table of Gold (Exod. xxv. 24), The Ark of the Covenant. And there are still more links—Thus the word for priest (Kohen) is the same word as used in Genesis for Melchizedek; in Exodus for Jethro; and for the priests of Israel throughout the Pentateuch. In like manner the expression translated "stranger within the gates," occurs in the sense of "guests of the gods." Then there are offerings for the Hearth (Lev. iv. 12). And the dead are known as "Rephaim" (cf. Job xxvi. 5).

A few pages back attention was drawn to the absence of reference to the seventh day or Sabbath in Egypt. Here on these tablets are abundant references to festivals of seven days, seven years' reign of the king, seven years' influence of departed spirits, and so on. There is a sentence of extraordinary interest on one of these tablets. It reads:

"Didst thou not smite Leviathan, the swift serpent, even the crooked serpent? Didst thou not break in pieces his seven heads?"

A parallel passage from the book of the prophet Isaiah reads:

"In that day the Lord with his sore and great and strong sword shall punish leviathan the swift serpent, and leviathan the crooked serpent," etc.

(Isaiah xxvii. 1.)

And again we find:

"Thou brakest the heads of leviathan in pieces."
(Psalm lxxiv. 14.)

This legend of leviathan has spread to the confines of the ancient world, and perhaps further. In the interior of Cambodia, the French have rescued from the growth of the tropical jungle the immense and magnificent ruins of the city of Angkor. Its many temples are built in square enclosures surrounded by square moats of water. These moats are crossed by long and spacious causeways; and the parapets sometimes consist of rows of eight-feet-high stone giants; each row holds up the body of one great stone serpent, one hundred feet or more in length. These serpents all have seven heads. Though Angkor was built seven centuries after Christ, it is evident that its builders, the Khmers, when they came from the interior of Asia brought the legend of leviathan with them.

But to return to the relationship between the first five Books of the Old Testament and the Ras Shamra inscriptions. [The people who wrote these inscriptions claim on them to be Arabs, whose forefathers came from the south of Palestine, from the district round the Dead Sea called the Arabah (Joshua iii. 16). And not only that, but they write of mystic rites in the same wilderness of Kadesh, where the Israelites sojourned for some time; and the birth there of Shalem Shassar, the moon god's son—Shalem Shassar—the seventh of the great gods, who "shall upbuild Ashdod."]

The distinguished French writer, M. Dussaud, relates the references on the tablet to a trade route from the upper end of the Gulf of Akaba on the Red Sea through

Kadesh to Ashdod—that is to say, a route from the Red Sea to the Mediterranean.

The tablets themselves were written after 1400 B.C., the year in which Moses died: we are confronted with the problem whether they connect with Israel's wanderings in the Wilderness, or whether they concern events, more or less mythical, long before this time. If the word Shalem is the same as the Salem in Jerusalem, then, since that city was in existence in the time of Abraham, an even earlier date must be postulated for Shalem. There is a reference in the Old Testament to Arabs associated with the Philistines at Ashdod (2 Chron. xxvi. 6, 7), but that would be six centuries or so after these tablets were actually written.

The date of 1400–1360 B.C., assigned to these tablets by the excavators, would mean that they were written at least some forty years after the Law was promulgated from Mount Sinai to the Israelites, and at most eighty years. Account must be taken of the fact that the manifestation in Sinai connected with this event must have become known to the Midianites. In course of time, their merchantmen would carry the news to the Theological College at Ugarit. The apparent fact that information did travel from Sinai there about that time is supplied by the alphabetical script itself. With the information at present at our disposal, the earliest alphabetical script has been found at the temple of Serabit, in Sinai, and dated by some in the very time of Moses, by others earlier. At Serabit it was not written in cuneiform characters at all, but in another form of script, to which reference will be made in due course. The inference is that the Theological College at Ugarit had heard of the alphabet, and tried to imitate it in the far more ancient cuneiform script which they already possessed at their college. At the same time the priests at the college composed and wrote in this alphabetical script a fresh ritual, in which they embodied then ancient rites and ceremonies, embellished them with what they had heard of rites practised in Sinai, and adapted the whole to suit their polytheism. It must be borne in mind that the Book of Genesis itself supplies ample evidence of ancient sacrifices resembling those ordained in the Wilderness.

If, on the other hand, we assume that the whole of the Ugarit rituals represent nothing that came from Sinai, except the alphabet in which they were written; and that they represent ceremonies in use among Hebrew-speaking people before Moses, then, like the Semitic legislation codified by Hammurabi, six centuries earlier, the ancient rites and ceremonies were reinstated in a modified form for the Israelites, but cleansed and purified of all polytheism.

Again let us recall how biographers love to trace the background for their great characters. Archæology has now indeed supplied us with a background for the Man Moses. Some of our readers must be aware how many centuries after Moses critics have dated the institution of the Ritual associated with his name.

And the Tabernacle and all connected with it was pronounced a myth! How ridiculous these conclusions now read in the light of these recent archæological discoveries. The background of 1500–1400 B.C. makes contact with Moral Laws, with Legislation, and with ceremonial Ritual, which in an astonishing manner suit the developments set out in the Books of Exodus, Leviticus, Numbers, and Deuteronomy.

A difficulty now arises for those of us who have been accustomed to regard the contents of these books as direct Commandments and Revelations of God. The Ten Commandments were spoken by God from Mount Sinai. And passage after passage begins, "The Lord said unto Moses." If from the historical side we recognize that the time was ripe for Moses to formulate the laws, legislation, and ritual, associated with his name, how do we reconcile that he did so with the religious side? Here we are entering into deep questions to be approached with profound reverence and humility. The narrative of the Giving of the Law from Mount Sinai, must be regarded as a unique Experience of a direct Manifestation from the Unseen. It is always referred to as such throughout the whole Bible. Other manifestations to Moses and Aaron were also from the Unseen, but more circumscribed. And lastly, the explanation of the oft-repeated expression "The Lord said unto Moses" involves the inquiry "What is the Nature of Inspiration?" How were all the Prophetic Books of the Bible written? Divine Inspiration must have been there, for some of the Prophecies, as already pointed out, are being fulfilled to-day before our very eyes.

But after accounting for all, either by the Direct Voice from the Unseen, or by Writing through the hand of Moses, the further objection may be raised that the Commandments, and the Laws, and the Ritual, were not altogether new. And, in the sense in which we have been accustomed to regard them as new, that objection is sustained. In the light of archæology it would seem as though the Mosaic dispensation restored Monotheism and other primeval Beliefs; and restated its Rituals, its Social and Moral Laws, and its Customs; and re-emphasized them all, perhaps with modifications, which we are not as yet in a position to distinguish. But the essential element in all these Books of Moses is, not the Law, nor the Ritual, but the COVENANT. That constituted the new element—God, the God of Abraham, of Isaac, and of Jacob, fulfilled His Promises to these patriarchs, and made a Covenant with their descendants—the twelve tribes of Israel. And associated with the Covenant was revealed the LOVE of God. This is clearly summed up in the passage:

"For thou art a holy people unto Jehovah thy God; Jehovah thy God hath chosen thee to be a people for his own possession, above all peoples that are on the face of the earth. Jehovah did not set his love upon you, nor choose you, because ye were more in number than any people; for ye were the fewest of all peoples: but because Jehovah *loveth you*, and because he would keep the oath which he sware unto your fathers," etc.
(Deut. vii. 6–8.)

It has been a common failing among modern preachers to represent Jehovah of the Old Testament as a God of Wrath, and Jesus of the New Testament as a God of Love. But a close study of the Bible reveals Them to be One and the Same Person. This should vastly enhance the value and wonder of the Incarnation in our human imaginations. Jehovah— the I AM—the BEING, who gave the stupendous Manifestation on Mount Sinai, on account of His Great Love for His Creation, humbled Himself and became Man. He did it in order to redeem humanity from the consequences of Sins and offences, recognized as such, from the beginning of the World; but re-emphasized from Mount Sinai, when Moses led Israel there, fourteen hundred and forty years before the Incarnation.

It may be pointed out that there are passages in the Epistles which do not entirely countenance the view that the sins and offences, as set out in the Books of Moses, existed before his time. But that may be part of the progressive Revelation which the Science of Archæology is imparting to us in these latter days. On the other hand, there is the allusion to the text:

"Thou art a priest for ever after the order of Melchizedek." (Psalm cx. 4.)

This, and other verses in the Epistle to the Hebrews, harmonize with the discoveries to which reference has been made.

## IV

## JOSHUA (1485–1375 B.C.) CAPTAIN OF THE LORD

THE biographies of the leading characters of the Old Testament are drawn with great ability. They are clearly and concisely portrayed. Neither their virtues nor their defects are concealed from us. These characters are indeed specimen characters, models, as it were, for all time for the study of the Science of Man. That of Joshua is not the least important among them. But the immediate purpose of this work concerns the historical setting, because the archæological contacts are reached through it.

Joshua, the son of Nun, succeeded Moses in the leadership of the Israelites; he belonged to the tribe of Ephraim. He had been the commander of the Israelites who fought against Amalek in Rephidim (Exod. xvii. 9, etc.); he had been one of the twelve men sent to spy out the land of Canaan, soon after the Exodus; and, with Caleb alone, had then favoured an immediate invasion of the country (Num. xiii. and xiv.). Lastly, he had been Moses' chief assistant on important occasions. His age, at the time he took over the leadership after the death of Moses, has been regarded as doubtful. But Josephus clearly states that he was the leader for twenty-five years (*Antiq.*, V, 1.29); and since he died at the age of one hundred and ten (Joshua xxiv. 29), Joshua was eighty-five when Jericho fell.

The camp of the Israelites had long been pitched on the Plain of Shittim when Joshua succeeded to their leadership. Shittim, situated on the east side of the Jordan, nearly opposite Jericho, and about an equal distance from that river. The anticipations of tourists are shocked if they first see the Jordan in this neighbourhood. They expect a river clear as crystal; instead, they face an opaque, earthy-coloured stream. Nevertheless the colour supplies the clue to the miracle of the crossing by Joshua and the army of Israel (Joshua iii.).

Some sixteen miles higher up, the Jordan flows through deep clay banks; and these, beside colouring the stream, have a way of crumbling into it, and impeding its course. When an earthquake shook Palestine as recently as A.D. 1927, these clay banks collapsed to such an extent that the Jordan ceased to flow for twenty-two hours. Similar seismic disturbances three thousand three hundred odd years earlier, on one day held back the river for the Israelites to cross its bed; and on another shook down the walls for the Israelites to enter Jericho.

The Walls of Jericho assume a vivid place in the memories of childhood. When Professor Garstang, with the author's co-operation, came to excavate them in 1930, they satisfied such imaginations, although the extent of the city they encircled did not do so. The walls proved to have been built of sun-dried bricks, some so large that a man can only carry one at a time. There had been two parallel walls fifteen feet apart, the outer one six feet thick, and the inner one twelve feet. Both walls were thirty feet high, and across their tops houses had been built. The plan of the city was an oblong, the length being about twice the breadth. At the north-west corner, facing the Judean hills, stood a tower or citadel. The walls abutted upon and enclosed this structure, which rose solid to their level and then upon and above them. This building, which is still standing to a considerable height, was not therefore overthrown with the walls, *indeed it held them up* in its immediate vicinity. Before the crossing of the Jordan, the Sacred Narrative tells us (Joshua ii.) that Joshua sent two spies into Jericho. They lodged in the house of a certain woman named Rahab, whose house was upon the walls; and from there, when the alarm was given, they were let down by a cord, and escaped to the Judean hills. It is evident, therefore, that Rahab's house adjoined the citadel. The point is important, because it is clear from the story that, when the walls fell, Rahab's house remained more or less intact (Joshua vi. 22, 25). These verses include a statement from which we infer that the narrative was written during Rahab's lifetime. The evidence of the excavations supports such a conclusion.

The fall of the walls through the agency of another earthquake, which succeeded the one that had dammed the Jordan by an interval of perhaps a fortnight, has been amply verified by the excavations. At first Professor Garstang inclined to the theory that the walls might have been undermined, and propped up by timbers, which were set on fire during the seven perambulations round the doomed city on the seventh day. In that case, Joshua would have been guilty of a pious fraud! But excavations, made beneath the foundations, proved that the soil had been undisturbed. They also disclosed the fact that the foundations themselves were defective. It would seem as though the citizens had relied upon the great width of the walls, and the fact that they were tied together, to neutralize this defect. But parallel earth tremors beneath the wide inner wall turned it over outwards on its faulty foundation. Tied though it was to the summit of the exterior wall, its great weight pushed the other over down the slope on which it stood, and fell on the top of it.

All through the subsequent conquest of Canaan, walled cities of the character of Jericho seem to have been a formidable obstacle to the Israelites. The raw levies that Joshua led possessed no experience of siege warfare. The Walls of Jericho must have appeared impregnable to them. Their numbers no doubt far exceeded those of the defenders; but in the face of those immense walls, numbers did not seem to count. No wonder then that the sudden overthrow of these huge fortifications was counted among the great miracles of their history.

The interior of Jericho supplied more evidence that the disaster was due to an earthquake. And it also yielded further confirmation of the Bible narrative. There it is stated that Joshua made a whole burnt offering of the city. Professor Garstang, like most excavators, is familiar with the strata of burnt cities. Indeed, in ancient times few cities escaped the flames at several stages in their histories. But Joshua's firing of Jericho must have been phenomenal; for the burnt strata was three or four times as thick as any normal one. It was as though the Israelites collected all the combustible materials immediately outside as well as inside the city, heaped them up in the streets, houses, and storerooms, set them alight, and made of Jericho one great holocaust.

This is singularly in keeping with the accounts of the burning; and another corroboration was found of even more value. It may be remembered that Joshua forbade the Israelites to touch anything except the silver, gold, and metal articles. In the rooms and store chambers of the city, have been found the scorched remains of foodstuffs—wheat, barley, lentils, dates, onions, olives, and pieces of dough. Despite the lapse of more than three thousand three hundred years, these mute witnesses remain to-day to testify that though Jericho was burnt, it was not plundered. Among the relics of Jericho is a charred piece of cord, which came from among the ruins of what might have been Rahab's house. People like to say that it is a piece of the one used to let the spies down from the wall—Perhaps? There have been less likely relics venerated.

So the discoveries made at Jericho confirm the Sacred Narrative, but the size of the city does not satisfy our conceptions of it. Although Jericho's walls were so great, they enclosed a city of only seven acres in extent. It is some compensation to know that the Jebusite city of Jerusalem, which David captured, was no larger; and that even Troy—that famous Troy, which Homer says withstood the Grecian armies for many years—was much about the same size. The heat of the Jordan valley, here no less than thirteen hundred feet below sea-level, makes it probable that, even in winter, most of the inhabitants of Jericho would live more comfortably in the shade of the beautiful palm groves outside the city. Jericho itself must have been an important centre of administrative Government, for it was alongside, and therefore controlled, the best water supply for many miles around it. Our excavations have proved it to be a store city. And lastly, it would be regarded as the place of refuge for the whole district, to which the people fled on the approach of enemies. In estimating its importance, and the size of its population at the time the Israelites besieged it, these considerations must be taken into account.

Intimations have already been given that the date of Joshua's destruction of Jericho has proved the basis for a surprisingly satisfactory Bible chronology from Abraham to Rehoboam. It is therefore of interest to refer to the evidence which established the approximate date of 1400 B.C. for the fall of the city. In the earlier part of this book an outline is given of the pottery system of dating. We know now, that quite a few earlier cities once stood on the same site as Joshua's Jericho. Their pottery strata give ample testimony as to their respective dates. But in consequence of the curse Joshua laid upon the spot, there has never been any complete occupation since his day. The Roman city of Jericho, mentioned in the New Testament, is on an entirely different site. The various layers of pottery have enabled Professor Garstang to distinguish one occupation from another. The stratum, of what may be described as the Great Burning, is associated with quantities and quantities of pottery fragments which belong to the middle of the late Bronze Age (1400 B.C.). Professor Garstang was so successful as to find the necropolis, outside the city, in which the inhabitants had buried their dead. The tombs contained numbers of unbroken pots, and among some of them Egyptian scarabs were found. The unbroken pots, and the scarabs, verified the dates of the quantities of fragments on the site; indeed, the scarabs carried matters rather further. They terminated with three of the reign of Amenhetep III (1413–1377 B.C.) in what appear to be the royal or official interments, and the tombs of the period come to an end at the same time. Professor Garstang was former

Director of the Department of Antiquities for the Palestine Government, and his authority as an expert in the dating of pottery, as well as in excavations, is unrivalled. Nevertheless, since the date of the destruction of Jericho was a key date for that of the Exodus, controversy was aroused among those who believed the Exodus must have occurred more than two centuries later. In order to finally settle the question, the author asked Professor Garstang to again verify his conclusions in the season of 1936.

Mr. Alan Rowe, who supervised the excavations in these levels at Beisan, was called in as another expert to join with the Professor in the work. And in due course the report was published in *The Times* of 21st April 1936, and the Quarterly Statement of the Palestine Exploration Fund for July 1936. It will be found on page 278 of the Appendix. It confirmed the date of 1400 B.C. with a possible alternative of any date not later than 1377 B.C. For reasons, discussed on page 280, there seem insuperable objections to 1377 B.C., which, however, decrease in proportion as the date is advanced to 1400 B.C., when they disappear. The discovery of this chronology revives the importance of another archæological find, and enhances the significance of the information gleaned from it.

In the year 1888, an old peasant woman in Egypt, rummaging about at a place called Tel el Amarna, lighted upon the ruins of a Pharaoh's Record Office. She found a collection of three hundred and twenty clay tablets inscribed with cuneiform writing in the

Babylonian language. The decipherment proved them
to have been written by the petty kings and governors
of Palestine and Syria, and sent to the then ruling
Pharaoh—Amenhetep III, and his successor, Amenhetep IV, better known as Akhenaton. They are
dated between 1400 and 1360 B.C. Our readers are
already aware, that the Egyptians had been conquering
and controlling Palestine, and Syria, while Moses led
the Israelites in the Wilderness; as a result, an Egyptian
suzerainty had been established over the conquered
countries. The Tel el Amarna Letters contained appeals
to Egypt for help against invaders from the other side
of the Jordan, named the Habiru and the Sagaz.

The decipherment, the translation, and the grouping
of these letters in their proper sequence, have presented,
and still present, many bewildering problems. But
the identification of the Sagaz with the Habiru is now
generally agreed. And reference has already been
made to the identification of the Habiru with the
Hebrews. This too is now meeting with general recognition. It has become clear that the Tel el Amarna
Letters contain enemy versions of Joshua's invasion,
written by Canaanite, Amorite, and Jebusite chiefs.
The trouble is to fit them into the course of events.
They extend over perhaps forty years, and numbers of
people, of whom we know nothing, are mentioned in
them. The name of Joshua actually occurs on one of
the tablets in the following setting:

"As the king my lord liveth, as the king my lord
liveth, Job is not in Pella. For two months he has

been in hiding. Ask then Benjamin, ask then Tadua, ask then Joshua."

This remarkable passage deserves our further attention. It was written by a certain Mut Baal, to an Egyptian official named Ianhamu, to confirm a previous letter that Job, king of Pella, had fled before him.

Now Pella was an important city on the east side of the Jordan. And the east side, or Transjordania, was occupied by the Israelites some time before they crossed the river, and took Jericho; and so presumably both before and after the writing of this tablet. What was the Egyptian interest in Pella? What was the Egyptian association with Joshua? The passage is enigmatical; it suggests that Benjamin, Tadua, and Joshua were friends of Ianhamu. Although it may contain the innuendo that, since the king of Egypt was not taking effective steps to drive out the Hebrews, their leaders were *assumed to be his friends*. Archæological discoveries in Palestine, taken as a whole, favour the hypothesis, that if the Israelites did not actually conquer and occupy Canaan with the aid of the Egyptians, they did so with their connivance. There are two passages in the Pentateuch (Exod. xxiii. 28 and Deut. vii. 20) which refer to a mysterious power, designated as "the hornet," which was to help the Israelites in their conquest of Canaan. Now the hornet was the badge of Thotmes III and his successors. And Professor Garstang has suggested that it is a symbolical allusion to Egyptian power. The way that the help of the hornet is finally recognized is also significant. Speaking through

Joshua's mouth, God tells the Israelites, after they had conquered Canaan:

"I sent the hornet before you, which drave them out from before you, even the two kings of the Amorites, not with thy sword, nor with thy bow."

(Joshua xxiv. 12.)

These two kings are specifically referred to as Sihon and Og (Deut. iii. 2, 3, and 8). And their defeat made the Israelites masters of the whole country east of the Jordan. If that were with Egyptian help or connivance, it would account for the fact that Mut Baal was referring the Egyptian official to Joshua, and others, for information about Pella, a city east of the Jordan in Israelite occupation. Further light is cast on the course of political events by the religious history of this period.

It is significant that about 1400 B.C. a unique religious revival began to manifest itself in Egypt. It was in the nature of a return to Monotheism. It has been associated with the name of Akhenaton; but we now know that it began some considerable time before his reign, in the days of his father, Amenhetep III. It may have come through the wives of one or both of these kings. Queen Thyi, the wife of Amenhetep III, was a great personality, and received peculiar honours. She was the daughter of Yua and Tuau, also two celebrated characters. Their origins are obscure; but the late Sir Arthur Weigall, once Chief Inspector of Antiquities in Egypt, wrote that Yua was probably a Syrian prince, whom the conqueror Thotmes III brought back with him to Egypt and educated. The name is not Egyptian, and may have been Yaa or Yau. He became a priest of Min, a deity which, in its form Min-Ra, was a sun-god. Yua's wife, Tuau, may have been a granddaughter of Thotmes III. The wife of Akhenaton was the daughter of Dushratta, king of Mitanni. Her name was Tadukhiba, which the Egyptians changed to Nefertiti. This royal house of Mitanni was of Indro-European descent, and worshipped the Indian trinity—Indra, Mitra, and Varuna.

Whatever the influence, the Egyptians almost reverted to their ancient Monotheism, while a new and wonderful art superseded the older conventional styles. A complete change had come over the court of Egypt since those days of forty years before, when Moses asked for the release of the Israelites. The process of driving out the Hyksos foreigners, and pursuing them into Palestine and Syria, had aroused a hard vindictive nationalism, which wrecked vengeance upon the Israelites because they were of Hyksos connection. A reaction had taken place in royal circles, a reaction which was favourable to the Israelites. It cannot be supposed that the Egyptian rulers lost all knowledge of the Israelites after they entered Sinai under Moses. Egyptian expeditions had visited the peninsula for ages, and left records behind that remain to this day. One such record even belongs to the reign of Thotmes IV (1423–1413 B.C.), a period which falls right into the forty years' wandering. Amenhetep III must have known something about the religious beliefs adopted by the Israelites under the leadership of Moses. They were more in harmony with his own than were the polytheistic practices of the petty kings of Palestine and Syria, as evidenced at Ras Shamra. Further, the Israelites observed the code of moral laws recognized in Egypt; they were *reliable* people; the contents of the Tel el Amarna Letters make it obvious, that the petty kings and rulers of Palestine and Syria who wrote them, were the reverse. No wonder they appealed in vain for Egyptian help against the Hebrews.

The main purpose of Old Testament history is to record God's dealings with His Chosen People, and to trace events to moral and spiritual causes. These are commonly passed over by world historians, who present external causes and ignore internal ones. It is due to the Science of Archæology, and the information it has gleaned from the monuments, that we now have knowledge of a number of external causes that throw light upon the Sacred Narrative.

The geographical position of Palestine rendered it peculiarly liable to become the battle-ground between Egypt, and any great military power who came down from the north. The country is only about the size of Wales. Its interior far more rugged and mountainous. But on the coast there is a strip of fairly flat land, about fifteen miles wide, along which ran a road parallel with the Mediterranean from south to north, until the flat land is blocked by the great mass of Mount Carmel. There the route passed inland over the lower slopes of that mountain, and debouched upon the great plain of Esdraelon. It has already been pointed out how, before the days of Abraham, the native dynasties that ruled in Egypt had been driven far up the Nile by the Hyksos invaders, who came through Syria and Palestine. When these invaders were at last driven out, the Egyptians, for strategic reasons, determined in future to hold the Plain of Esdraelon in the north. So the flat coastland corridor of Palestine became an Egyptian line of communication. It was necessary to clear this route, to keep it clear, and to safeguard it. That had been the aim and object of all Egyptian conquests of Palestine, before Joshua and the Israelites entered the country. And that continued to be the aim and object of the Egyptians all through Old Testament history. It was never an easy task, because the steep and rocky hills and valleys that ran parallel with the route afforded excellent shelter to marauders. It became necessary, therefore, that the people who occupied these districts should be friendly to Egypt. Such was the strategic position, and such it continued to be for many centuries. In the latter part of this volume it will be noted that eight hundred years later, in the days of Jeremiah the prophet, Babylon carried Judah into captivity because it sided with Egypt.

Bearing these facts in mind, it is not surprising that one of the most significant discoveries in Biblical Archæology is the persistent presence of Egyptian remains upon and near this route through Palestine. They belong to the period covered by the Books of

Joshua and Judges. On the other hand, if Bible students search to see what the Old Testament has to say about Egypt during these periods, they will find—NOTHING AT ALL. The silence in face of archæological facts is so remarkable that it must have a meaning. Authorities have tried to escape from the dilemma by suggesting that the Israelites did not leave Egypt till two centuries later. But this does not account for still later evidences of Egyptian occupation, still not recorded at all in the Old Testament. If the facilities, to use no stronger expression, which the Egyptians gave the Israelites for the conquest of Canaan really took place, they must have been regarded by the latter as Providential. And since the purpose of the Old Testament is to provide a historical account of God's dealings with His Chosen People, the Israelite scribes omitted all references to Egypt. There is a monument of the Pharaoh Mernepthah (1223 B.C.) which claims that he severely chastised Israel. Nothing is said about the incident in the Book of Judges. One can only assume it to be omitted because at other times the Egyptian rule had been helpful.

Professor Garstang has pointed out that, on the basis of the Jericho chronology, the periods of Rest which the Israelites enjoyed, as recorded in the Book of Judges, were precisely the periods in Egyptian history when the power of the Pharaoh dominated their country. Even apart from the fact that no nation's historian cares to record help that his country received from outside sources, there is an even stronger reason why the history of Israel should omit all reference to Egyptian help. It is a religious one. Year by year, at the great ceremony of the Passover, the Israelites were reminded of their deliverance from Egypt. Their scribes did not dim the glory of this event by recording that forty years afterwards, and indeed for succeeding centuries, Egypt was of considerable service to them. Yet there are reminders of an indirect character. The Psalmist, singing of the events associated with Israel's conquest of Canaan, says:

"For they gat not the land in possession by their own
            sword,
  Neither did their own arm save them:
  But thy right hand, and thine arm,
  And the light of thy countenance,
  Because thou hadst a favour unto them."

                                    (Psalm xliv. 3.)

So the Egyptian assistance was taken as part of the Divine Plan. Egypt did not help the Israelites for their sakes, she helped them for her own. They were peace-loving and reliable people, as compared with the idolatrous Canaanites, Hittites, and Amorites, etc., therefore it suited Egypt's purpose that they should settle there and enjoy her protection.

The supposed site of Ai, the next city that Joshua captured, was examined by Professor Garstang, who claims to have found there some similar Late Bronze Age fragments to those at Jericho. So apparently did other explorers. But as a more recent excavator claims that the city was destroyed in the early Bronze

Age, or the time of Abraham, difficulties have arisen which have not yet been cleared up.

The Sacred Narrative then goes on to record the diplomacy by which the Gibeonites contrived to conclude an alliance with the Israelites (Joshua ix.). This incident, or similar ones, is reflected in the Tel el Amarna Letters. The writers of them complain that various chieftains are from time to time betraying Egypt by going over to the Habiru. Again, if the identification of the Hyksos with the Hebrews before Abraham is correct, there would still be men of Hyksos descent in Canaan who would be likely to go over to the Israelites, for they would recognize a common ancestry.

The names of some of the ringleaders in the rebellion —such as Milki-ilu, Aziru, Abd-Ashirta, Abimilki, and Zimrida—seem to be Babylonian renderings of Hebrew names. As are also those of Yank-hamu and Dudu, the very officials of the Pharaoh in Palestine and Syria.

According to the Book of Joshua, after the Gibeonite alliance, a confederacy of five kings—Adonizedek king of Jerusalem, Hoham king of Hebron, Piram king of Jarmuth, Japhia king of Lachish, and Debir king of Eglon—attacked the Gibeonites, who appealed to Joshua for help. He defeated the confederacy, and slew these kings; and when Horam king of Gezer went to the help of Lachish, he also slew him.

The names for the kings of these places in the Tel el Amarna Letters do not at first sight seem to correspond with the Bible ones. On the tablets the cuneiform characters, that stand for the name of the king of Jerusalem, have been interpreted to represent the name Abdi Hiba. Those for the governor of Lachish first stand for the name Yabni-ilu, and then for that of Zimrida. And lastly the king of Gezer is Yapahi. But it has been pointed out by several distinguished scholars that Abdi Hiba should be read Arta Hiba. And that the word "arta" signifies "righteousness," and is equivalent to the Semitic word Zedek. There always existed a special association of Jerusalem with "righteousness" (cf. Heb. vii. 2).

Hipa is the name of a Hittite goddess. The prophet Ezekiel taunted Jerusalem with its Hittite origin. It is improbable that the author of Joshua would be familiar with such a name as Hipa, so he substituted for it the title Adonai=Lord, and Zedek, the equivalent of Arta.

When the other names are compared, it will be noticed that the king of Gezer is Yapahi. This is the exact equivalent of Japhia mentioned in Joshua as the king of Lachish. It is known that the two cities were connected with each other; and reference has just been made to the attempt of Horam of Gezer to come to the rescue of Lachish. The Tel el Amarna tablets record the capture by his foes of Zimrida of Lachish. After that event, it is probable that Yapahi, or Japhia, took on the government of both Gezer and Lachish. When he was slain by Joshua, after the battle of the five kings (Joshua x. 23), then his successor at Gezer, Horam, tried in turn to save Lachish. This would tend to reconcile the two narratives.

The fact of the matter is that those who have sought the proper sequences, the proper associations, and the proper dates, of the Tel el Amarna Letters, have laboured under grave difficulties and embarrassments. They have tried to the best of their ability to put tablets in their right order in their particular group, and assign that group's relation to other groups. But it has been work of a highly speculative character. To make matters worse, all attempts to correlate such conclusions with the statements made in the Book of Joshua, were rendered still more difficult and even impossible. There was no sort of certainty about the Bible chronology of this period. The Jericho excavations have now definitely fixed the date of the Israelites' entry into Canaan. This fact alone calls for an entirely fresh examination of the Tel el Amarna tablets. And to be satisfactory, it should be made by men whose minds are not obsessed with ideas about the "mythical" character of the Sacred Narrative. The excavations of Jericho have proved there was nothing mythical about *that* story. There would seem to be no doubt whatever that really unprejudiced scholars can now throw a great deal of light on the conquest of Canaan by the Israelites. That light may not be entirely in accordance with our past ideas of what we supposed happened, but it will supplement the Sacred Narrative and not violate it. There is a vast distinction between these two forms of treatment. The one is constructive and the other is destructive. It may be that the grave mistake of academic authorities has often been that they have recognized and accorded preference to the latter. It has been already suggested that the Gibeonite alliance with Joshua, may have played a much more important part in the Israelite conquest of Palestine, than we have been accustomed to assume was the case. And when as young people we read our Bibles, we supposed that those events recorded in the earlier chapters of Joshua followed at short intervals one upon another.

But it is quite probable that some years elapsed before the king of Jerusalem formed his confederacy to attack the Gibeonites. Such an interval would be occupied by Abdi Khiba in writing constant letters of appeal to the Pharaoh for help. In such letters he, and others, refer to those who are in league with the Habiru to betray them and their cities. These might well be the Gibeonites.

The excavations now proceeding at Lachish will no doubt ultimately throw considerable light on events. But it is a long way down to the Joshua level of the city. Meantime, it is worthy of notice that a great Egyptian scarab has been found there, in a ruined temple outside the city. This scarab definitely dates itself to 1403 B.C. It probably belonged originally to the still earlier temple, which lay beneath the one in which it was found. The fact that the scarab was preserved, and used to adorn a temple destroyed a century later, testifies that the Egyptian connection was recognized by the Israelites. Lachish is mentioned several times in the Tel el Amarna tablets, and further reference will be made to them in the account of its excavations.

Professor Garstang has suggested that the sentence on tablet No. 289, which reads:

"Labaya and the land of Shechem have gone over to the Habiru,"

refers to the secession of Shechem to the Hebrews. The place became a centre of Israelite worship, and from there Joshua made his farewell address to the assembled tribes. The bones of Joseph, which the Israelites had brought up with them from Egypt, were buried at Shechem.

Joshua's campaign in the north of Palestine is described in the eleventh chapter of the Book that bears his name. A confederation of nations covering a large area around the Sea of Galilee, and extending even to the snow-topped Mount Hermon, united against him. Joshua suddenly surprised and attacked them by the waters of Merom. This place does not seem to have been Lake Huleh through which the Jordan flows to the Sea of Galilee. It is called in the Septuagint "the waters of Maron," and Professor Garstang places it at the foot of a high mountain —Jebel Marun, where there are copious springs of water. He points out, in his book, *Joshua—Judges*, that to this day the natives of Galilee, and of southern Lebanon, meet here once a week for market purposes. And the nature of the ground is of such a character, that though the horses and chariots mentioned in the narrative could be transported there, they could not there be used against the Israelites in battle.

The defeat of the confederation led to the capture and burning of Hazor. The site of this city was unknown until it was identified by Professor Garstang under its modern name of El Kedah. It stands on the present main road ten miles north of the Sea of Galilee in the direction of Lake Huleh. In the year 1928 the author collaborated with Professor Garstang in an expedition there, and an examination and some excavations were made. The site is one of the largest in Palestine, being twelve hundred yards long and six hundred yards wide. It was surrounded by sloping ramparts of beaten earth, no less than sixty feet high, evidence of the Hyksos occupation. On its south side this enclosure was dominated by the mound of the city proper, rising one hundred and sixty feet above the level of the neighbouring road. It was estimated that the city itself would contain a population of four thousand people, while the camp enclosure would hold thirty thousand, along with quantities of horses and chariots.

Hazor was in a highly flourishing condition about 1800 B.C. when the Hyksos were ruling Egypt, and when Joseph was governor of that land. A great stone wall had been added to its other defences, and houses had encroached upon the camp enclosure. But the ruins supplied evidence that later on Thotmes III, in his Megiddo campaigns, had captured Hazor and bespoiled it, even as he records in his inscriptions. Hazor had risen to power again about a century later, when Joshua overwhelmed and burnt it. Ample evidences of this conflagration have been left behind, and the examination of two thousand five hundred pottery fragments associated with it, satisfied Professor Garstang that the camp must have been destroyed about 1400 B.C. And that though the city proper was inhabited again, the destruction of the camp enclosure was complete and final. There is a record of the destruction in the Tel el Amarna tablets, contained in the reminder of an Egyptian envoy:

"Let my lord the king recall what Hazor and its king have already had to endure."

The pursuit of the Israelites, after the battle with the confederation, brought them into Syria as far north as Sidon. The tribes of Asher and Zebulon occupied these northern territories. It is significant that their names occur in the Ras Shamra tablets (1400–1350 B.C.) although associated with a mythological story of Abraham's time of a much earlier date. There are other mentions of the tribe of Asher in the Egyptian records between 1317 and 1229 B.C., where it is located at its correct place in the Promised Land. The ingenious theory that not all the tribes of Israel went down into Egypt, was used to account for their presence in Palestine, when the Exodus was believed to have occurred in 1220 B.C. With the Exodus fixed at 1440 B.C., such deviations from the Sacred Narrative are no longer necessary.

Tourists who go to the Holy Land all visit the Lake of Galilee. It is associated with the Ministry of Our Lord Jesus Christ. And an atmosphere of peace exists there which is lacking in Jerusalem. The various traditional sites mentioned in the New Testament are pointed out; and among them the Horns of Hattim, said to have been the Mount of Beatitudes.

On a memorable occasion in March, some three or four years ago, the writer left the excellent motor road from Nazareth, some miles or so before it descended below sea level to Tiberias, in order to visit this place. The way lay across fields covered with varieties of beautiful wild flowers.

Somewhere hereabouts the last great battle of the Crusaders was fought, which led to their expulsion from the Holy Land. A short but steep climb at the finish led over a pointed rocky ridge down into a great amphitheatre. The place was obviously the crater of an extinct volcano. Some projecting pinnacles of rock, that rose above the rim, gave the title of the Horns of Hattim. There is a wonderful view of the deep blue Lake of Galilee from one side of the crater's edge. The spot is peculiarly peaceful, and lends itself to Beatitudes. But long before the time of Christ, before the days that Joshua captured Hazor, the crater had housed a Bronze Age settlement and encampment. The name occurs in the lists of Thotmes III as one of the places he captured. One can almost trace a route by which the chariots and horses could have found shelter there. All this district abounds in ancient Bronze Age camps, whose exploration may throw further light upon the battles once waged around and beyond the plain of Esdraelon.

The Israelite conquest of South Syria, which was included in the upper part of Canaan, presents even more problems than their occupations of Palestine. The Bible account is vague, and the Tel el Amarna Letters involve us in a medley of nationalities. We are hampered by inadequate knowledge of the history of the time. Authorities have emphasized the view that the Hittites led this invasion. Indeed they have been puzzled as to how the Sagaz, or Hebrews, came to take part in it at all.

Further problems arise in connection with the people of the Mitanni. It is true that their kings were Aryans, but there seems a good deal of mystery associated with their subjects. It will be remembered that Amenhetep IV (Akhenaton) married a daughter of the king of Mitanni, and it has been suggested that influences from there may have brought about his monotheism. And then again the father of that Pharaoh's mother, Queen Thyi, came from Syria. Did the Egyptian monotheism come through such channels? The situation appears to be rendered more difficult by the fact that the king of Mitanni ruled over people who did not belong to his race. And indeed it has been suggested that he assumed the title of king of the Hittites, and wrote letters under several different names. Then the Arameans have also been associated with the Mitanni; and the patriarch Jacob was called an

Aramean. It will be remembered that he married the daughters of his relative Laban. And that his mother Rebekah was Laban's sister. The word Laban is related to Lebanon. In the days of Moses when an Israelite made an offering of first fruits he was required to say:

"An Aramean (Syrian) ready to perish was my father." (Deut. xxvi. 5.)

One could have understood the expression if the words had been, "A Hebrew ready to perish"—but why an Aramean?

The very words of Psalm civ., which is closely related to an Egyptian poem known as Akhenaton's hymn, link both up with Syria. It is rather singular that authorities, in attempting to unravel this tangle of the Syrian invasion, seem to have overlooked the fact that the Israelites had previously occupied the Amorite kingdoms on the far side of the Jordan. And that this northern territory gave them an excellent approach to Syria. The accounts on the Tel el Amarna tablets confuse the Israelites with the Amorites. This is amply accounted for by the fact that they came from the former Amorite land. Again the Letters indicate that the king of the Mitanni sided with the Israelite invaders; which of course he would do, if the influences favourable to them in Egypt had come through his relatives there.

The Book of Joshua tells us that the Israelites' invasion reached Tyre and Sidon, but does not say that they captured these cities. The Tel el Amarna tablets, on the other hand, assert that they were captured by such hostile forces. Thus, the ruler of Sidon writes to Amenhetep:

"Behold all my cities which the king has given into my hands have fallen into the hands of the Habiru."

The ruler of Gebal reports:

"Abdasherah has conquered beyond the land of the Amorites; the city of Sidon has submitted to the occupation of his allies, the lands are for this Habiru so now there is none who is a friend to me."

The Book of Joshua's account of the invasion of Canaan records his battles and his victories. The Tel el Amarna Letters record the results of those victories in the defection of the native population from their nominal rulers. For some time it would seem as though the covenant with the Hivites, or Gibeonites, obtained by strategy, was the only example of compromise (Joshua xi. 19). But later on other covenants were made. These were sternly reprobated by "the Angel of the Lord" (Judges ii. 1–4). But they corroborate the evidence of the Tel el Amarna Letters in regard to northern Palestine and Syria.

# V

## LACHISH (1400–587 B.C.), JUDAH'S CHIEF FENCED CITY

THE excavation of this important place began in the autumn of A.D. 1932, under the direction of Mr. J. L. Starkey, and has been continued in each succeeding winter. The funds for carrying on the work of the Expedition have been largely found by the late Sir Henry Wellcome, and since his death by his Trustees. A fuller reference to those who have contributed to this great exploration will be found in the Preface.

The now definitely established site of the city of Lachish is the mound of Tell Duweir in the low hill country of South Palestine. The usual route is by motor-car from Jerusalem, along the main road towards Hebron. Immediately before entering that city, the road to the site branches off sharply to the right. There follows a steep descent from the Judean highlands to the Shephelah, or low hill country, and on to Beit Jibrin, once the Roman town of Eleutheropolis. Then a left turn to the south is made, and Tell Duweir is reached after six miles over a rough road. The journey all the way at present occupies about two hours. An alternative route from Jerusalem is westwards along the Jaffa road, and by turning south at Bab al Wad.

—— Tell Duweir is some twenty-three miles east of Gaza and about twenty miles inland from the sea. Its summit is <u>nine hundred</u> feet above sea level. It commands an extensive view, in one direction right over the Philistine plain, to the blue waters of the Mediterranean; and in others over bare, rugged, hilly country. The Tell itself is an extension of a limestone ridge, which is surrounded on four sides by valleys that isolate it from adjoining hills, and make it almost an island site. In ancient times these hills must have served as a natural barrier between the Philistines on the coastlands below, and the more elevated territory of the tribe of Judah. The area on the top of the Tell Duweir is twenty-two acres, and its base covers thirty-nine acres. Its mean height, above the valley in which it rises, is one hundred and thirty feet. A cross section, cut into the side of the mound, showed that there were no less than sixty feet of debris below its present summit down to bed-rock. This great mass represents the accumulated remains of many cities built one upon the other. The earliest must belong to a very remote period of time, probably between 4000–3000 B.C. That would actually be one or two thousand years before Abraham entered Canaan. And it is surprising to find that, judging from the surroundings, the site enjoyed its halcyon age in those early days. Then the Tell itself seems to have been used as the citadel, or acropolis, of a much larger settlement without defences beneath it. Like ancient Jericho it must then have been a place for refuge on the approach of enemies, rather than a permanent lodging place.

This very remote period of time may have been the golden age of Palestine as well as Egypt. It would be before Sargon of Accad, and his successors, brought their Semitic Sumerian civilization from the Euphrates, to trouble a pastoral and peaceable folk, who only desired to be left to mind their own business. Reference has been made, in the chapter on Moses, to the writings on the interior of the pyramids of Sakkara in Egypt. The religious and moral atmosphere there indicated, may have been shared with Palestine, for they date back to this period. Perhaps we shall know more when the sixty feet of debris that remain of Lachish have been excavated and examined; but that may take a long time.

The identification of this site of Tell Duweir, with the Bible city of Lachish, may puzzle those who recall the excavations made in Palestine before the Great War. And those who look for Lachish on most of the older maps of Palestine will experience a similar bewilderment. As long ago as 1890, the Palestine Exploration Fund began to excavate a site further south in Palestine, and only sixteen miles from Gaza, named Tell el Hesy. This came to be regarded as the site of Lachish. And a cuneiform tablet was found there that mentions the name of Zimrida, already familiar to us as associated with Lachish in the Tel el Amarna Letters. But the identity of Tell el Hesy with

Lachish, came to be regarded as doubtful, because it was not a ruin of sufficient size. At length the distinguished American archæologist, Dr. Albright, drew attention to the fact that the great mound of Tell Duweir was seven miles from Eleutheropolis (Beit Jibrein), stated to be the distance of Lachish by Eusebius in the *Onomasticon*, while Tell el Hesy was more than twice as far away. As will be seen, the excavations at Tell Duweir have now definitely established its identity with Lachish. So maps that still place it at Tell el Hesy need correction. Tell el Hesy may represent the Old Testament city of Eglon.

The earliest mention of Lachish occurs in the Book of Joshua (Joshua x. 3). Reference has been made to it in an earlier chapter. The identification of its king Japhia, with the Yapahi of the Tel el Amarna tablets, has been also pointed out. There are half a dozen references to Lachish in this correspondence, which is dated between 1400–1360 B.C. Zimrida, the Egyptian governor, would seem, from the Letters, to have been seized and perhaps murdered there. Lachish is represented in some of the Letters as siding with the Habiru or Hebrews. That may have either been before or after Joshua's capture. It is recorded in Joshua x. 32 that the siege only lasted two days. As yet the excavators have no knowledge of the strength of its defences at that time. But if they were of a formidable character, the inexperience of the Israelites in siege operations suggest that internal dissensions may have led to its rapid fall. That would be quite in accord with the

Tel el Amarna accounts of the attitude of its inhabitants to the Habiru. In writing of the defences of Lachish in the days of Joshua, one is reminded of discoveries already made on the slopes of the Tell. The sloping glacis, or ramp, characteristic of the Hyksos occupation, must have then been, as it still is to-day, a prominent feature of the defences. Such fortifications resemble those sometimes used in this country before the Roman occupation. Maiden Castle in Dorsetshire, recently excavated by Dr. Mortimer Wheeler, is an example. The Hyksos glacis at Lachish constructed at an angle of about 35°, with a hard slippery surface of limestone plaster, must have been a formidable position to scale. It exposed its assailants to a direct hail of arrows, stones, and other missiles, at every stage of their approach. Some shelter from missiles can be found close to a high perpendicular wall, and it could also be breached with siege engines. But there was none for those who assailed a Hyksos glacis, and it could not be battered down. The Egyptians learned in course of time how to deal with these sloping fortifications; and the evidence of their method has been found at Lachish.

Along the interior of the glacis, and parallel to it, there runs a low subterranean tunnel, some four feet in width and height. It has a floor beaten hard by the passing of many feet. The tunnel was entered from a point low down in the moat. There would be a number of exits from it on the city side. These passages through the glacis were probably the work of one of the armies of Thotmes III, which thus passed through the Hyksos defence of Lachish, in the days when Moses was living in the land of Midian.

Lachish may have been a chariot city, or posting station, of the Egyptians as far back as the time of Joshua. The Old Testament tells us that in later centuries Solomon had a great number of horses and chariots. We read:

"And Solomon had forty thousand stalls of horses for his chariots, and twelve thousand horsemen. And those officers provided victual for king Solomon, and for all that came unto king Solomon's table, every man in his month; they let nothing be lacking. Barley also and straw for the horses and swift steeds brought they unto the place where the officers were, every man according to his charge."

(1 Kings iv. 26, 27, 28.)

The existence of a vast system of wheeled transport in such ancient times, is surprising, and almost unbelievable; yet stalls for four hundred and fifty horses have been found in the excavations of Megiddo, on the plain of Esdraelon in northern Palestine.

Although Joshua conquered Canaan more than four centuries before Solomon, the Egyptian records prove that, even then, a complete system of transport and postal service between Egypt, Palestine, Syria and beyond, was in existence. It has already been suggested that the Hyksos first introduced horses and chariots into Egypt. It would be during their rule that the transport of the patriarch Jacob and his household in wagons from Canaan to Egypt took place (Gen. xlv. and xlvi.).

The later records of Thotmes III contain the account of the capture of many horses and chariots at Megiddo and elsewhere. And still later, the horses and chariots of the Pharaoh of the Exodus pursued the Israelites into the Red Sea. So it is natural to find that vehicles were being used by the Egyptians, for peace as well as for war, in a transport service throughout Palestine, before and after, Joshua invaded the country. The excavations inside Lachish have not yet reached the remains of Solomon's city, much less that of Joshua; so it is uncertain whether stables are there like those at Megiddo. But the remains of a building outside the city walls may prove to be related to this ancient Palestine horse transport and posting service. The Expedition has described it as a Khan or Inn, and the site of its ruins proved to be admirably suited for the camp-house of the Expedition. An alignment of tall standing stones and flagged floors suggest stabling. The neighbouring pottery indicates that it was built about 2000 B.C. or earlier, the very time that horses came into general use. Like the city itself, it finally met its fate through fire. Its incendiaries were probably some of Nebuchadnezzar's soldiers.

The Israelites themselves, after their occupation of Canaan, would be guided by the prohibition of Moses:

"Only he (the king of Israel) shall not multiply horses to himself, nor cause the people to return to Egypt, to the end that he should multiply horses;

forasmuch as the Lord hath said unto you, Ye shall
henceforth return no more that way."

(Deut. xvii. 16.)

After the days of Joshua, the Old Testament tells us
nothing about Lachish for nearly five hundred years.
But the excavations have already brought some evidences to light of the intervening period. Thus, the
ruins of three temples, superimposed one above the
other, and situated outside the city walls, have yielded
a great deal of valuable information, as well as other
relics from tombs of that period. In the city itself,
however, with some exceptions, the levels of occupation
below Nebuchadnezzar's destruction have not yet been
dug out. The five centuries of silence in the Sacred
Narrative is ended by the statement that Rehoboam,
the son of Solomon, fortified Lachish among other
cities of Judah (2 Chron. xi. 9). This would be in the
years 923–919 B.C. It would seem that this fondness
for fortifications aroused the wrath of Shishak, king of
Egypt, who came up against him with his own army
of twelve hundred chariots, and sixty thousand horsemen, as well as a great force of auxiliaries. The fenced
cities of Judah fell before these overwhelming numbers,
and Rehoboam had to make his peace with Shishak by
parting with all the gold of Jerusalem (2 Chron. xii.).
Rehoboam's work at Lachish appears to be contained
in a double defence wall round the city, which formed
the basis of the fortifications of later times. The lower
courses of this wall are made up of large blocks of the
local limestone of the district, laid dry without mortar,

and wedged in position by small stones at a pronounced batter. The middle courses are more nearly vertical, and are faced with a thick lime plaster. They are in regular sections and run back obliquely from the lower courses. The recurring angles convey the effect of panelling. The upper courses are of unbaked mud brick. These defences had been buttressed and strengthened by flanking towers.

Wherever it has been examined the revetment itself goes down to bed-rock; and in places fourteen courses of stonework still remain to a height of over twenty-five feet. It completely encircles the Tell, and is built of large limestone blocks in regular courses. In the north-east corner, in an angle at the turning of this revetment, the excavators came across a well, lined with stone to a depth of twenty-six feet; and then cut down through the rock to the water level, some hundred and twenty-two feet from the surface of the soil. At the north-west turning there are five large buttresses; and at the south-west corner the revetment joins on to a great bastion, which contained both an outer and inner gateway. A steep roadway led up to this entrance to the city, flanked on its east side by three tiers of fortifications, which dominated and protected it. This brief description gives some idea of the exterior of the fortifications of Lachish as revealed by excavation. But they would not all be the work of Rehoboam, and it is as yet uncertain whether the city withstood a siege from the soldiers of Shishak, although grim evidence has been left of later ones.

Lachish is next mentioned as the refuge to which a king of Judah—Amaziah by name—fled from a conspiracy laid against him in Jerusalem. The escape served him no purpose for he was followed and slain there (2 Kings xiv. 19). The narrative recounts that his body was brought back on horses, and there is a further reference to the city, by one of the prophets, which again associates it with horses:

"Bind the chariot to the swift steed, O inhabitant of Lachish: she was the beginning of sin to the daughter of Zion: for the transgressions of Israel were found in thee."                                    (Micah i. 13.)

But the most important event associated with Lachish in the Old Testament was its siege by Sennacherib the great king of Assyria. He has left to posterity a detailed account of his doings at Lachish. The stone Bas-Reliefs depicting his siege, which he had carved to adorn the interior of his palace at Nineveh, are now in the British Museum. Some reproductions of them are used to illustrate this volume, and they will be described in detail in Chapter XI. It will be seen from a study of the illustrations that Sennacherib both attacked the city by direct assault, and breached its walls. These still bear ample traces of his handiwork. Against the face of one of the walls, near the gateway, there has been found the bronze crest of a helmet similar to those worn on the helmets of Assyrian spearmen, as illustrated on the Bas-Reliefs.

The account of Sennacherib's invasion of the kingdom of Judah, and the demands he made upon its king Hezekiah, constitute some of the most dramatic passages in the Old Testament. It would seem as though Lachish bore the brunt of this Assyrian invasion. Thus:

"Now in the fourteenth year of king Hezekiah did Sennacherib, king of Assyria, come up against all the fenced cities of Judah, and took them. And Hezekiah king of Judah sent to the king of Assyria *to Lachish*, saying, I have offended; return from me; that which thou puttest on me will I bear."

(2 Kings xviii. 13–14.)

Sennacherib thereupon demanded three hundred talents of silver, and thirty talents of gold. Later, the Assyrian king thought he could obtain the surrender of Jerusalem as well. Thus:

"And the king of Assyria sent Tartan, and Rabsaris, and Rabshakeh *from Lachish* to king Hezekiah with a great army unto Jerusalem." (Verse 17.)

The names of Sennacherib's emissaries are not personal names, but the titles of his three chief officials. There follows the arrogant speech of Rabshakeh familiar to all Bible readers. It suggests that Hezekiah was involved in the war because he had sided with Egypt. Hezekiah then appealed to Isaiah the prophet for Divine Help, which was promised him. The Narrative continues:

"So Rabshakeh returned, and found the king of Assyria warring against Libnah, *for he had heard that he was departed from Lachish.*" (2 Kings xix. 8.)

# LACHISH (1400–587 B.C.)

When Sennacherib heard that Tirkhakah, king of Ethiopia, was come out to fight against him, he again sent messengers to Hezekiah, this time with a letter. After he had read it, the king "spread it before the Lord" and prayed. Then Isaiah came and told him that his prayer was heard, and that he would receive Divine Protection. Whereupon a calamity overtook the Assyrian Army of one hundred and eighty-five thousand men, which it is thought consisted of an outbreak of virulent plague; and Sennacherib returned to Assyria.

The account of events in the Book of Chronicles commences:

"After this did Sennacherib king of Assyria send his servants to Jerusalem (*now he was before Lachish and all his power with him*)." (2 Chron. xxxii. 9.)

The narrative is much abbreviated as compared with the one in Kings, and the subsequent destruction of Sennacherib's army is limited to the mighty men of valour, and the leaders and captains (verse 21).

A third account, in the Book of the Prophet Isaiah, resembles the account in the Book of Kings, but the opening verses, concerning Hezekiah's original acquiescence, are omitted. The salient passage referring to Lachish is as follows:

"And the King of Assyria sent Rabshakeh *from Lachish* to Jerusalem unto king Hezekiah *with a great army*." (Isaiah xxxvi. 2.)

It has even been suggested that, since there is no direct statement in these narratives that Sennacherib captured Lachish, he may have failed to do so. But what is known to-day does not leave the matter in any doubt. Afterwards, judging from the Sacred Narrative, Sennacherib moved on to the siege of Libnah, and the disaster probably overtook his army in his camp there.

It is possible that Sennacherib had the Bas-Reliefs of the siege carved after his return, for people to forget the subsequent failure of this Expedition. It is evident that Lachish must have been of such importance to him, that he could not leave its siege to go himself to Jerusalem. It guarded the route to Egypt. Libnah lay at the mouth of the Vale of Elah, some fifteen miles north of Lachish. It was perhaps at the time the key to an advance with Sennacherib's whole army on Jerusalem. Its possession would have protected his rear from an Egyptian army coming to the rescue of Jerusalem.

Now as it happens, what is known as the Taylor prism in the British Museum records Sennacherib's account of this campaign. It is a matter of considerable interest to compare it with the Old Testament references. For the comparison is a similar one to that of the Tel el Amarna Letters in their relation to the Book of Joshua. Sennacherib's account describes the external course of events, but is silent about his subsequent disaster. The Bible account is reticent concerning the extent of Hezekiah's initial surrender;

and the investment of the city is only implied in the words that Rabshakeh came up *with a great army* against Jerusalem. The emphasis of the Sacred Narrative is laid on the fact that the city was saved by prayer, and by Divine Aid in answer to prayer. And according to his own account, though closely invested, Sennacherib never took Jerusalem. The incident is used as an example for all time of the Deity's intervention on behalf of those who humble themselves, and put their trust in Him, rather than rely on external help.

Sennacherib's version informs us that the inhabitants of the Philistine city of Ekron had made their king Padi captive, and sent him bound to Hezekiah at Jerusalem. This Padi, king of Ekron, along with Mitenti, king of Ashdod, and Silli-bel, king of Gaza, were allies of Assyria. In other words, they controlled the trade routes into Egypt for Sennacherib, which the Egyptians desired to have in their own hands.

Sennacherib marched down from Syria with his army, and defeated the Egyptian and Ethiopian forces, sent to help the Ekronites, at "Altaku." He besieged and captured that place and Timnah. He then impaled the leaders of the Ekron rebellion round their city. Padi was brought back from Jerusalem, and reinstated as king of Ekron. It may be assumed Hezekiah gave him up to Sennacherib as part of the ransom. Hezekiah was probably regarded by Sennacherib as responsible for this attempt to shut off the Assyrian route into Egypt.

Sennacherib records the punishment he meted out as follows:

"As for Hezekiah, the Jew, who did not submit to my yoke, forty-six of his strong walled cities, I besieged by escalade, by bringing up siege engines, by storming, by mines, tunnels, and breaches. I took two hundred thousand people, great and small, male and female; horses, mules, asses, camels, cattle, and sheep without number. As for Hezekiah himself I shut him up in Jerusalem, his royal city, like a caged bird. I threw up earthworks against him. I turned back to his misery anyone coming out of his city gate. . . . As for Hezekiah the splendour of my majesty overcame him, and the Arabs and his mercenary soldiers which he had brought in to strengthen Jerusalem deserted him. Thirty talents of gold, and eight hundred talents of silver, gems, antimony, jewels, precious stones, ivory couches, and chairs, elephants' hide, ivory, maple, cedar, all kinds of treasures, beside his daughter, his harem, and his musicians, male and female, he had them brought after me to Nineveh my royal city."

It has been pointed out that there is no mention of Lachish in this account. The name of the place that figures most prominently in the fighting is transcribed "Altaku"; Sennacherib defeated the Egyptians there, and afterwards besieged and captured it. It may be suggested that the characters transcribed and interpreted as "Altaku" represent Lachish. All this happened in the year 701 B.C.

But to return to what the excavations tell us. Although at the time of writing the Expedition has not reached the level of the interior of the city of Sennacherib's time, yet in two rock tombs underneath the mound they have come across the remains of some two thousand bodies, indiscriminately thrown in after his siege. These tombs proved on examination to have been originally used for interments of a much earlier date. So far as is known at present, a hundred years elapsed before Lachish had to face another siege. In the meantime the excavations reveal that the wide breaches in the walls made by Sennacherib's soldiers were repaired. And a great mass of masonry, built across the road near the gateway, made it proof against the approach of battering rams. A cuneiform tablet from Nineveh records that the Assyrians had a military governor at Lachish for twenty-five years after its capture, and a Philistine garrison.

In the year 604 B.C. Nebuchadnezzar ascended the throne of Babylon. And the age-long conflict between the northern nations and Egypt began again. If reference is made to the last chapters of the Second Book of the Kings, it will be seen that Pharaoh-Nechoh made Jehoiakim king of Judah (2 Kings xxiii. 34) and put him under tribute to him. But in the fourth year of his reign Nebuchadnezzar invaded Judah, doubtless on account of differences with Egypt, and Jehoiakim served him three years, and then rebelled against him (2 Kings xxiv. 1).

There ensued a period of considerable disruption in the rule of Jehoiakim. It is important to notice it, because the excavations of Lachish disclose two distinct layers of burnt debris, sufficiently close to each other to render it improbable that one of them may be identified with Sennacherib's conquest of the city a century earlier. The Sacred Narrative records that:

"The Lord sent against him (Jehoiakim) bands of the Chaldeans and bands of the Syrians, and bands of the Moabites, and bands of the children of Ammon."

(2 Kings xxiv. 2.)

The Book of Chronicles tells us that Nebuchadnezzar came again in the eleventh year of Jehoiakim's reign, and bound him in fetters to carry him to Babylon (2 Chron. xxxvi. 6); but judging from the account in the Kings (2 Kings xxiv. 6) he died before his transportation. Further details concerning his end will be found on page 215. He was succeeded by his son Jehoiachin, whom Nebuchadnezzar also removed, and superseded with an uncle, Zedekiah. He in turn rebelled, and Nebuchadnezzar besieged Jerusalem from the ninth to the eleventh year of his reign, and then carried him to Babylon (2 Kings xxv. 1–7).

It would seem to have been at this time that Nebuchadnezzzar besieged and finally destroyed Lachish. The event is recorded thus:

"Then Jeremiah the prophet spake all these words unto Zedekiah king of Judah in Jerusalem, when the king of Babylon's army fought against Jerusalem, and against all the cities of Judah that were left, against Lachish and against Azekah, for these alone remained of the cities of Judah as fenced cities."

(Jeremiah xxxiv. 6, 7.)

There are no details extant of the final sieges and

captures of Lachish by the Babylonians. But from the evidence that remains of them, they must have been of a different character to the Assyrian siege of a century earlier. Sennacherib's Bas-Reliefs display the battering of the walls, and the storming of the place. These may be said to be orthodox methods of overcoming a city's defences. But the Babylonians adopted a different plan. They cut down the olive, the oak, and the fig trees, that flourished in the surrounding neighbourhood, and with other combustible material, they piled them in places at the foot of the walls, especially at the bases of the repaired breaches. They then set fire to them; and these great bonfires were kept burning night and day, till they reduced to powder the limestone blocks of which the walls were built, and caused their collapse.

A tour of the exterior of the Tell supplies impressive evidence of the intense conflagrations which have raged outside its defences. In places the ruins of the lower wall are overlaid with great heaps of lime. The south-west corner of the city's exterior suffered most from this attack, and it was perhaps from thence that the fire enveloped the whole city.

The remains of burnt olive stones among the charred pieces of wood outside the city walls, indicate that the burning down of the defences occurred in July or August, which corresponds with the "fourth month" when Jerusalem also fell.

Such was Nebuchadnezzar's terrible handiwork in South Palestine. Perhaps it saved his army from the slaughter attendant on storming the defences of Lachish after the manner of Sennacherib. But it was done at the cost of the city and its contents, which, like Jericho, would be burnt but not plundered. And at what a cost to the city's defenders, to its inhabitants, and to the surrounding countryside! More than two thousand five hundred years have passed over those hills round Lachish since Nebuchadnezzar denuded them of their oaks, and their olives, and their fig trees. They are still bleak, desolate, and bare. The Wellcome Expedition has spent five winters there, winters when rain fell in abundance. But there are no trees left to retain both soil and rain, and to shade the bare heights from the scorching summer heat.

The digging up of any ancient site used to involve its being left in a more desolate condition than before. But a better memory is in store for the Wellcome Expedition's work. Even as excavations proceed, the slopes of Tell Duweir are terraced by stones from the ruins, and the terraces filled with fresh earth. At least on the Tell itself, something is being done to bring beneficent nature back to the bare slopes.

The earlier chapters of the Book of Daniel take up the story of Nebuchadnezzar after his return home from the destruction of Lachish, Azekah, and Jerusalem. The end of the Babylonian Dynasty came some forty-seven years after these events. The Fall of Babylon itself is dramatically recorded in the story of Belshazzar's Feast (Dan. v.). Without taking account of their limited knowledge of the period, and relying on

classical history, some critics and commentators used to
deny that Belshazzar ever existed, and others that he
ever ruled. The classics had told them that Nabonidus
was the last king of Babylon. Hundreds and even
thousands of cuneiform tablets of the period have now
been found in Babylonia. Their evidence has established the fact that Belshazzar was made co-regent with
Nabonidus, his father, in the third year of the latter's
reign; they further suggest that Belshazzar's mother
was probably a daughter of Nebuchadnezzar. And
lastly, they demonstrate that this chapter of Daniel
excels all classical and other historical accounts in its
knowledge of the period.

Cyrus, king of Persia, succeeded to the Empire that
had belonged to Nebuchadnezzar. The coming of
Cyrus, as a restorer of the Jews from their captivity,
had been foretold by Isaiah the prophet, two hundred
years before his time. Now that the reality of prediction is being recognized by Science as an established
fact, we are justified in placing more emphasis on this
event, than has been customary for a very considerable
time. Isaiah's prophecy ran as follows:

"I am Jehovah that maketh all things; that stretcheth
forth the heavens alone; that spreadeth abroad the
earth by myself; that frustrateth the tokens of the liars,
and maketh diviners mad; that turneth wise men
backward, and maketh their knowledge foolish; that
confirmeth the word of his servant and performeth the
council of his messengers; that saith of Jerusalem,
She shall be inhabited; and of the cities of Judah,
They shall be built, and I will raise up the waste places

thereof; that saith to the deep, Be dry, and I will dry up thy rivers; *that saith of Cyrus, He is my shepherd*, and shall perform all my pleasure: even saying of Jerusalem, She shall be built; and to the temple, Thy foundation shall be laid."

(Isaiah xliv. 24–28.)

And the prophecy goes on:

"Thus saith Jehovah to his anointed, *to Cyrus*, whose right hand I have holden, to subdue nations before him, and I will loose the loins of kings; to open the doors before him, and the gates shall not be shut; *I will go before thee*, and make the rugged places plain; I will break in pieces the doors of brass, and cut in sunder the bars of iron; and *I will give thee* the treasures of darkness, and hidden riches of secret places, that thou mayest know that I am Jehovah, *which calleth thee by name*, even the God of Israel. For Jacob my servant's sake, and Israel my chosen, *I have called thee by name, I have surnamed thee* though thou hast not known me. I am Jehovah, and there is none else; beside me there is no God: *I will gird thee*, though thou hast not known me: that they may know from the rising of the sun and from the west, that there is none beside me: I am Jehovah, and there is none else. I form the light and create darkness; I make peace and create evil; I am Jehovah that doeth all these things."

(Isaiah xlv. 2–7.)

Josephus, the Jewish historian, recounts how the attention of Cyrus was drawn to these ancient and splendid prophecies concerning himself, and how he then gave the Jews leave to return to their land, and to rebuild Jerusalem and their temple. The proclamation of Cyrus is recited in the Old Testament in the following language:

"Thus saith Cyrus, king of Persia, All the kingdoms of the earth hath the Lord, the God of heaven, given me, and *he hath charged me to build him an house in Jerusalem, which is in Judah.*"

(2 Chron. xxxvi. 23; Ezra i. 2; 1 Esdras ii. 31.)

Josephus gives more exact details, and even recites the official documents Cyrus sent to the Persian governors in Syria.

The Persians have left the mark and evidence of their occupation on the summit of Tell Duweir, above the earlier ruins of Jewish, Israelite, Canaanite, and Hyksos cities. The work of the Expedition has brought to light a double gateway, a market square, the ruins of houses, a temple, and the residency and offices of the Persian governor. This last was built upon the remains of a great stone building belonging to the Judean kingdom, and of considerably larger dimensions. The residency was oblong in shape, the private apartments formed the southern half of the buildings; while the northern consisted of an open courtyard, or atrium, with a series of offices round the three outsides. The remains of the rooms were full of the collapsed barrel vaulting of their roofing. The private apartments were complete with bathroom, lavatory, and a proper drainage system. There were also the remains of columns that had supported the porticos opening on to the atrium. The abandonment of this building, about the year 400 B.C., was followed by a

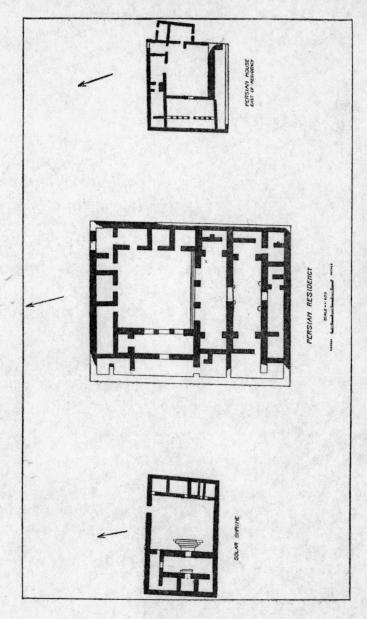

PERSIAN HOUSE
EAST OF RESIDENCY

PERSIAN RESIDENCY

SCALE 1:200

SOLAR SHRINE

GROUND PLANS OF PERSIAN BUILDINGS EXCAVATED AT LACHISH

period of squatter occupation. And two large lime-kilns create apprehension as to what valuable records of the past may have there been reduced to dust. They would presumably belong to the Persian occupation.

The temple devoted to sun worship was in the north-east quarter of the Persian city. Like the residency, it was oblong in shape. Its orientation is East and West, and it was entered through a square open courtyard. There was an ascent of six steps up to the antechamber, while three more led to the inner shrine. A drain in the centre of the entrance to the latter, indicated that libations were offered there. The raised position of the sanctuary, facing the east, admitted the first rays of the rising sun in accordance with solar worship. Two altars were found, and an interesting bronze lamp.

Sun worship, among other idolatries, was practised in the Temple at Jerusalem before the Nebuchadnezzar destruction. Thus it is written:

"And he brought me into the inner court of the Lord's house, and behold, at the door of the temple of the Lord, between the porch and the altar, were about five and twenty men, with their backs toward the temple of the Lord, and their faces toward the east; and they worshipped the sun toward the east."

(Ezekiel viii. 16.)

The Persian religion approached much more nearly to original Monotheism, than the other idolatrous religions practised in the East in Old Testament times. Like Moses and the prophets, Zoroaster (1000 B.C.?), the great exponent of it, taught the existence of a single Deity—Ormuzd or Aura-Mazda. Evil was personified in Ariman or Angra-Mainu. The two principals were in eternal conflict, and humanity was involved in it. But man was responsible for what he did, whether good or evil. He had free will to choose. If he fought against evil he would share in the final victory, and secure a place in Heaven among the righteous.

It is interesting to notice how a great conqueror like Cyrus, with such belief as this, would respond to the strains of Isaiah's splendid prophecy which has just been quoted in these pages. Cyrus would identify Jehovah the God of Israel with Aura-Mazda, though he had not known Him before under the former name. The very words, "That they may know from the rising of the sun and from the west," were in harmony with Cyrus's belief. Or again, "I form the light and create darkness; I make peace and create evil." The sentences expressed the very Faith to which Cyrus gave allegiance. People have thought that some of the Christian Faith was borrowed from ancient religions like the Persian. They were perhaps unaware of the original Monotheism of the World, and how these ancient faiths may have preserved and reflected certain aspects of the original.

## VI

## EXCAVATIONS AT LACHISH

FIVE seasons of excavations of the mound of Tell Duweir, of the cemeteries which surround it, and of their rock-cut tombs, have brought to light a vast number of objects. It has been fortunate that our remote—our very very remote predecessors —used to bury lasting objects of their culture with the bodies of their dead, otherwise so much less would be known about them. The articles discovered in any excavation of an ancient settlement of man, resemble pieces of an incomplete jigsaw puzzle. It is usually difficult, and often impossible, to give them any sort of coherence, much less fit them together. Many do not even attempt to do so, but content themselves with recording their finds, leaving to others the task of evolving some sort of coherent and consecutive narrative. It makes it harder when periods of time are expressed in involved language, and a foreign system of measurement is used. Complications do not really represent erudition; nor do they help to interest the general public in archæology; they tend to make reports read as dry as the bones whose discoveries they record; and cause people to ask, "What is the good of Archæology?"

# EXCAVATIONS AT LACHISH

There was a time when a knowledge of history was treated as almost as essential for education as reading, writing, and arithmetic. It is really as important as ever, because it enshrines past experience of the working of human nature. And Science is now directing our attention to facts of experience as the basis of true knowledge. The call to the study of the Science of Man, referred to in the opening chapter, is a call to study human experience. It thus becomes abundantly evident that a knowledge of history is essential for this study of Man.

But Archæology is the handmaid of History. To-day it is an invaluable handmaid, for it is supplying the evidence that is confirming ancient history; and is sweeping away the doubts that have been cast upon tradition. So an endeavour is made in this volume to escape from a dry-as-dust presentation of facts, and to correlate the evidence found at Lachish with the Old Testament. And it will be seen that, while some discoveries need but passing notice, the importance of others calls for a complete chapter.

During five winters of continuous work, the Lachish excavations have furnished ample remains of man's handiwork which are more than two thousand five hundred years old. They represent an assortment of the wares, and of the products, of one hundred generations of people, who lived, and loved, and worked, and worshipped, and fought, and died, before the birth of Christ.

The pottery system of dating, described earlier,

enables us to place these people, and their handiworks, in somewhere near the different periods of time in which they lived.) Allusion has already been made to the analogy of a jigsaw puzzle. In order to carry the comparison a stage further, let us suppose that the man who has to fit together the pieces for a picture of an English town, is given, as a guide for his selection, a view of a native African village. It would not take him many minutes to recognize that a mistake had been made; he would see pieces that did not fit. Now the Old Testament narrative goes into detail, and in places into minute detail, of the circumstances and mode of existence of the people whose lives it purports to portray. The Lachish finds fit that picture; they rarely, if ever, differ from it. It is true that gaps remain. Some of the gaps are due to the absence of those things which have not survived the ravages of time: all the woodwork, and the textiles, the writings on papyrus, and skins, and such like. Even these occasionally survive in Egypt, thanks to the exceeding dryness of the climate. But Palestine is more humid, and the joint effects of air and water cause decay. Among the objects on which they make least impression are seals or scarabs. They are of peculiar interest because they sometimes carry evidence of identification. References are often made to seals both in the Old and New Testaments. In those times the art of writing was not in general use, it was the profession of the scribe; and seals were employed instead of signatures, by kings and all prominent men.

Seals were used in Babylonia long before the days of Abraham. Some beautifully engraved cylinder seals have been found there, with curious pictures of deities and mythological characters. The Temptation of Adam and Eve, with the tree of knowledge between and the serpent in the background, forms the subject of one of them (Plate 9). Cylindrical seals of this character, pierced lengthways, and suspended by a cord round the necks of their owners, would be used by Abraham and his descendants. Indeed we read that Jacob's son Judah wore such a seal (Gen. xxxviii. 18, 25). Specimens of this type have been found at Lachish, and one depicts the Tree of Life, with a seated Deity, two human figures, and other emblems. Again, we read how the king of Egypt gave his signet ring to Joseph (Gen. xli. 42). The seal of this ring would perhaps be of the scarab type. This Pharaoh, who reigned about 1880 B.C., would belong to one of the Hyksos dynasties; and a number of their scarabs have been found at Lachish. One of these bears the cartouche of Aahetep-Ra with those spirals engraved round it which are character-istic of the Hyksos; only four other scarabs of this Pharaoh are known. Another rare royal Hyksos scarab is that of Apepa or Pepa, who is said to have belonged to the XV Dynasty, and another of Kheper-Ra. These scarabs of early Hyksos kings all testify to their association with Palestine in patriarchal times, and they support Petrie's views about the length of time that must be allowed for their dynasties.

The royal scarabs of the Pharaohs of the XVIII

Dynasty—the native Dynasty which drove out the Hyksos—also abound at Lachish. Reference will be made in the next chapter to the discovery of several of Amenhetep III, who ruled Egypt when Joshua conquered Canaan. Scarabs of nearly all the other kings of this Dynasty, as well as some of the nineteenth, have come to light. They illustrate the close relationship which existed between Israel and Egypt from patriarchal times. The Jews themselves at a later date imitated such seals. The Expedition found, close to a robbed tomb, a large steatite scarab, carefully made, bearing on its under side the name Ahimelek, which means, "brother of the king," written in Hebrew script, below an emblem of the four-winged scarabeous beetle.

The royal seal impressions found on the handles of pottery vessels also bore a representation of this insect. Many have been found in the remains of the city of Zedekiah's period. They belong to the later days of the Jewish kingdom after Josiah. Stamped above the beetle on such handles are the words, "for the king," and below it the name of the towns, "Hebron," or "Socoh," or "Memsheph." The device of a bird with outstretched wings sometimes replaces that of the beetle. The two types of seals may differentiate the contents of the jars, possibly olive oil and wine. We read:

"These were the potters, and the inhabitants of Netaim and Gederah: there they dwelt with the king for his work." (1 Chron. iv. 23.)

The last half-dozen words, paraphrase the expression "For the king," inscribed on the handles. When these inscribed jar handles were first found in excavations many years ago, there was a good deal of discussion as to their significance. It is now suggested that the badge was a royal trade mark, and the name beneath, the place of origin. At Lachish the names of private individuals are frequently found stamped on the handles of the large storage jars.

Lastly seals, or seal impressions, of some prominent Jews have come to light in the ruins. Most important of these may be the seal impression of Gedaliah. It is of pink red clay, and bears an impression which reads "For Gedaliah," and underneath the words "He who is over the house." At its back there can still be seen the imprint of the papyrus fibre of the document to which it was once affixed. The title, attached to the name on this seal, corresponds to our title—the lord chamberlain. One of Solomon's ministers bore it (1 Kings iv. 2, 6). And in Hezekiah's day, when Rabshakeh demanded the surrender of Jerusalem to Sennacherib, it was Eliakim "which was over the house" that headed the deputations to meet him. There was a Gedaliah who was very prominent at the time of the downfall of the Jewish monarchy, and it is probable that this is his seal impression. The evidence that he was "over the house," though circumstantial, is strong. He was the grandson of Shaphan the celebrated scribe of King Josiah. And when Nebuchadnezzar finally captured Jerusalem in the days of King Zedekiah, Jeremiah, at his own request, was given into the charge of Gedaliah. Nebuchadnezzar then appointed Gedaliah governor of Judah; and to judge from the Bible accounts, he was admirably carrying out his commission when he was murdered. (Jer. xli. 2). It is said that unto this day the Jews keep a fast for him. This seal impression was found near the Persian gateway below the outer defence wall.

Another seal of the scarab type, bore the inscription "For Shallum the son of . . . ." There is a Shallum mentioned in the Lachish Letters. Then a small clay seal, bearing the name of "Hilkiah the son of Mas," was found also in the upper burnt layers of the city. Hilkiah was the name of Jeremiah the prophet's father, but we seem to have no knowledge of "Mas." The last seal to mention is that of Shebnah Ahab. It is made of pink limestone and was found in a tomb, the contents of which date it between 800–600 B.C. It is of an oval lozenge shape, and is pierced with a hole for a cord. It is divided into two equal parts by a line: on the upper it reads "Belonging to Shebna," and on the lower occurs the word "Ahab." It is thought to be an Israelite seal rather than a Judean one.

Some five hundred yards to the north-west of the city proper, the Expedition found a suburb or settlement which belonged to 3000 B.C., when copper was only just beginning to supersede flint. There came to light here quantities of hand-made pottery, mixed with flint knives, daggers, and scrapers. Some of the flints

were from five to seven inches in length; they were
found in groups among the undisturbed rubbish of the
settlement. There were also pear-shaped mace heads
of limestone, as well as flint adzes and borers. A
feature of this collection were the ledge-handled pots
made of clay paste, mixed with limestone and flint.
And from them, and their surroundings, Mr. Starkey
has evolved an interesting story of the beverage in
vogue among these early Palestine settlers. Although
wine is often mentioned in the Bible, beer is not. Yet
in times that were remote when Abraham entered
Canaan, Mr. Starkey postulates beer as the beverage
of these flint workers; beer such as the natives in the
interior of Africa, and especially in the Sudan, brew
and drink to this very day. Mr. Starkey writes:

"1. The commonest form of handle on the larger
pots is the wavy ledge handle, which only gives an
effective grip when the pot is inverted. The complete
inversion of a pot would only be necessary where the
contents would tend to adhere to the inside of the
vessel, and with this type one could tip up and shake
out a porridge-like mass with ease. These same ledge-
handled jars are frequently found with spouts and also
with a small loop handle at the rim to allow for the
normal tipping of the vessel to pour off liquid, for
which purpose the inverted ledge handles would not
be required. This would fit in well with the necessity
to drain off the brew from the pounded germinated
grain.

"2. The frequent occurrence of hard limestone
mortars in these cave dwellings has been noted. It is
possible that these receptacles may have been used for

the crushing of the dried grain, preliminary to the final brewing process. It is interesting to note that in this early period, we have no forms from which the later wine jar could have developed. This vessel which is so characteristic of the post-Canaanite culture would seem to herald the arrival of fundamental changes in the domestic life of the people. One thing is certain, that after the arrival of the two-handled wine jar, the inverted wavy ledge handle disappears, and also spouted vessels are rarely found."

Another liquid which must have played an important part in the lives of these early settlers, as it has done in those of their successors in all ages, was the olive oil, which was extracted from crushing the berries of the olive trees. Groups of cup holes have been found, cut in the limestone rock, with connecting channels that drained from one into another. These were once used for crushing the olives and squeezing out the oil, even as is done to this day.

These numerous cup marks at Lachish, testify that olive trees once flourished in this region. They probably covered the now bare hills, until the day that Nebuchadnezzar's soldiers cut them down in order to burn their way into the city. The olive is little known in this country, for our climate does not suit it. Its native lands are Syria and Palestine, where it has made bountiful contributions towards the needs of humanity. It is often referred to in the Bible, indeed it is the first tree mentioned in Genesis, for it figures in the story of the Flood (Gen. viii. 11).

An olive grove makes a beautiful break in the bare

landscape of Palestine—some half-dozen miles or so before reaching Tell Duweir, the road takes travellers through a very ancient one. The gnarled and hollow trunks testify to the great age of these trees; they were probably planted about the time that our Richard Cœur de Lion was fighting there in the Crusades.

Olive trees rarely grow to more than thirty feet high, but their trunks often measure twenty feet and more in circumference, and some in this grove have attained such dimensions. In Old Testament times olive oil served a great number of purposes. It was used in place of butter for cooking; it was used in lamps for lighting and heating; it was used for rubbing over the body; it was used in the Temple Ritual for anointing and other purposes; indeed, it was even poured on the carcases of the beasts and animals sacrificed for burnt offerings.

The olive tree has been peculiarly associated with the Semitic Race; the Phœnicians are said to have transplanted it from the shores of Syria, to Spain and Greece, and other western lands. Olive wood has a beautiful grain and takes a fine polish; when burned it gives out a great heat. Since the tree has always been associated with peace, it is the more pitiful that Nebuchadnezzar used it for war and for destruction. May the bare hills round Tell Duweir be replanted and their trees thrive yet again! May Palestine become once more a land of vines and olives, of oil and honey!

The food eaten at Lachish in Old Testament times would presumably be much the same as what was eaten at Jericho. We learned from those excavations that they had wheat, barley, lentils, dates, and onions, and that they made bread. Many bread ovens have been found at Lachish. It was Esau who sold his birthright for bread and pottage of lentils (Gen. xxv. 34). Beside honey there would be grapes and figs, and sheep and goats' flesh for meat. The goat has not been an unmixed blessing to Palestine; it is peculiarly destructive of all forms of vegetation, and is said to be responsible for much of the barrenness of the hills. In the matter of clothing, piles of loom weights, made of clay, have been found among the ruins of houses inside the Lachish destroyed by Nebuchadnezzar. The remains of old wood looms and dyeing vats have also been brought to light. So there was weaving and dyeing of cloth in, at least, the later days of the city. But whether that industry was carried on there in much earlier times, remains to be seen when the lower levels are excavated. Still, there is Bible evidence of the use of the loom in the near neighbourhood of Lachish as far back as 1100 B.C. One of the "experiments" that Delilah made on Samson was to weave his hair into the web of a loom (Judg. xvi. 13, 14). And it is clear that linen garments were in common use then, since this "strong man" wagered thirty of them with the Philistines over the solution of his riddle. The impress of finely woven textiles, was found in the early copper-age settlement to which reference has just been made. And since these would have been worn a thousand years before Abraham, it is unlikely that the people of Canaan would be naked savages in patriarchal times. When Jacob deceived his father, the blind patriarch Isaac, into the belief that he was Esau, we read that Rebekah, in Esau's absence, took "goodly raiment of Esau" and put it upon Jacob (Gen. xxvii. 15). There was also the coat of many colours, or a long garment with sleeves, that Jacob made for his son Joseph, which excited the jealousy of his brethren (Gen. xxxvii. 3). It is recorded of these times that Laban went to shear his sheep (Gen. xxxi. 19). This may be said to indicate that the woollen industry was established in Syria by 1900 B.C., while goats' hair was also used in the earliest forms of weaving, particularly perhaps for tent coverings. It would be hard to assign a sufficiently early date for the manufacture of textiles in Egypt, and in Babylonia, and even in Syria. Silk may come much later in Bible lands, though Ezekiel refers to it in his prophecies during the Captivity (Ezek. xvi. 10, 13).

So far as head coverings are concerned, it is interesting to notice that the pattern of turban on the heads of captives depicted in the Siege Bas-Reliefs (700 B.C.), is still worn by some of the local inhabitants. The mention of heads brings about a further reference to a multitude of skeletons discovered in two rock tombs that testified to this siege. The operation of trepanning has been performed on several of these skulls. Rectangular apertures had been made in them by intersecting saw cuts. It is hard to conceive how any

victim of this primitive operation, presumably under-
gone without any form of anæsthetic, could have
survived.

The ornaments, which had been buried with the
deceased in the Lachish tombs, were of a less abundant
character than those in Egyptian tombs. These people
had a more primitive culture and enjoyed a simpler
life. Near the Khan, or Inn, a bronze mirror came
from a tomb that dates back to the days of Moses.

Since it has been the only mirror that has yet come
to light, we may wonder whether it formed part of
the toilet of a lady tourist who died on a visit. With it
was a small circular alabaster stand.

In the same tomb that contained the iron trident,
or priests' fork, referred to in the succeeding chapter
on the temple, was an ivory calendar with thirty
holes arranged in three columns of ten. It had a
pierced boss at the top, so that it could be suspended
by a cord. It probably belonged to the priest's servant who owned the fork, and had been used by him
to record the fasts and feasts. There were four iron
knives with it, which may have served for cutting up
sacrifices in the days when Solomon was reigning over
all Israel at Jerusalem.

From another tomb came an ivory duck's head,
similar in type and size to one found in the temple,
and with it a scarab of Thotmes IV (1423–1413 B.C.).
Here were also bronze earrings, and faience playing-
pieces, resembling those used in the modern game of
Halma.

One of the prize finds made at the start of the excavations, was a bronze Maat feather. The feather of Maat is used as a hieroglyphic sign to represent the goddess Maat or Truth, in the Egyptian hieroglyphic script. This one is certainly of Egyptian manufacture; it came from the ruins of a private house, which had pottery ovens for making bread; and it lay with the fragments of a large fluted bronze ewer. Mr. Starkey thinks they had both been taken from a temple. The feather measures five and a half inches, from its tip to the broken end of the quill, and both sides are engraved to make it resemble an ostrich plume. Once it had been overlayed with gold leaf; and its last owner had wrapped it in a piece of fine linen cloth, for traces of texture still adhered to its surface (Plate 9).

A number of copper daggers of the pre-Hyksos period came to light in another burial. They seem to be made of pure copper, without the addition of any tin which would entitle it to be called bronze. It is doubtful whether the word copper should not be substituted for bronze in the expressions, "Early— Middle—and Late *Bronze* Ages." Copper is translated Brass in the Old Testament, and frequent references are made to it under that name. But brass is technically an alloy of copper and zinc. The earliest use of copper, under the name of brass, is placed in the Old Testament long before the Flood (Gen. iv. 22). Tubal Cain is there represented to be the first artificer in metals, a worker both in copper and iron. Attempts have been made to dispute the great antiquity of iron, because the Egyptians used copper. But recent excavations at Tell Asmar in Mesopotamia, made by Dr. Frankfort, have unearthed a copper-handled dagger with an iron blade. An iron axe was found by Sir Leonard Woolley at Ur, though it is claimed that it had been forged from a meteorite; but this dagger blade was the product of ordinary smelted iron, and carries the use of that metal back to 3000 B.C. Sixteen small instruments of iron were found in the tomb of Tutankhamen by Dr. Carter, and an iron dagger with a gold handle and sheath. But it is probable that the Egyptians had carried the alloying and tempering of copper to a high pitch, and preferred it to iron, for they were a conservative people. Sir Flinders Petrie dates the introduction of copper into Palestine before 3200 B.C., when he says that bronze, the alloy of copper and tin, was introduced. Recent discoveries of Dr. Nelson Glueck, reported in the "Bulletin of the American School of Oriental Research," have proved the extensive mining of copper in Edom before the time of Abraham. The mineral wealth of their Promised Land was portrayed to the Israelites in the words:

"A land whose stones are iron, and out of whose hills thou mayest dig brass." (Deut. viii. 9.)

After the Exodus from Egypt, an altar of burnt offering was overlaid with brass (Exod. xxxviii. 2–8). And we read of the brazen serpent that Moses made (Num. xxi. 9). It would seem that the word copper should be substituted for brass in all these cases. There is an interesting passage in Job, which suggests that the scene of his adversities was near the copper mines in Edom, or Midian, where tradition placed it; it runs: "Brass is molten out of stone" (Job xxviii. 1-2). In the time of David it is stated that Goliath of Gath was clad in armour of brass (1 Sam. xvii. 5). It would be interesting to know when tin was first used as an alloy to harden copper, and where it was found. If Sir Flinders' contention is correct, that Irish gold ornaments were brought to Old Gaza as early as 2300 B.C., then one may reasonably assume that tin was brought from Cornwall at the same time. Another notable discovery at Lachish are the toggle pins, such as Sir Flinders Petrie has found at Old Gaza, and other sites on the borders of Egypt. This pin is made of copper, and the centre is pierced with an eye. It would seem as though such pins were used for fastening the cloak or outer garment; their origin is traced to the Caspian side of the Caucasus. Those found at Lachish belong to the Hyksos period (Plate 13).

The red burnished pottery found in the tombs of the Israelite period is very good, but the bulk of their ware is coarse and ungainly; it presents a marked contrast to the pottery in use before their invasion. A number of images of Astarte, the Bible Ashtaroth, have come to light. There are models in pottery of couches and chairs, like those found in Mesopotamia, and pottery rattles. These may all have been children's toys (Plate 19).

Quantities of beads, some blue glazed, others in

carnelian, garnet, and crystal, have been found in the tombs. These had once been strung in neck-laces.

Most of the pots have flat rather than the conical-shaped bases. The latter are frequent at Jericho, where the climate was much warmer, and the people mostly lived outdoors, and stood them in the light soil.

An ivory comb came from an interment to which a date of 1400 B.C. has been assigned, along with ivory and pottery rods (Plate 18). These were probably used for curling the hair into ringlets, such as are depicted on the heads of captive Jewish elders in the Lachish Bas-Reliefs of Sennacherib. The custom of wearing their hair with side ringlets prevails to this day among the orthodox Jews.

Lachish was a fenced frontier city of Judah to keep out the Philistines. The nearest Philistine centre—Gath, the most easterly of their five main cities—was only six miles away from Lachish. On a hill to the west of Tell Duweir, overlooking the frontier, are the ruins of a small military outpost, which is connected to Lachish by a road that recalls the reference, "From the tower of the watchmen to the fenced city" (2 Kings xviii. 8).

The Philistines, those armed warriors who so often fought with Israel, were not so well equipped for taking fenced cities as the Egyptians, or Assyrians, or Baby-lonians. It would appear that Lachish, with its chain of neighbouring fenced cities, proved an effective barrier. Much more will be known of its history when the Wellcome-Marston Expedition penetrates deeper into that sixty-odd feet of debris. Meanwhile it is evident that what has been brought to light is consistent with, and confirms, the Old Testament Narrative.

# VII

## THE TEMPLE RUINS OUTSIDE LACHISH
### (1500–1263 B.C.)

ARCHÆOLOGICAL work in Palestine has brought many disappointments in the past, and will perhaps bring more in the future. It is not like unearthing the exotic civilizations of Egypt or Syria, of Babylonia or Assyria. Palestine possessed a more primitive culture. It lacked the libraries of inscribed clay tablets found elsewhere. Like ourselves the Israelites preferred paper, or rather papyrus its predecessor, to clay tablets; though it was much more tractable it was less permanent. But the importance of Palestine as the scene of most of the events recorded in the Bible, makes its discoveries compensate for its disappointments. Since our lives are largely spent in anticipations, so Biblical Archæology deserves wider advertisement : it is one of the most unexpected of all the Sciences.

The temple ruins outside Lachish represent the remains of three temples superimposed one above another. They were built on the filled-up moat at the foot of the Hyksos sloping earth ramp, or glacis. At present we can only conjecture why such a site was selected for a temple. It may be that the interior of

Lachish was overcrowded. It may be that the worship at this temple was foreign to that of the city. Or again, the evidence that suburbs sprung up outside the walls and in the surrounding valleys, after the expulsion of the Hyksos by Thotmes III, may account for its presence. The shrine would be more accessible to these outside dwellers than if they had to mount up the Tell and go inside the walls.

The Wellcome Archæological Expedition first struck treasure trove in its second season, in the shape of the ruins of the topmost of these temples. The excavators were clearing the western slopes of the Tell when they came across the remains of some substantial walls. As usually happens on these occasions, the importance of the find was not immediately evident. But when a niche in an east wall was found to contain a stack of thirty-five bowls, the staff of the Expedition suspected something important. Their anticipation proved to be fully justified; for they unearthed a small temple whose contents never seem to have been disturbed since it was finally destroyed by fire, and its ruins overwhelmed by streams of liquid mud, from the city rubbish thrown out upon the slopes above it. Imagination pictures the work of a great thunderstorm whose lightnings set the temple on fire, and whose torrents of rain washed the liquid mud down over the ruins. Those who witnessed the catastrophe might well treat the remains of the temple and its contents as accursed, and so leave them untouched. Soil from the foundations for a new city wall was afterwards thrown down on to the ruins. Whatever the cause, after the temple was burnt, its contents remained undisturbed to the day that the excavators uncovered them.

Among a quantity of temple furniture, there was found a great scarab of the Pharaoh, Amenhetep III, lying face upwards in the mud on the floor of the shrine. The inscription on the scarab, in Egyptian hieroglyphics, recorded the fact that this king had slain one hundred and two lions with his own hand in the first ten years of his reign. And since Amenhetep III began to reign in 1413 B.C., it is evident that the scarab was cut after 1403 B.C., which would be near to the time that Joshua and his men were taking Jericho. This Pharaoh, who was such a lion killer, is one of the three or four outstanding figures in Egyptian history. He has already been repeatedly referred to in these pages. He was on the throne of Egypt when Joshua captured Jericho. He was the Pharaoh to whom many of the Tel el Amarna Letters, asking for aid against the Hebrews, were addressed. He, and his wife Thyi, were the parents of Amenhetep IV, or Akhenaton. It was in his reign, after he had killed the hundred and two lions, that he seems to have turned from Sport to Religion, and to Art. He became the protector of the Egyptian religious revival of Monotheism, and the patron of its art renaissance. Since it has become known that Jericho had fallen to Joshua in his reign, there was something quite appropriate in finding his great scarab on the floor of this temple (Plate 14). Its surroundings satisfy our conception of what an Israelite temple of the time might be like.

As the earth and the overlaying mud were cleared away, a building and its furniture were brought to light which remind Bible students of a certain scene in the Sacred Narrative. There on the south side was a brick altar, approached by three steps. Behind the altar a raised platform, on which a shrine or "ark" might have stood. Facing the altar, on one's left hand, was a great earthenware cauldron for meat offerings. And on the right a tall pottery stand holding a bowl for drink offerings. Beside the latter lay a decorated pottery censer, and at the foot of the three altar steps was a foot bath for ablutions. Surely it was in some such place as this, that the child Samuel was laid down to sleep in the temple before the ark of God (1 Sam. iii. 3); and where he heard the Divine voice pronouncing the doom of Eli and his sons.

The great cauldron may be a replica of that cauldron of meat offerings into which Eli's servant plunged the flesh hook in order to bring out the priest's share (1 Sam. ii. 13, 14). One of these iron tridents, or flesh hooks, was afterwards found in a neighbouring tomb (Plate 18). Two small rooms behind the altar, served as a treasury, and a retiring room for the priest. We can imagine Samuel going to wake Eli in one of them. The temple had nine brick benches ranged against its walls on its other three sides, and was approached through an ante-chamber. It measured eighty-one feet long by forty-one feet wide. Its roof had been supported by four

wooden pillars, for their stone bases were found set in
the white plastered floor. This latter was strewn with
quantities of pottery, and before the base of the altar
there was a small curb surrounding an oval hearth,
where charcoal would have been burnt for kindling
purposes. Upon the raised platform there were found
glass toilet vases, ivory rods, gazelle heads, an ivory
statuette of Horus—the child, a couchant bull, and the
head of a duck. These had probably been ornaments
for objects of ritual, and had pegs or sockets for attach-
ment. There was a perfume flask which had been
carved from a single tusk. Its form is that of a lady
with a long skirt, loop handles represent the arms and
shoulders, and a stopper the head. A hole through
this stopper connected with an open hand rising above
the head, which served as a spoon (Plate 16). Syrians
are depicted, on the Egyptian tombs of the eighteenth
and nineteenth dynasties, presenting such objects to
the Pharaoh.

There were also two ivory spoons, a circular toilet
box ornamented with lions attacking bulls in low relief
of exquisite workmanship (Plate 14); a blue-glass faience
vase some seven inches high, and four more large scarabs
of Amenhetep III, as well as the great lion-hunt scarab
already described.

The temple was built of undressed stone, and unbaked bricks, the whole covered with white plaster,
including the floor. Around the great cauldron, which
had four handles, were a quantity of small open bowls
or saucers, that had been used to present the offerings

of the worshippers. And the soil there was littered with small bones of goats, birds, and fish.

The large bowl for drink offerings on the other side of the altar had a drain to it. This sacrifice seems to have been presented in a small saucer with a raised central well, and a lip on the outer rim. The bath for ablutions had also a raised bridge across the centre to act as a foot-rest. Perhaps one of the most significant finds, was a small faience plaque, poorly moulded, which bore the name of Rameses II. The room, which has been termed the temple treasury, at the back of the altar, contained a large collection of faience beadwork which belonged to the Tel el Amarna, or renaissance, period of decoration. It included pendants of corn-flowers, of daisies, pomegranates, bunches of grapes, mandrake fruit, and palmettes, together with fragments of many glass perfume vessels.

Outside both the north and east walls of the temple, were many circular pits, which had been used for the temple rubbish. These contained quantities of bones that were remains of offerings, and pieces of worn temple furniture and decoration. There were hundreds of beads and broken bowls, and among the latter, forty fragments of a decorated water jug. When these were fitted together, they formed the ewer, about eighteen inches high, which will go down to history, because the first discovered specimen of the Sinai Hebrew script is painted round its shoulder.

One may not conclude the enumeration of these castaways without reference to a beautiful ivory hand of a girl, about two-thirds life-size. The upper part of the wrist suggested it had fitted into a socket. Was it the hand of some image which had once stood upon the platform behind the altar? Or could it have served as a decoration or symbol elsewhere? These ivory carvings were probably the work of Syrian craftsmen. Several centuries later, Ahab, king of Israel, married a Syrian princess, the infamous Jezebel, and built himself an ivory palace—presumably a building decorated with ivory—pieces of which have been found in the excavations of Samaria. And before Ahab's days there are references in the Old Testament to the use of ivory. Thus, for example:

"Out of ivory palaces stringed instruments have made thee glad." (Psalm xlv. 8.)

But the ivory work in the Lachish temple was executed some four hundred years before that Psalm was composed. A great hoard of ivory work, dating perhaps a century later than the Lachish find, has just been discovered at Megiddo.

The prevalence of glass articles, among these ruins and rubbish pits, also prompts us to desire some information about glass-making in these very ancient times. There is a tradition in Palestine that glass was first made underneath Mount Carmel, on the banks of that river Kishon which dealt so roughly with the fugitives of Sisera's army (Judges v. 21). And this tradition is confirmed by the classical historian, Pliny.

The date of the destruction of this temple is derived

from the presence in its ruins of articles belonging to
the period of Rameses II (1295–1229 B.C.). Mr. Starkey
places it as having occurred about 1262 B.C. But the
lion-hunt scarab, and many other objects, belong to over
a century and a half earlier. Why were the scarabs of
Amenhetep III preserved as precious relics in this
temple during all that time? Why were there so many
relics from Egypt to the south, and Syria to the north?
Both Amenhetep III and his son Akhenaton were
closely related to Syria by marriage; and if they had
connived in the Israelite conquest of Palestine by
Joshua, it would explain the presence of these relics
in an Israelite temple. In due course this edifice
was removed by the Expedition, and its duplicate
was found underneath it. In the words of the excavators:

"We have lifted the plaster floor of the temple
sanctuary, and immediately below it we struck the tops
of narrow benches precisely similar to the upper layout which we found last season. Against them we
found further offering bowls and lamps. . . . It was
surprising to find this earlier layout so perfectly preserved, with no sign of fire or destruction, just filled
in with soil and re-levelled to take the latest plastered
floor."

And again:

"The priests' chamber to the east behind the shrine
is now being worked, and already we see pottery
vessels preserved against the foundations of the north
wall."

158

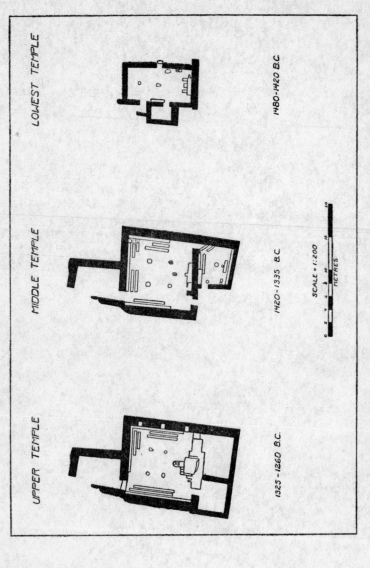

UPPER TEMPLE      MIDDLE TEMPLE      LOWEST TEMPLE

1325 - 1260 B.C.      1420 - 1335 B.C.      1480 - 1420 B.C.

SCALE = 1:200

METRES

GROUND PLANS OF LACHISH TEMPLES FOUND SUPERIMPOSED ONE ABOVE THE OTHER

The repetition occurred again in the case of the four column bases of the middle temple; they were directly below the upper ones. And so was the hearth in front of the altar. Underneath both this high altar and its platform, were found small gold pendants with crudely executed repoussé figures of the goddess Astarte, familiar to us in the Old Testament as Ashtaroth. There was no altar in the middle temple, and instead of the raised platform behind, there was a low narrow stone bench. On the outer side of the sanctuary wall there was but one room, instead of two as in the upper temple.

Several new forms of goblets and bowls, with polychrome decoration, were found in the middle temple level; as well as some gold objects, including a larger gold star pendant, and a small scarab of Amenhetep III and Queen Thyi his wife. Perhaps the most important find in this area was a hæmatite cylinder seal, which is thought to be of Syro-Hittite manufacture, and is dated just before 1400 B.C. Grouped with several figures of men and animals is the Tree of Life. The engraving is extremely delicate, and it must have been a prized possession (Plate 9).

The third or lowest temple was much smaller than those above it, and had only two pillars to support its roof instead of four. In place of the rooms behind the altar, there were outside rubbish heaps; but there was a small room on the west side of the building. Beneath the bench of the middle temple, which had a single square projection, there was a long mud bench with three square projections. It is suggested that these may either have been bases for images of the three Syrian deities—Shur, Mut, and Alat—referred to in the next chapter; or stands for the offerings of incense, food, and drink.

A quantity of pottery stacked against the east end of the altar bench, and sealed in below the masonry foundation of the middle temple altar bench, supplied evidence of date. It was a very interesting deposit, for it consisted of seventy small dipper flasks, many broken bowls, and one large bread platter. There were also a decorated milk bowl from Cyprus, a red burnished flask and goblet, and a remarkable specimen of Mykenean ware. This latter was a buff-coloured goblet some six inches high, decorated with ivy leaves in black and red. It belonged to what is known as the late Helladic II period (1500–1400 B.C.), and is the only complete specimen found so far in the country (Plate 16). Here were also found a small bronze statue of Reshef, the Syrian war god, three and a half inches high, some small twisted gold ornaments, similar to those found at Gaza, which Sir Flinders affirms are of Irish manufacture; and buttons and beads.

Mr. Starkey provisionally dates the three temples as follows:—

The lower temple, after the conquest of the Hyksos city by Thotmes III, about 1480 B.C.

The middle temple, 1400 B.C.

And the upper temple, 1300 B.C.

He remarks that only the upper temple shows evidence of having been destroyed by fire.

The religious history of the temples must be a matter of speculation, but the presence of some few evidences of idolatrous worship, by no means negatives the idea that the middle and upper temples were used for Israelite worship. Judging from the evidence found in the lowest temple, the offerings there were of a different character from those in the upper ones. They took the form of food, and libations, and possibly incense, rather than the flesh of birds or animals. It might be possible to identify the cult from these peculiarities. The whole evidence of the three temples associates them with Egypt and Syria, and the two upper ones with Amenhetep III and his Syrian wife, Thyi. If the lower temple was not destroyed by fire, why was it superseded for the middle one? And the middle for the upper? Did the three temples denote different forms of worship? It is noticeable that the high altar and platform of the upper temple are absent in the middle one. That suggests a primitive and less ornate form of ritual than was practised in the upper one. Underneath the altar and platform were gold emblems of Astarte. This was Ashtaroth, the goddess of the Zidonians, of the Old Testament. And the children of Israel are said to have forsaken Jehovah and served her, after the death of Joshua, and after the death of all the Elders that outlived Joshua (Judges ii. 7–13).

Does that give us any date for the erection of this temple, and its prominent altar and platform? It will be seen on reference to the chapter on Joshua that he died about 1375 B.C., and the Elders that outlived him would represent another fifteen years. That would make the date when the Israelites began to worship Astarte, or Ashtaroth, about 1360 B.C. It would appear as though the upper temple, with Astarte emblems beneath its altar and platform, may have been built after that time.

The small statue of Reshef found in the lowest temple is of special significance (Plate 16). He was worshipped at the period both in Egypt and Syria; and forms another connecting link between the two countries, among the many others found here.

The suggestion that the worship of Shur, Mut, and Alat was carried on in the lowest temple is problematical. The identification of the three names on the broken ewer from the rubbish heap of the upper temple is not certain. Allat as a goddess is well known. There were fifty gods worshipped at Ras Shamra (Ugarit) in North Syria, and twenty-five goddesses; presumably this triad may have come from there. It is interesting to notice that none of these temples appear to have been used for burnt offerings. In the upper temple there is the cauldron for the boiled-meat offerings, as there was in the case of the temple where Samuel ministered at Shiloh. If the altar had been used for burning incense, it may be noted that until recently Old Testament scholars disclaimed the use of a fixed altar for burning incense before the fifth century B.C.

To sum up, the evidence is consistent, and even
suggests that the lowest temple belonged to a Syrian
cult which offered incense, bread, and wine. It is
possible that this first temple was replaced by an
Israelite temple soon after Joshua captured Lachish.
And that in turn was replaced by another temple,
where the worship of Ashtaroth was prominent, as may
be suggested by the ivory hand found in the refuse pit.
This last temple was destroyed by fire, perhaps deliber-
ately, perhaps by a great thunder-storm, in the days
of Rameses II, when Shamgar ben Anath judged
Israel. Professor Garstang has suggested that Shamgar was a sea captain of that Pharaoh. In that case
the ox goad with which Shamgar slew six hundred
Philistines was probably the name of his ship. His
association with the sea, would account for the chaotic
conditions on land, portrayed in the Song of Deborah:

"In the days of Shamgar the son of Anath . . . the
highways were unoccupied and the travellers walked
through byways."                                    (Judges v. 6.)

It seems clear that the wonderful lion-hunt scarab of
Amenhetep III, and his other scarabs, together with
the finer ivories, originally belonging to the middle
temple, remained in use in the later one. Was it
because the Israelites venerated this Pharaoh as their
benefactor? Was it because Lachish was still a chariot
city used by the Egyptians, and the worshippers
regarded the presence of his scarabs as a token that
they enjoyed the protection of that power? There is

ample evidence at Beth Shan (Beisan), that the Pharaoh Seti I (1317–1295 B.C.) engaged in warfare in the north of Palestine round the plain of Esdraelon : he had to guard his line of communication. Egyptian troops would be constantly in touch with the cities in control of the foothills, Lachish may have been used by them.

Perhaps we shall obtain more light on these problems when the excavators reach the corresponding levels in the interior of the city.

# VIII

## THE STORY OF THE ALPHABET

THE story of ancient writing is a long story; for it would seem as if civilized man could always write; and civilized man may have existed as far back as primitive man. The problem was to reproduce sounds that came from the mouth, by permanent visual symbols.

The alphabet and its origin constitute a story in themselves. So far as human knowledge goes at present, writing was in existence for thousands of years before the alphabet was invented. The man who discovered how to simplify writing by the substitution of about a couple of dozen signs, for the hundreds and thousands of characters which were used to reproduce a language, conferred a great benefit on literature. Let us set down in a few words what has been discovered about the origin of our own alphabet, and the signs that express it. It is a matter of general knowledge that these signs are derived from the Greek, and that those who formulated them borrowed in turn from the Phœnician. Until lately the Phœnicians enjoyed the credit of being the originators. The archæological evidence now suggests that the Phœnicians derived the alphabet from the Israelites. The course of events which has led to this discovery ran as follows—

In the winter of 1904-5, Sir Flinders Petrie led an Expedition of some thirty people into the centre of the peninsula of Sinai. The region was then little known on account of its inaccessibility. The peninsula is the traditional scene of the wanderings in the Wilderness of the children of Israel under the leadership of Moses. And the nature and character of the country satisfy the impressions we receive of it from reading the Bible account.

It is a wild waste barren land of black and red rocky hills with splashes of green; mountains interlaced with deep defiles, and gorges among occasional oases. Distances which look short on the map are made long by these rugged conformations. The difficulties of obtaining proper supplies of drinkable water, which beset the Israelites in their wandering, have still to be faced by expeditions which go there.

Petrie's Expedition started from Suez, and after going by boat a few miles up the Canal, landed on the shores of the peninsula at a convenient spot to start for the interior. They found that they had then to follow a route for some considerable distance that was parallel with the shore. Most of the members of the Expedition walked all the way, but they had a few camels to carry provisions, water, and baggage. The rocky hills of hard black marl, rising many hundred feet above the sea, testified to the presence of copper, for their fissures were stained with verdigris. In the last few years manganese has been extracted by the Sinai Mining Company, who have a railway that runs about twelve miles inland. Manganese was unknown to the ancients, but there is no doubt that in olden times Egyptian expeditions had, from time to time, sought copper in this forbidding country. The miners they employed were Semites—Midianites and Edomites, from the other side of the neighbouring Gulf of Akaba, which was a great copper-mining district. It has already been pointed out that in Midian, Moses spent many years of exile. But in Sinai, the mining of copper was quite subordinate to the mining of turquoises. These jewels were much prized by the Egyptians from the early days of their first Dynasty. They were known under the name of "mafkat." They must surely be mentioned among the many jewels in the Bible, but by a name which has been incorrectly translated.

The Petrie Expedition visited Maghara and Serabit, districts where these turquoises had once been dug out of the rocky crags and hills. Many of the ancient mine workings have caved in, either through lack of support, or more probably through the crumbling away, in the course of a few thousand years, of their wooden pillars or props. But there is still sufficient evidence remaining, of the extensive and elaborate way in which the mines were being operated before and after the days of Moses. For example : near Serabit are the remains of a tunnel cut right through a ridge, a distance of over seventy yards. It was ventilated midway by a square well. There are inscriptions in Egyptian hieroglyphics, at either entrance, as well as inside the ventilating shaft.

There is a graphic description of mining in the Book

of Job (xxviii. 1–18). A reference is made there to the " stones of obscurity," which may very well be a poetic expression for the turquoises. A postscript to the Septuagint translation of Job, describes him as living in a land on the borders of Edom and Arabia. This position of course suits the land of Midian. Job is also stated there to be a descendant of Esau (Gen. xxxvi. 34) in the fifth generation from Abraham. Now that the critical conclusions concerning the Old Testament have gone to pieces, it may be worth while to revive the traditional belief that Moses wrote the Book of Job when he was sojourning in the land of Midian. In that case it may even contain this reference to these Sinai turquoise mines.

Besides being dedicatory, some of these hieroglyphic inscriptions record the Egyptian officials of the expeditions—the leader, the comptroller, the treasurers, the storekeepers, and the coppersmiths: these last to keep the copper chisels used by the miners, in working order, and in good repair. The monuments of the earliest Egyptian expeditions supplied dates from about 3000 B.C., the latest to about 1150 B.C. The expeditions had always been intermittent, the dry barren land permitted no permanent settlement.

The seat of worship of the miners, was a temple on the top of a rocky plateau, two thousand five hundred feet above sea level, and three or four days' journey from the coast. The Expedition found the ruins of this temple, and of an extensive settlement, which had once been fortified, perhaps against the intrusion of wild beasts rather than against men. The place is a day's journey from water at the present time. This temple of Serabit contained a shrine which was dedicated to Hathor, the mistress of turquoises. There were a number of inscriptions in Egyptian hieroglyphics; and from these it was ascertained that one of the builders and adorners of the temple had been the Princess Hatshepsut, who there is such good reason to believe was the patroness of Moses. Her work there had been done at the time she was associated on the throne with Thotmes III (1501–1486 B.C.), and that was also the time when Moses was a full-grown man at her court.

Evidence that at this temple a form of worship was carried on, which resembled that of the Israelites, was manifested in a number of ways. This was a great high place. Here were immense heaps of wood ashes, and the fuel must have been carried up to this rocky plateau from places a thousand feet below. And these ashes testified to the burnt offerings, which it was the custom of Abraham's race to sacrifice on the summits of high hills and mountains. Here there were many portable stone altars for burning incense, and no less than four successive great lavers, or tanks, for ablutions. A feature of the settlement itself, was a number of stone sleeping-shelters with monoliths, or large standing stones, which may be associated with dreams, like the one erected by Jacob at Bethel (Gen. xxviii. 18). The Egyptian inscriptions testify that the locations of the precious turquoises were believed to be revealed by dreams.

Though the Egyptian expeditions had built and adorned the temple with their inscriptions, the cult practised was not an Egyptian one. The evidence that had been left behind, identified the religious ceremonials of its worshippers as similar to those practised by the Israelites. And the inscriptions of the miners themselves, carved on stone sphinxes, and cut on rocks both inside and outside the turquoise mines, prove that they used an alphabetical script in their system of writing. So far as is known, these Serabit inscriptions represent the oldest examples of alphabetical writing in the world. It is now more than thirty years since they were found by Petrie. It is only during the last ten years that other archæologists have visited the place, and have collected, and brought back to the Cairo Museum, all the inscriptions that they could find in this mysterious script.

Of the earlier attempts made by scholars to decipher these inscriptions, the most important was that of Dr. Alan H. Gardiner in 1916. He suggested that certain signs signified " Baalat." He was followed by K. Sethe in 1917, and R. Eisler in 1919. Professor H. Grimme, of Münster, in 1923, claimed that he had deciphered the name of Moses on one of the inscriptions, but this interpretation does not seem to be favourably regarded by later students of the writings.

The date of these writings is not regarded as corresponding with those recorded by the earlier Egyptian expeditions to Serabit. Sir Flinders Petrie, who found the writings and first examined their surroundings, was

confident that they were written about 1500 B.C. It
has already been pointed out in this chapter that this
is a time which we now know corresponds with the life
of Moses when he lived in Egypt as the favourite of
Hatshepsut. On the other hand, Father Butin of the
Harvard Expedition, which visited the ruins in 1930,
ascribes them to the eighteenth century B.C., and he
suggests that they are distantly related to the Egyptian
hieroglyphics.

In December 1929, a bit of pottery was discovered
at Gezer in South-West Palestine, with three letters of
this Sinai script written upon it. While still earlier, at
the excavations of Tel el Hesy before the Great War,
three letters were found painted on the fragment of a
pot which belonged to the thirteenth century B.C.

A third example of the Sinai Hebrew script was found
by Dr. Grant at Beth Shemesh in 1930, written in ink
on an ostrakon. Dr. Albright insisted from the first
that this writing belonged to the fourteenth century
B.C., and the later discoveries at Lachish tend to confirm his conclusion.

So matters stood until the second season's work at
Lachish brought to light the ruins of a temple outside
the walls, which have been described in the previous
chapter. There, among the debris in a rubbish pit,
was found the remains of a water jug or ewer. On the
shoulder of this ewer, intertwined with conventional
figures of a lion, a bird, gazelles, and trees, were eleven
letters or signs belonging to this same Sinai alphabetical
script. There is no agreement as to the correct

decipherment of the whole inscription, but the Hebrew word "Matan," meaning "Gift," has been generally accepted as forming part of it. The last two letters are thought to represent L T or P T. Father Burrows has suggested that the whole inscription probably read: "A gift (or offering) to Shur, Mut, and Alat"—three deities whose names are associated in the same order in the Ras Shamra Tablets.

The next example of the Sinai Hebrew script, was found the following year at Lachish on a red pottery bowl in a tomb. The letters were painted across the outside of the bowl in white paint. They looked at first sight as though they had been made in chalk, and the Expedition leaders wondered if someone was playing a practical joke on them. But the inscription proved to be even more important than that on the ewer. Several attempts to decipher it did not seem to produce very satisfactory results. Finally, in a letter to *The Times* of 5th October 1935, the late Dr. Langdon of Oxford suggested that the photograph of the inscription had been printed upside down. And that when read from left to right, which was the original direction of this script, the sentence seemed to be complete, although the last four letters are uncertain. His decipherment was: Z—D—Q—W Q—T—.—Y W —(?)—Y—(?)—H. This he read, "Zidqo qati we" . . . which meant, "His righteousness is my hand (or support) and . . ."

The learned Professor went on to point out that, while the language is identical with the Canaanite glosses in the Tel el Amarna Letters, which are written in the old cuneiform script, yet the phraseology is strikingly similar to that of the Hebrew Bible. And that this inscription, as well as the one on the ewer, indicates that the Hebrews had already invented the system of pointing vowels. Dr. Langdon went on to state that the discovery makes it entirely believable that literature, before Moses, also existed in alphabetical script. He wrote:

"These are not traditions handed down the ages by memory only. They were actually incorporated into written documents as early as the thirteenth century. Obviously we have here the most important discovery of modern times in respect to Biblical criticism."

Dr. Langdon's letter will be found, quoted in full, on page 275 of the Appendix.

The expression, "His righteousness is my hand (or support)" corresponds with the passage, "Be thou their arm every morning" (Isa. xxxiii. 2); and it further reminds us of the lofty sentiments expressed by Moses in his farewell address to Israel:

"The Eternal God is thy dwelling place, and underneath are the everlasting arms."    (Deut. xxxiii. 27.)

The third Sinai Hebrew inscription, is on a fragment of a bowl found on the floor of the upper level of the temple. In a further letter published in *The Times* of 17th October 1936, Dr. Langdon deciphers this inscription to read:

"Baallil" or "Lord of the Night."   He says that it

is strikingly like the name of a pagan Canaanite deity referred to in the Old Testament—Beliyā'al or Belial. The one allusion in the New Testament appears to establish the identity of this deity with the Lord of the Night. St. Paul writes:

"What communion hath light *with darkness*? And what concord hath Christ with Belial?"

(2 Cor. vi. 14-15.)

The fourth example of this Sinai Hebrew script was found inside the lid of a small burnished pottery censer. This shapely circular vessel is made of the same quality clay and finish as the ewer. The loose lid has two pierced lugs which fit corresponding ones on the vessel. The upper side of the lid is decorated with incised ornaments of trees or plants; on the underside are three letters of this alphabet painted in red ochre. Mr. Theodor Gaster suggests that it reads, "This is the back" (or underside).

Four pictographic characters have also been recently found at Lachish engraved on the blade of a Hyksos dagger. These may be related to the earlier history of the Sinai Hebrew script before 1600 B.C.

There is therefore no longer any doubt that this writing was in general use in Palestine after Joshua had conquered the country. The date provisionally assigned for these early evidences of alphabetical writing at Lachish is 1295–1262 B.C., but some of the objects, like the ostrakon found at Beth Shemesh, may be earlier. Thus the ewer was in a rubbish heap of the temple destroyed at the above date, but other objects found in use in the temple when it was destroyed date back to 1400 B.C. It is true that they were scarabs of Amenhetep III and not so perishable as the ewer. But even if this rough provisional dating is accepted, we are face to face with the fact that, within about a century of the conquest of Canaan, a script that was employed in Sinai in the days of Moses was in general use at Lachish. The obvious suggestion is that the Israelites learned to use the script when in the Wilderness of Sinai, and brought it with them into Palestine when they conquered the country under Joshua.

The circumstances surrounding the initial use of this script at Serabit, in the peninsula of Sinai, as they present themselves to us, are significant in themselves. Here is the best system of recording human speech in writing, first found in common use among turquoise miners in the centre of the inaccessible peninsula of Sinai. We ask ourselves—Why among miners of all people? And why in the centre of an inaccessible land like the peninsula of Sinai? The invention of such a system was worthy of the trained imagination of a great human genius. The place of its birth some great Union Theological Seminary or College, like that recently found at Ras Shamra, the ancient city of Ugarit, in highly civilized northern Syria. Instead "illiterate folk" like miners, and an illiterate mining camp in Sinai. Sinai, the wilderness into which Moses led the twelve tribes of Israel—Moses, learned in all the wisdom of Egypt—Moses who had lived for many years in Midian, the centre of the mining fraternity. There is small need to stress the evidence. The facts speak for themselves. Their emphasis is reminiscent of the Revelation, and of the Voice of Thunder, which the Israelites saw and heard in that same peninsula.

Some scholars, in their haste to prove the Israelites were illiterate, have not even noticed the instructions of Moses to the Israelites to write things down. For how could they write anything down? The crushing answer now seems to be—How could the miners at Serabit, at that very time, be writing things down? But the fact remains that they did. And with such evidence, it becomes obvious that the Israelites, under the leadership of Moses, might most certainly do the same. So the task assigned to His Chosen People in the following inspired passage was not an impossible one:

"Hear, O Israel: Jehovah our God is one Jehovah: And thou shalt love Jehovah thy God with all thine heart, and with all thy soul, and with all thy might. And these words, which I command thee this day, shall be upon thine heart: And thou shalt teach them diligently unto thy children, and shalt talk of them when thou sittest in thine house, and when thou walkest by the way, and when thou liest down, and when thou risest up. And thou shalt bind them for a sign upon thine hand, and they shall be for frontlets between thine eyes. *And thou shalt write them upon the door posts of thy house, and upon thy gates.*" (Deut. vi. 4-9.)

No need, then, to assign these injunctions any longer to the time of the Jewish king Josiah—just a mere matter of seven centuries later! The stones of Sinai are testifying to the fact that alphabetical writing was in common use in the region through which the Israelites had previously passed, at the very time Moses addressed these words to them. And if anyone has desired evidence that the Israelites ever learned to use the writing language of the Midianite miners, it is now supplied him by the Lachish discoveries. These prove that they did so, and suggest that they introduced it into both Palestine and Phœnicia. It is interesting in this connection to recall the instructions that Moses gave to Joshua:

"It shall come to pass that in the day when ye shall pass over Jordan unto the land which Jehovah thy God giveth thee, that thou shalt set thee up great stones, and plaister them with plaister; and *thou shalt write upon them all the words of this law* . . . and it shall be that ye shall set up these stones in Mount Ebal, and thou shalt plaister them with plaister. . . . *And thou shalt write upon the stones all the words of this Law very plainly.*" (Deut. xxvii. 2-8.)

In accordance with these instructions we further read:

"Then Joshua built an altar unto Jehovah the God of Israel in Mount Ebal. . . . *And he wrote there upon the stones a copy of the law of Moses.*"

(Joshua viii. 30-32.)

As we study these verses with the new evidence now at our disposal, it seems natural and reasonable to suppose that Joshua used the Sinai Hebrew script. The plaster on the stones would prove a more tractable surface on which to inscribe its characters than that of the stones themselves.

Authorities agree that the specimens of this script found at Lachish, and elsewhere, constitute the connecting link between the Sinai and the Phœnician alphabet and characters. Some years ago a date of about 1200 B.C. was ascribed to an inscription in these characters on the tomb of a Phœnician king named Ahiram. It was not then evident that so early a date was justified; there is no longer any doubt that it was correct. On the other hand we know, from the Ras Shamra inscriptions, that the Phœnicians were reproducing this alphabetic script in cuneiform characters between 1400–1350 B.C. It would seem as though they discarded these in favour of the Sinai Hebrew script at a later date. It is always possible that further discoveries may modify previous conclusions; but at present it seems clear that the Israelites possess a claim, prior to that of the Phœnicians, for the introduction of the alphabet. And those characters which represent that very ancient alphabet have, with many modifications, become the alphabet we use at the present time.

To us, who are mere outsiders, it seems strange that neither the Egyptians, nor the Babylonians, nor the Assyrians, nor other ancient civilizations, ever adopted this simple alphabetical system of writing. It may be that we overlook a curious kink in human nature, which treats complications as indicative of culture and learning, and takes less account of the simpler and more direct ways of life. The Chinese illustrate this tendency in the case of their writing; the Chinese alphabet still contains thousands of characters. The Phœnicians, who so readily adopted and used the alphabetical script, became, as we know, the greatest commercial nation of their day. It is probable, to say the least, that some of the northern tribes of Israel were intimately associated with them in their maritime and other adventures. The relationship that existed between Solomon, and Hiram king of Tyre, supplies an example. But as the Phœnicians learned their writing from the Israelites, so the Israelites, fresh from the Wilderness wanderings, seem to have learned their idolatry from the Phœnicians. That may be regarded as another inference from the Lachish excavations.

It is clear that the Sinai Hebrew characters were a primitive form of writing, which could either be carved on rock, or painted on pottery. But they did not lend themselves to writing on papyrus sheets, which was the medium used for paper in ancient times. It is evident that the flowing characters of the Phœnician Hebrew script, used to write the Lachish Letters, were invented for this purpose.

These Letters, whose discovery and decipherment are recorded in the next chapter, were written about 600 B.C. That is some seven centuries after the specimens of the Sinai Hebrew were painted on the pottery found in the earlier deposits of the city. But there is evidence that this Phœnician Hebrew writing dates back many centuries before 600 B.C. More will be said about it in the following chapters. So far as is known at present, it would seem as though the Sinai Hebrew script usually reads from left to right, like our own writing, while the Phœnician Hebrew reads from right to left, like modern Hebrew.

In conclusion it may be said, that the circumstances surrounding this Sinai alphabetical script supply yet another clue to the mystery of Inspiration. They suit the Old Testament Narrative, and they suit the tradition concerning its authorship. Indeed they do more, they dovetail into them. As we gaze upon the complete picture presented to us, we feel compelled to infer from it, that *the Bible began to be written when, and where, alphabetical writing began to be written*. And that there may be an even closer relationship than has yet been brought to light.

## IX

## THE LACHISH LETTERS

THE 29th of January 1935, is a date to be remembered by those who are interested in the Bible. For on that day the Lachish Letters were found in the debris of the gate tower of the city. And the finding of these written documents of the time of Jeremiah, bridges the gap between the writings of that prophet, and the writing of the oldest Hebrew manuscript of the Bible in existence. This latter is thought to be the one in the Karaite Synagogue in Cairo; and the date assigned to it is A.D. 895. Since the date of the Lachish Letters is approximately 600 B.C., they were written no less than fifteen hundred years before the Cairo Manuscript. There are however, copies of the Greek, or Septuagint, version of the Old Testament that are five hundred years older than the Hebrew. They reduce the interval to one thousand years; but even that is a very long period of time; we realize how long when we consider that it is less than a thousand years since the days of William the Conqueror; or that it is little more than seven hundred since Magna Charta was written. It is evident, from an inspection of this historical document in the British Museum, that many changes have taken place both in language, and in caligraphy, since the days of King John.

Until the Lachish Letters were found, there was little knowledge of the script in which the Old Testament would be written in the time of Jeremiah, and no certainty that it was written in the Hebrew language. That may have caused some to doubt whether it was even then written down at all; others to suggest that it was written in Aramaic. The uncertainty rendered possible that wide field for speculation, to which references have been made. The Lachish Letters are written in ink; in carbon ink, ~~similar to what was used for the Codex Sinaiticus~~, and with a reed pen. They are written on pieces of broken pottery, which are called "potsherds" in the Bible. They were found in the rubbish on the floor of the gate tower, of the Lachish destroyed by Nebuchadnezzar, king of Babylon. This was below the remains of the eastern tower of the outer Persian gateway. When those ruins were removed, there was found the cobbled floor of an earlier chamber, with a layer of four inches of black mud and ash on its surface. Debris to the height of two feet lay upon this floor, debris of burnt limestone, burnt brickwork, and blackened fragments of pottery. A portion of the latter which were covered with soot, when they were washed, showed lines of ink writing upon them; some of it as clear as the day it was written, others indistinct, and some illegible. The group constitute the famous Lachish Letters; they are called Letters because, with one exception, they prove on decipherment, to be personal letters from one man to another. There are eighteen of them in all, and together they contain ninety lines that are readable. Their decipherment and translation have both been carried out by Professor Harry Torczyner, Bialik Professor of the Hebrew University at Jerusalem. His difficult task has been done in a most painstaking and scholarly manner; it has evoked expressions of admiration and appreciation from all quarters. Scholars who desire to read a complete and technical treatise on these Letters are referred to *The Lachish Letters*, by Professor Torczyner, published by the Oxford University Press. The writer of these lines has been privileged to see an advanced copy of this learned work, and is indebted to it for much that appears in this chapter and the next.

We now know that the Phœnician Hebrew script, in which the Letters are written, was the script used by the Jews, and indeed by the Israelites as well, up to the time of the Babylonian captivity. It was superseded by the Assyrian Hebrew script, which is used to-day, and seems to be a product of the Babylonian captivity. The family of Maccabees who delivered the Jews from oppression between 175 B.C. and 100 B.C., or long after they had returned from Babylon, unsuccessfully sought to revive the older script, and used it on their coinage. In the course of succeeding centuries it fell into complete disuse, and has been so forgotten that some of its characters were unknown. The Samaritans who live at Nablus (Shechem) show a copy of their Pentateuch to visitors, which they affirm dates almost back to the days of Aaron. Some scholars seem to have decided that it is later than the Jewish Hebrew text. But since the Phœnician Hebrew script of the Lachish Letters resembles the writing of the Samaritan Pentateuch, it is evident that the latter represents a far older version than has been accredited to it. Other writings that have been found in Palestine in the Phœnician Hebrew, are the Siloam inscription of the time of Hezekiah (700 B.C.), a few potsherds recording sales of wine and oil found at the excavations of Samaria and dated 850–750 B.C., and a single sherd found in the excavations of Ophel (600 B.C.).

A superficial study of what has been written about the Old Testament and its surroundings in the time of Jeremiah, seems sufficient to demonstrate the revolutionary changes that will be made by the discovery of the Lachish Letters. They appear to open up fresh avenues of approach to all manner of problems. In recognition of this fact, Professor Torczyner has pointed out that any future work on the textual criticism of the Old Testament will have to start with the Lachish Letters.

It has already been pointed out that the Phœnician Hebrew script, with its flowing characters, would have been developed through writing on papyrus. The Egyptians used this material for writing from remote antiquity. We have it, on the authority of Sir Frederick Kenyon, that the earliest extant example of writing on papyrus was found at Sakhara in 1893. It contained accounts dated in the reign of the last

king of the V Dynasty (3360 B.C.) Proverbs of
Ptah-hotep, preserved in the Papyrus Prisse, were
copied down about 2500 B.C. There can be no doubt,
therefore, that Moses would be acquainted with
papyrus writing when he became learned in all the
Wisdom of Egypt. The Sinai Hebrew script, described
in the previous chapter, was probably used for writings
on stone, like the "Tables of the Law" (Exodus xxxiv.
1, 27, 28). But there are several references in Exodus
and Numbers, and half a dozen and more in Deuteronomy, to writing in a book. There is a curious
passage, from which one may infer, that the writing
of a book could be dissolved into water (Numbers v. 23).
Leather and skins were also used in Egypt as material
for writing, long before the days of Moses. Indeed,
it is probable that the Old Testament had always
been written on skins. Josephus states that the copies
brought to Egypt, to be translated into Greek for the
Septuagint about 300 B.C., were written on membranes.
There is a passage in one of the Lachish Letters where
the writer says: "I have written upon the sheet"—
which is an obvious reference to papyrus. But what
is meant by the words—"writing in a book"—as
applied to the days of Moses? Such an expression cannot now be confidently explained away as belonging to
an age that was many centuries after his time. The
evidence of the common use in Egypt of papyrus, and
skins, for writing purposes before the time of Moses,
combined with the discoveries of the Sinai Hebrew
and Phœnician Hebrew scripts, have made such

assumptions quite inadmissible. The book might have consisted of a bunch of skins fastened together, or a roll. And it would seem as though the writing must have been made in ink. Several centuries later David wrote:

"In the roll of the book it is written of me," etc.
(Psalm xl. 7.)

There are later allusions to this form of book. Isaiah is told to take a great roll (Isaiah viii. 1). Baruch, the scribe, wrote in "a roll of a book" all the words of Jeremiah's prophecy. This roll, king Jehoiakim cut with a penknife and cast into a fire (Jeremiah xxxvi. 23). It is interesting to reflect that this incident possibly occurred the very year some of these Lachish Letters were written. Sir Frederick Kenyon has suggested that the fact of a knife being used by Jehoiakim to cut the roll, is an indication that it was probably made of skin or vellum.

Whether the medium employed was papyrus, or skin, or vellum, it is evident that the Phœnician Hebrew script of these Lachish Letters was peculiarly adapted for rapid writing in a flowing style. It is clear that it was in common use in the days of Jeremiah, for the Letters are written in several different hands. Professor Torczyner is of the opinion that this form of writing had taken many centuries to develop, and might even go back to the time of Moses. So Historians, and Lawgivers, Psalmists, Prophets and Priests, all possessed in this Phœnician Hebrew script, a superb instrument for literary expression.

This running script would lend itself to inspired writings—writings that, like a radio, transmit vibrations other than one's own. What is known to-day as automatic writing is probably related to this class of phenomena. King David seemed to have possessed the gift (1 Chron. xxviii. 19, Rev. Version). It would be in this Phœnician Hebrew script he would write those wonderful Psalms associated with his name, but containing evidence of Divine Inspiration. Solomon, his son, could also write (2 Chron. xxxv. 4). He has left us the Proverbs, and other books, including perhaps the Wisdom of Solomon, relegated in mistake to the Apocrypha. It would be interesting to try to ascertain if all the Old Testament authors learned this Phœnician Hebrew script, or whether, like the author of the Lachish Letters, they dictated to scribes. It may be that Bible critics have already pronounced on such questions; but if they were unaware of the very existence of the Phœnician Hebrew script, as well as other matters of first-class importance, their judgments will need revision.

Professor Torczyner considers the discovery of these Lachish Letters to be the most valuable that has yet been made in connection with the Archæology of the Bible. The previous evidence that has been brought to light by this branch of Science, concerning Israel or Judah, has come from enemies—such as Sennacherib's account of his treatment of Hezekiah quoted in a previous chapter—or from men who were only partly of Jewish birth, as in the case of the papyri found at

Elephantine in the interior of Egypt. But the Lachish Letters are contemporary correspondence between orthodox Jews, written in the last days of the kingdom of Judah.

Professor Torczyner affirms that their language is pure Biblical Hebrew; and that it corresponds in phraseology, spelling, style, and composition, with that used in the Second Book of the Kings, and the Book of Jeremiah. The Letters therefore furnish direct confirmation of the authenticity of these particular books, and indirect confirmation of the Old Testament as a whole.

When the Lachish Letters were first found, it was assumed that they were copies of original letters written on papyrus, which had been sent by the Governor of Lachish to the King at Jerusalem. As their contents were deciphered this theory became untenable. It was then recognized that the Letters themselves were not copies at all, but original documents; and it was suggested that they were dictated by some subordinate officer in command of an outpost, to the captain of the guard of the city of Lachish. This supposition still prevails subject to some further modifications and developments.

The name of the subordinate official, who was the writer, or, to be more correct, the author, or dictator, of most of the Letters, is recognized to be one Hoshayahu, or Hoshaiah. He states his name in the opening sentence of Letter III. Sons of Hoshaiah are mentioned in Jeremiah xlii. 1 and xliii. 2, it is quite uncertain whether it would be the same person. This name was also borne by a man who must have been prominent after the Captivity in Babylon (Neh. xii. 32). The Letters are addressed to "my lord Ya'ush" or Jaush. The idea that Jaush was captain of the guard at Lachish, originated from the fact that the correspondence was found in the guardhouse. The abject terms in which Hoshaiah addresses him in these Letters, lead one to conclude that he was a very high official, probably the military governor of Lachish. Next to Jerusalem, Lachish was perhaps then the most important place in the kingdom of Judah. If he were military governor of Lachish, then Jaush must certainly have been an important person. The name does not occur in the Old Testament, so he may perhaps have been a foreigner, or a descendant of a mercenary soldier.

The purport of these Lachish Letters is not evident at first sight; they demand more than a superficial study. While some few statements in them are clear, the rest seem wrapped up in the repetition of fulsome phrases of flattery. So it is hard at first to master the contents, or form any clear idea of what Hoshaiah was intending to tell his lord Jaush. A study of Professor Torczyner's book makes it clear that we should approach the whole correspondence with the recognition that it was of a highly confidential character. That will help to explain its vagueness. And we are further handicapped by the fact that we possess so little knowledge of public events of the period in which the Letters were written, much less of confidential ones. There may be yet another reason for the cryptic character of many of these sentences, and for their repetition. If all the Letters were penned by Hoshaiah himself, and were read by none except Jaush, we should then have something more like the kind of direct correspondence that passes between two people in these times. Yet even then, in handling a very confidential subject, a certain amount of reticence would be observed.

But while it is evident, both from the Book of Jeremiah as well as from these Letters, that writing was in common use in the kingdom of Judah during its last days, it is equally evident that scribes were employed as intermediaries, even as they are in the East to this day. Thus some of Jeremiah's prophecies were dictated by him to Baruch, the scribe, who in turn wrote them down on a roll (Jeremiah xxxvi. 4). And in due course Baruch himself read aloud what he had written to the princes (verse 15). After the roll had been laid up in the chamber of Elishama the scribe (verse 20), Jehoiakim the king sent another scribe named Jehudi to fetch it. Then Jehudi read its contents aloud to the king and to the princes (verse 21). We are not entitled to suppose that the correspondence between Hoshaiah and Jaush was of a more direct character. Hoshaiah would probably dictate what he had to say to a scribe, who would write it down for him. If Hoshaiah was writing about confidential matters, it is obvious that he would have to express himself in a roundabout sort of way, in order to prevent the scribe from knowing too much.

The writings indicate that several scribes were employed by Hoshaiah, perhaps for this very reason. When the contents of the Letters are discussed in the next chapter, it will be seen that in Professor Torczyner's opinion, Hoshaiah was actually refuting charges of divulging confidential information.

But even supposing the scribes employed by Hoshaiah were entirely trustworthy, there was the further danger that the scribe who in turn read his communications to the military governor of Lachish, might reveal them to outsiders. So there may be ample excuse for vagueness on the part of Hoshaiah, and for the continual repetition of compliments; which may have been used to conceal the real import of a particular letter; or they may even have been part of the stock in trade of words of the scribe, rather than those of Hoshaiah. It is suggested that these considerations must be kept in mind when a detailed study of the Letters is made.

The constant use of the Divine Name is another feature of this most ancient correspondence. Those who read the Old Testament account of the downfall of the Jewish monarchy, derive the impression that its idolatries persisted and were accentuated at its close. The Lachish Letters perhaps only represent to us the religious views of its commander and its garrison. But there are indications in the personal names as well, that there had been a Reformation. During the past ten years it has been made clear that the Divine Name, with which we are familiar as Jehovah, was originally

Jah or Yah. This came to be represented in verbal form by the Hebrew letters YHWH—that is to say Yahweh or Jahweh, which means "He causes to be."

The word Jehovah is said to have been an altogether later creation, which has come about by pointing the vowels of the Hebrew word "Adonai" or Lord. Readers are doubtless aware that the name "Jehovah" is translated "lord" in our authorized English versions. But the original is not Jehovah at all, although that Divine Title has been used in the previous chapters of this book. It is Yahweh or Jahweh, as it is written in these Lachish Letters. So to make it quite clear, wherever Yahweh or Jahweh occurs in this chapter and the next, it must be understood to represent the word Jehovah, which is the more familiar through long usage. Then again the Divine Title, as above, is compounded with personal names, in the form of the suffix "Iah." Thus Hosha-yahu, the writer of the Letters, is known to us as Hoshaiah. There is much significance in the fact that in these Letters the Divine Name, always used, and constantly appealed to, is "Yahweh." And there is further significance in the personal names. It is an exception to find a man's name that lacks the suffix "iah" to which reference has just been made.

In this respect the Letters are a testimony to the Monotheism of the kingdom of Judah immediately preceding its Fall; and a further testimony to the worship of Jehovah at that time. This has been attributed to the strenuous religious reformation carried out by Josiah, the father of both Jehoiakim, and of Zedekiah, the last king of Judah. It is said of Josiah:

"And like unto him was there no king before him that turned to Jehovah with all his heart, and with all his soul, and with all his might, according to all the law of Moses; neither after him arose there any like him." (2 Kings xxiii. 25.)

The tragic end of this good king has some slight bearing upon events with which the Lachish Letters are associated. It is described as follows:

"When Josiah had prepared the temple, Neco king of Egypt went up to fight against Carchemish by Euphrates: and Josiah went out against him. But he sent ambassadors to him saying, What have I to do with thee, thou king of Judah? I come not against thee this day, but against the house wherewith I have war; and God hath commanded me to make haste: forbear thee from meddling with God, who is with me, that he destroy thee not. Nevertheless Josiah would not turn his face from him, but disguised himself, that he might fight with him, and hearkened not unto the words of Neco, from the mouth of God, and came to fight in the valley of Megiddo. And the archers shot at king Josiah; and the king said to his servants, Have me away; for I am sore wounded. So his servants took him out of the chariot, and put him in the second chariot that he had, and brought him to Jerusalem; and he died, and was buried in the sepulchres of his fathers. And all Judah and Jerusalem mourned for Josiah. And Jeremiah lamented for Josiah": etc.

(2 Chron. xxxv. 20-25.)

The fate of Josiah, king of Judah, recalls that of Ahab, king of Israel, who fell at Ramoth Gilead in battle with the Syrians (1 Kings xxii.). Josiah had endeavoured to intervene in a war between Egypt and Assyria, presumably on behalf of the Assyrians, the same people who had captured Lachish, and threatened his great grandfather, Hezekiah. The Assyrian Empire fell soon after Josiah's death. Henceforth the closing years of the Jewish monarchy are concerned in the struggle between Egypt and Babylonia. After his victory at Megiddo, Pharaoh Necho deposed Josiah's son Jehoahaz, and made his brother Eliakim king, and changed his name to Jehoiakim. But Nebuchadnezzar, king of Babylon, defeated the Egyptians, invaded Judah, and compelled Jehoiakim to serve him. It is probable that Nebuchadnezzar first burnt Lachish at this time, and again a dozen years later in the reign of Zedekiah. The fullest account of what happened is set out in the following passage in Josephus:

"But when Nebuchadnezzar had already reigned four years, which was the eighth of Jehoiakim's government over the Hebrews, the king of Babylon made an expedition with mighty forces against the Jews, and required tribute of Jehoiakim, and threatened on his refusal to make war against him. He was affrighted at this threatening, and bought his peace with money, and brought the tribute he was ordered to bring for three years." (Josephus, *Antiq.*, X, 6.1.)

Anarchy ensued in Judah, and despite the warnings of Jeremiah the prophet, Jehoiakim turned to Egypt.

This caused the further intervention of Nebuchadnezzar, and the death of Jehoiakim. Nebuchadnezzar then placed on the throne his brother Zedekiah, who in turn rebelled against him, in the hope of Egyptian help, which failed to come and save Judah. This led to the final destruction of Lachish and Jerusalem and the carrying of the Jews away captives into Babylon.

The Lachish Letters were most likely written in the last three years of Jehoiakim, when he was paying tribute to Nebuchadnezzar; that is to say between 600 B.C. and 596 B.C. They were found lying between two layers of burnt debris, implying two distinct destructions; and there is marked evidence from other ruins in the city of these two different destructions. Nor can the lower one be possibly dated back to Sennacherib's siege. We may speculate whether the earlier was the work of Pharaoh Necho, or to this earlier invasion of Nebuchadnezzar; or whether it happened during the time of anarchy that occurred in the last years of Jehoiakim when:

"Jehovah sent against him bands of the Chaldeans, and bands of the Syrians, and bands of the Moabites, and bands of the children of Ammon."

(2 Kings xxiv. 2.)

The Letters convey the impression that the Lachish garrison and its governor, to whom they were addressed, sympathized with the utterances of Jeremiah and other prophets, and favoured their religious policy rather than that of the king, court, and priesthood.

A few other general remarks about the Letters may

be made before considering them in detail. It has been observed that nearly all of them seem to be attempts on the part of the author to exonerate himself from accusations that have been made against him. What those accusations were, are matters of inference which will be dealt with in the next chapter.

The Wellcome Expedition were fortunate to find definite literary proof in Letter IV, for the identification of the ruins of Tell Duweir with those of Lachish, at such an early stage of their work. And the simultaneous association of Azekah with Lachish, is of additional interest in view of the passage in Jeremiah xxxiv. 6, 7, already quoted in Chapter V. That passage associates Nebuchadnezzar's attack on Lachish and Azekah with the final siege of Jerusalem. This began in the ninth year of Zedekiah's reign, and lasted for eighteen months. But there is a paragraph in the writings of Josephus the Jewish historian which gives a more detailed account of the course of events. It runs as follows:

"Now when Zedekiah preserved the league of mutual assistance he had made with the Babylonians *for eight years*, he brake it and revolted to the Egyptians, in hopes by their assistance of overcoming the Babylonians. When the king of Babylon knew this, he made war against him: he laid his country waste, *and took his fortified towns*, and came to the city Jerusalem itself to besiege it: but when the king of Egypt heard what circumstances Zedekiah his ally was in, he took a great army with him, and came into Judea, as if he would raise the siege. Upon which the king of Babylon departed from Jerusalem and met the Egyptians, and joined battle with them, and beat them, and when he had put them to flight, he pursued them, and drove them out of all Syria. Now as soon as the king of Babylon was departed from Jerusalem, the false prophets deceived Zedekiah."

(Josephus, *Antiq.*, X, 7.3.)

Josephus goes on to relate how Jeremiah endeavoured to confute the predictions of the false prophets that the king of Babylon would not return; and he tells how Jeremiah, when he was going to visit his native city of Anathoth, was arrested and imprisoned (cf. Jer. xxxvii. 11, 12). After that incident Josephus continues:

"Now in the ninth year of Zedekiah, on the tenth day of the tenth month, the king of Babylon made *a second expedition* against Jerusalem, and lay before it eighteen months," etc. (Josephus, *Antiq.*, X, 7.4.)

This is clearly the siege of Jerusalem referred to in 2 Kings xxv. 1–3.

According then to Josephus, Lachish probably fell in the ninth year of Zedekiah, before Jerusalem was finally invested. The mystery of the two burnings of Lachish so close together might be explained by the supposition that Nebuchadnezzar destroyed it twice in these last three years, but that does not seem possible. And it is more consistent with the evidence of the Letters themselves to place the earlier burning in the eighth year of Jehoiakim. The sentence "for these alone remained of the cities of Judah as fenced cities" (Jerem. xxxiv. 7), implies that there had been an earlier destruction of other fortified cities, including probably Lachish.

So with the evidence at present at our disposal let us regard the two burnings, between which the Lachish Letters were found, as having occurred, the one in the eighth year of the reign of Jehoiakim, and the other in the ninth year of Zedekiah, or about a dozen years apart.

Mr. Starkey has pointed out that the Letters numbered II, VI, VII, VIII, XVIII are all pieces from the same pot. In that case one may assume that they were all written about the same time, and emanate from the same source. Professor Torczyner claims that the handwriting of XVIII resembles that of VI and XII, as well as II and III. And that XVI bears internal evidence of coming from the same source.

He also points out that the writing of No. I resembles that of VIII. The handwriting gives no indication of the order of date, though it does of identity. There is therefore sufficient evidence to enable us to believe that the Letters are all from Hoshaiah to Jaush. They were probably originally packed together in one pot. In that case other archives may have been kept at Lachish, and there is hope that more writings on pottery fragments may be brought to light. They may still lie stored in the ruins of some of the official buildings of the city destroyed by Nebuchadnezzar. But the immediate problem that confronts us is: How did these fragments come to be strewn in the ashes on the stone-paved floor of the guardroom?  The contents of the documents, to be discussed in the next chapter, suggest that they belong to the reign of Jehoiakim. Although Professor Torczyner presents an alternative explanation in his book for dating them in the time of Zedekiah.  There are difficulties to either dating. But the more likely course of events would seem to have been as follows:  The hostile invasions in Zedekiah's reign may have caused Hoshaiah to take refuge in Lachish, long after he had written to say he was observing its signals rather than those of Azekah.  In these old times, and in these ancient cities, the gateway was a recognized place for a judicial inquiry. When Hoshaiah was tried, the pot containing his Letters would be brought there from the archives, and left there.  Later the city was attacked, captured and burnt.  During the burning and collapse of the gate-tower, the pot would become broken and the inscribed potsherds strewn among the debris.

The problems created by the whole correspondence, and the surrounding circumstances, are extremely interesting but involved.  Professor Torczyner, who deciphered the Letters, and Mr. Starkey who found them, have, of course, a more intimate knowledge of them than anyone else.  And the writer's own views here expressed, where they may differ from these authorities, are advanced with some diffidence.  The potsherds, on which the Letters have been written, were exhibited at the Wellcome Research Institution in London in the summers of both 1935 and 1936.  Various attempts were made to restore the ink writing where it was uncertain or had faded completely, but without success.

In the winter of 1935 a meeting of the Palestine Oriental Society was held in Jerusalem, at which Professor Torczyner presided. The Lachish Letters formed the subject of discussion, and criticisms were offered both of Professor Torczyner's readings and his conclusions. They appear to have been mainly concentrated on his translation of the characters which stand for the word " prophet," and on his identification of the prophet. So far as the decipherment and translation of the Letters are concerned, Professor Torczyner should be the best judge. Scholars who are interested in those issues are referred to his full publication now in the press. The present writer can only judge on the basis of the Professor's translation, on the basis of the archæological facts, and on the basis of the internal evidence of the Letters in their relation to the Old Testament. If these are correct, and their significance correctly appraised, our readers can decide whether there is any room for reasonable doubt on the identification of the prophet, to which reference will be made in the next chapter.

## X

# MORE ABOUT THE LACHISH LETTERS

THE order in which the Letters are numbered is a purely arbitrary one, and carries no significance. Letter No. I may even be the last of all. That would be the case if it is Hoshaiah's list of witnesses, as Professor Torczyner has tentatively suggested:

*Letter No. I.*

> " Gemeriah son of Hissiliah
> Jaazaniah son of Tobshillem
> Hagab son of Jaazaniah
> Mibtahiah son of Jeremiah
> Mattaniah son of Neriah."

As an alternative suggestion, this list of names may represent adherents of the prophet mentioned in Letter VIII, which perhaps accompanied it, for the two seem to be in the same handwriting. No. I is taken first in this chapter because it is detached in a sense from the remainder. There is only this list of ten names, yet they serve as a good introduction to the whole correspondence. There are, however, really only nine names, since Jaazaniah occurs twice. Seven of these are mentioned in the Old Testament, and no less than six in the time of Jeremiah the prophet.

Gemariah is a name familiar to Old Testament readers. Gemariah, the son of Hilkiah, was sent as an ambassador by Zedekiah to Nebuchadnezzar; Jeremiah the prophet entrusted a letter to him unto the Jews in captivity in Babylon (Jer. xxix. 3). And there was beside Gemariah the son of Shaphan the scribe, mentioned several times in connection with the incident of Jehoiakim's burning of the roll (Jer. xxxvi. 10–12, 25).

Jaazaniah was a common name at this period. No less than four bearers of it are mentioned, and all contemporary with the time the Lachish Letters were written. There is Jaazaniah the Maachathite, a captain mentioned in 2 Kings xxv. 23. There is Jaazaniah, the son of Jeremiah, one of the chief Rechabites (Jer. xxxv. 3). There is Jaazaniah, the son of Shaphan, an idolatrous priest (Ezek. viii. 11). And there is Jaazaniah, the son of Azzur, one of the princes (Ezek. xi. 1). So the name was quite a favourite one. It means, "Jah is hearing."

The name Tobshillem does not occur in the Old Testament. It would seem to be a combination of "Tob," meaning "fruitful" or "good," and the word "shillem" which means "recompense." There was a family of Shillemites (Num. xxvi. 49). The name Tobshillem occurs also in Letter XVIII, where he is apparently to be the bearer of a letter from the governor of Lachish to Jerusalem, probably to the king.

The next name is Hagab, the son of Jaazaniah. If

it is the same Jaazaniah who was in turn the son of Tobshillem, the bearer of the letter to Jerusalem, then three generations figure in this list. The expression "children of Hagab" occurs in Ezra ii. 46, as belonging to the Nethinim, a class of servants employed as assistants to the Levites. Professor Torczyner says the word Hagab means "Locust."

Mibtahiah is another name that does not appear in the Old Testament. He is represented on the list as the son of Jeremiah. But which Jeremiah? There are half a dozen or more individuals of that name mentioned in the Old Testament; but only three in the period of the Lachish Letters. These are Jeremiah of Libnah, whose daughter Hamutal was the wife of King Josiah, and mother of the last king Zedekiah; Jeremiah, the son of Hilkiah the prophet, who was of the line of Abiathar; and Jeremiah the Rechabite (Jer. xxxv. 3), the father of one of the Jaazaniahs. This name Jeremiah is believed to occur also in Letter XVII. So far as is known, Jeremiah the prophet had no son named Mibtahiah.

Mattaniah is a name familiar to us. The last king of Judah bore it before Nebuchadnezzar made him king, and changed it to Zedekiah (2 Kings xxiv. 17). It was also the name of a Levite who lived about that time (Neh. xiii. 13).

The name Neriah, the father of this Mattaniah, recalls Baruch, the son of Neriah. Baruch was the scribe who was closely associated with Jeremiah the prophet (Jer. xxxii. 12), and became his amanuensis (chap. xxxvi., etc.). Baruch had a brother named Seraiah who was chief chamberlain (Jer. li. 59); but there is no mention of Mattaniah. At the same time Neriah is an unusual name, and does not occur elsewhere. It means, "Jah is light."

At the time of writing, no name on this list can be definitely identified with men mentioned in the Old Testament, but in some instances they may be the same. The certain fact is that more than half belong to the time of Jeremiah.

Since Letter VIII is said to be in the same writing as this list, and may have accompanied it, let us take it next.

*Letter No. VIII.* Illegible, but contains the word "prophet"; while on the reverse side the words, "I am writing," are discernible.

As previously stated, Professor Torczyner thinks "I am writing" may refer to the list of names in No. I, for the handwriting is alike. Here it will be noticed that there is writing on both sides of this piece of pottery. That is the case on other pieces, and it is gratifying to observe that some yield better results. The mention of the word "prophet," associates this letter with the rest of the correspondence, in which the affairs of the prophet occupy a prominent place.

There are two prophets to which reference is made in the Bible narrative of this period. The best known is, of course, the prophet Jeremiah. Strange to say, he is not mentioned at all in the Second Book of the Kings;

but a reference is made to him in the Second Book of Chronicles. The Book of Jeremiah contains a detailed record of his prophecies, and his sufferings. He displayed great courage and fortitude from first to last, remained at his post, and escaped with his life. The other prophet was Uriah, the son of Shemaiah, who fled to Egypt to escape the wrath of the king. For reasons which are convincing, Professor Torczyner has identified this Uriah with "the prophet" mentioned on this and the other potsherds. It is interesting to notice that the expression "open-eyed" is used to designate the prophet. The words take us back eight centuries to the dramatic occasion when Balaam was summoned to curse Israel, and blessed them. There Balaam describes himself as, "The man whose eyes are open" (Num. xxiv. 3).

The next Letter to be introduced to our notice is No. II. Again there is no particular reason to regard it as in its proper sequence; it is quoted now because it supplies a further introduction to what follows:

*Letter No. II.*

1. To my lord Jaush: may Jahweh let hear
2. My lord tidings of peace (well being)
3. Even now, even now. Who is thy slave
4. a dog, that my lord has remembered his
5. slave, may Jahweh investigate (and punish)
6. my saying something which I did not (even) know.

Here we begin to encounter the mystery which is a feature of these Letters. This communication seems to imply that Hoshaiah has received a despatch from Jaush, which suggests that he has been revealing confidential information; and he replies, in effect, that he could not have revealed it because he did not know it. The expression, "Who is thy slave, a dog," etc., is met with several times in the Old Testament. Here it is an Oriental way of expressing the honour that has been conferred upon the recipient in receiving a message from a superior. When Elisha the prophet, told Hazael the Syrian, that he foresaw the evil that he would do to the children of Israel, Hazael replied:

"What is thy servant, which is but a dog, that he should do this great thing."      (2 Kings viii. 13.)

Because it is a fragment from the same piece of pot, Letter VI may be associated with the one that has just been quoted. It reads as follows:

*Letter No. VI.*
1. To my lord Jaush.   May Jahweh let see (us)
2. my lord (while) thou (art) even now in peace. Who is
3. thy slave, a dog, that my lord has sent the (lett)er
4. of the king, and the letters of the offic(ers say)
5. -ing.   Read I pray thee, and (thou wilt) see the words of the (prophet)
6. are not good, (liable) to loosen the hands (to make)
7. sink the hands of the coun(try and) the city . . . .
8. . . . . . . . . . . . . . My lord wilt not thou
9. write to (them saying) :  why should ye do
10. thus ! . . . . . . . . . . . . . . . . . . . . . . . . .

11. . . . . . . . . . . . . . . . . . . . . . . . .
12. . . . . . . . . . . . . . Jahweh lives thy god
13. and my l(or)d lives (to punish) if any sla-
14. ve has read the letter and (anybody has tri)ed
15. to rea(d it to him or has s)een (of it)
16. (anything)

From this Letter the further information is derived that Jaush had sent Hoshaiah letters of the king and of the officers complaining that the words of a certain person were detrimental to the national interest. Similar expressions are used in connection with Jeremiah and his prophecies:

"Then the princes said unto the king—'Let this man, we pray thee, be put to death; forasmuch as he weakeneth the hands of the men of war that remain in this city, and the hands of all the people,'"

(Jer. xxxviii. 4.)

It will be observed that the first half of line 8 on this potsherd VI is indecipherable. Perhaps, like the passage just quoted from Jeremiah, it read: "Let this man be put to death." That would accord with what follows: "My lord wilt not thou write to them saying why should ye do thus." There follows another tantalizing blank, and a repetition, in a slightly different form, of the denial in Letter II. There Hoshaiah says he knows nothing about it. Here he writes as though he has been asked to explain how the contents of some letter have become known.

*Letter No. VII.*—Another of the pieces from the same pot, but it is indecipherable.

*Letter No. VIII* was referred to in conjunction with the list of names at the beginning of the chapter. It will be remembered that it alludes to the prophet, but that is all.

*Letter No. XVIII.—*

1. Until the evening (when comes Tob)shillem shall send thy slave the letter which
2. my lord has sent, from here into the city.

Which would seem to mean that, on the arrival of Tobshillem in the evening, Hoshaiah would send Jaush's letter, or one that Jaush had sent on to him, into the city. It will be remembered that the name of Tobshillem, occurs as the father of Jaazaniah, in the list of names on Letter No. I. The word "Shillem" is closely related to "Shallum," a name which occurs in another letter. The words "the city" undoubtedly refer to Jerusalem, and probably to the king. Perhaps this letter, sent to Jerusalem, was the result of Hoshaiah's appeal to Jaush to use his influence to save Uriah (see Letter VI). This exhausts the Letters that come from pieces of the same pot.

The handwriting of the next Letter resembles that of Letter No. II which has already been recited, but that supplies no indication of its place in the series:

*Letter No. III.*

1. Thy slave Hoshaiah has sent to
2. tell my lord Jaush may
3. Jahweh let hear my lord tidings of peace
4. (and now) thy slave has sent a letter to the open eyed

5. (And in it) referred thy slave to the letter which
6. my lord had sent to thy slave yesterday (and has said) that
7. thy slave's heart is sick, since thou has sent to thy slave
8. And that he says ; my lord I do not know (it)
9. to read a letter. Jahweh lives (to punish me) if anybody has tried
10. to read me a letter for ever. And also
11. whatever letter came to me I
12. Have not read it and even have not seen of it
13. anything. And to thy slave it has been told
14. saying : Down went the commander of the army
15. (Yi)khbariah the son of Elnatan to come
16. to Egypt. And
17. Hodaviah the son of Ahijah and
18. his men he sent (ordered) to take (bring) from here
19. And the letter which Nedebiah the grandson of the king had brought
20. to Shallum the son of Jaddua from the prophet saying
21. Beware ! has thy slave sent to my lord.

Line 18—*i.e.* " he sent (ordered) to bring Hodaviah and his men from here."

This letter contains more information than any other. It was evidently a very important despatch, and Hoshaiah begins it with his own name as sender. He goes on to state that he has sent a letter to the prophet, which referred to the one that Jaush had sent him the previous day. And in that letter, he has expressed his mortification that Jaush had accused him of divulging the contents of another letter, or letters, which presumably concerned the prophet. Hoshaiah, according to his own account here, has sent a letter to the prophet, which referred to the one that Jaush had sent him the previous day. And in that letter, beside expressing his mortification that Jaush had accused him of divulging the contents of letters, denies emphatically that he has done so. Since Hoshaiah says he has sent a letter to the prophet, we infer that he knew the prophet's address. He then reports information concerning the commander of the army going to Egypt, and taking with him Hodaviah, and his men "*from here*," wherever "here" was. And lastly he tells Jaush that he had sent him a warning letter from the prophet brought by Nedebiah, the grandson of the king, to Shallum the son of Jaddua. Let us consider these statements in the light of a short passage in Jeremiah. It reads as follows:

"And there was also a man that prophesied in the name of Jehovah, Uriah the son of Shemaiah of Kirjath-jearim ; and he prophesied against this city and against this land according to all the words of Jeremiah : and when Jehoiakim the king, with all his mighty men, and all the princes, heard his words, the king sought to put him to death ; but when Uriah heard it, he was afraid, and fled, and went into Egypt : and Jehoiakim the king sent men into Egypt, namely, Elnathan the son of Achbor, *and certain men with him*, into Egypt; and they fetched forth Uriah out of Egypt, and brought him unto Jehoiakim the king ; who slew him with the sword, and cast his dead body into the graves of the common people."

(Jer. xxvi. 20-23.)

The relationship between what Hoshaiah tells Jaush, and this passage, is obvious. The scribe who wrote Letter III has clearly made a clerical error in transposing the name Elnathan, the son of Achbor, into Yukbariah, the son of Elnathan. Similar mistakes occur in places in the Old Testament. The sentence in the passage quoted from Jeremiah, that Elnathan took "certain men with him," entirely fits the passage in the letter—that Elnathan ordered Hodaviah and his men "from here" to accompany him. A supposition of Professor Torczyner that Kirjath Jearim was actually the place from which Hoshaiah wrote, becomes highly probable. It was the native town of Uriah; so Elnathan would take from thence men who could identify this prophet. We read in 2 Kings xxiv. 8 that a certain Elnathan of Jerusalem was the brother-in-law of King Jehoiakim. Long before these Letters were found, he was identified with the Elnathan the son of Achbor, who is mentioned both in this connection, as well as in Jeremiah xxxvi. 12 and 25, in the incident of the burning of Jeremiah's roll.

It is evident from Hoshaiah's communication that he suspects, but does not say, what was the object of this mission to Egypt. He concludes his despatch with the statement that Nedabiah, the grandson of the king, has brought a warning letter from the prophet to Shallum, the son of Jaddua, which he, Hoshaiah, had sent on to Jaush.

This warning letter may have led Jaush to suspect that Hoshaiah had divulged to others where Uriah had taken refuge. The reference to "Nedabiah grandson of the king" needs to be read in conjunction with the following passage:

"The sons of Josiah; the firstborn Johanan, the second Jehoiakim, the third Zedekiah, the fourth Shallum. And the sons of Jehoiakim: Jeconiah his son, *Zedekiah his son.* And the sons of Jeconiah, the captive; Shealtiel his son, and Malchiram, and Pedaiah, and Shenazzar, Jekamiah, Hoshama *and Nedabiah.*" (1 Chron. iii. 15-18.)

There seems to be some confusion in this passage. It will be noticed that the name Zedekiah is repeated as though he were a son of Jeconiah, whereas in the previous sentence he is an uncle. Then the name Nedabiah is the last of seven others, presumably of the sons of Jeconiah. But the Royal Genealogy in St. Matthew states that Jeconiah (Jehoiachin) begat Shealtiel after the carrying away to Babylon (Matt. i. 12). Malchiram and Pedaiah were therefore born later, the latter being apparently the real father of Zerubbabel the son of Shealtiel. There remain three other names beside that of Nedabiah. If these four represent men who were born still later in Babylon, then the Nedabiah there, cannot be Nedebiah of the Lachish Letter. But it seems likely that these four names have been added to the Royal Genealogy, not because they were sons of Jeconiah, but because they were also grandsons of Josiah. The Old Testament tells us nothing more of them; they do not appear in the genealogies. They were probably either brothers or cousins of Jeconiah. Since Nedabiah, according to this Lachish Letter, brought a letter from the prophet, he presumably brought it from Egypt, where the prophet had fled. Nedabiah may possibly therefore have been a son of Johanon (Jehoahaz), whom Pharaoh Necho deposed and took to Egypt (2 Kings xxiii. 34), and he would perhaps be come up out of Egypt to visit his relatives. We further read, from this Letter III, that the prophet's letter was first passed on to Shallum, the son of Jaddua. There are a good many Shallums mentioned in the Old Testament; most of them were Levites. One Shallum was the uncle of Jeremiah the Prophet (Jer. xxxii. 7 and xxxv. 4), also a Levite. Jaddua was also a Levitical name. Curiously enough, Hodevah or Hodiah, which may or may not be identified with Hodaviah, whom Elnathan took with him to Egypt, was another Levite name.

The contents of this Letter No. III, compared with the previously quoted Letter No. VI, fit with one another into the Uriah story. And it is possible that Jaush, first suspected Hoshaiah of telling Uriah of the king's threat against him, to which reference seems to be made in Letter VI. Hoshaiah's warning to the prophet, may have led to the latter's flight to Egypt. Meantime Hoshaiah implores Jaush to use his influence with the king to spare the prophet. The passage quoted in Jeremiah xxvi. tells us that Shemaiah was the name of Uriah's father. It will be seen that the name Shemaiah occurs in Letter No. IV, which is further evidence in favour of the place being Kirjath

Jearim. If the Shemaiah referred to in a later letter
as working with Hoshaiah, was the father of Uriah,
that would supply another link in favour of the
conclusion that Hoshaiah warned the prophet.

Those who seek to place the incident of Uriah in the
reign of Zedekiah, point out that in the chapter of
Jeremiah following the one where the incident of Uriah
is mentioned, the name Jehoiakim has been inserted
in mistake for Zedekiah (see Jer. xxvii. 1 and 3). This
is probably correct, and, in the first verse of the twenty-
sixth chapter, the same mistake has been made. But
the alteration, instead of transferring the incident of
Uriah to Zedekiah's reign, establishes the view that
has been expressed here. Every one who will read
through Jeremiah xxvi., must admit that the affair of
Uriah the prophet had *happened before the events that led
to the mention of it.* Those events were the arraignment
of Jeremiah for prophesying against the temple, and
against Jerusalem. Then when the priests called for a
death sentence, Jeremiah warned them, "If ye put me
to death, ye shall bring innocent blood upon your-
selves." Then "certain of the elders" instanced two
precedents: First, the case of a prophet who had
prophesied in a similar strain, to whom King Hezekiah
had given heed instead of punishing him. Up to this
point the elders are clearly on Jeremiah's side. Then,
secondly, they narrate the case of Uriah, where the
prophet was put to death by the king. On the face of
it, this precedent told against Jeremiah. But in reality
it was immensely in his favour. Jehoiakim, *on his own*

*responsibility*, not on that of the princes, or priests, or people, beside shedding innocent blood in the case of Uriah, had not even allowed Uriah's body honourable burial. The affair must have aroused great indignation. Jeremiah prophesied:

"But thine eyes and thine heart are not but for thy covetousness, and for *shedding innocent blood*, and for oppression, and for violence, to do it. Therefore thus saith the Lord concerning Jehoiakim, the son of Josiah, king of Judah: They shall not lament for him saying, Ah my brother! or, Ah sister! They shall not lament for him, saying, Ah lord! or, Ah his glory! He shall be buried with the burial of an ass, drawn and cast forth beyond the gates of Jerusalem."

(Jer. xxii. 17-19.)

The prophet again takes up the theme after the burning of the roll by Jehoiakim:

"His dead body shall be cast out in the day to the heat, and in the night to the frost."

(Jer. xxxvi. 30.)

The Sacred Narrative in both Kings and Chronicles is vague about the fate of Jehoiakim; but Josephus describes his end as follows:

"Now a little time afterward, the king of Babylon made an expedition against Jehoiakim, whom he received into the city, and this out of fear of the foregoing predictions of this prophet, as supposing that he should suffer nothing that was terrible, because he neither shut the gates, nor fought against him; yet when he was come into the city he did not observe the covenants he had made, but he slew such as were in the flower of their age, and such as were of the greatest dignity, together with their king Jehoiakim, whom he commanded *to be thrown before the walls without any burial.*"  (*Antiq.*, X, 6.3.)

If the incidents described in chapter xxvi. occurred in the beginning of Zedekiah's reign, the fate of Jehoiakim would be a vivid memory in the minds of all—princes, priests, and people. To them the moral was obvious. Jehoiakim's death, and lack of burial, was a punishment for the innocent blood of Uriah and his lack of proper burial. Let them beware lest they incurred similar punishment by putting Jeremiah to death. Apart from this simple explanation of a difficult context, the attempt to date the affair of Uriah in the reign of Zedekiah, is entirely contrary to what we know of the characters of the two men; Jehoiakim, malignant and autocratic, Zedekiah afraid of his principal men and irresolute. The king who burnt the roll was obviously the king who slew Uriah.

There seems some doubt as to the site of Kirjath Jearim. Professor Garstang has placed it at Der el Azur, above Kiryat el Anab. The *Onomasticon* places it as being nine miles from Jerusalem. Professor Torczyner, on the other hand, identifies it with Tell Zakaria, which is usually thought to be Azekah, and is further off from Jerusalem. This Azekah lies between Lachish and Der el Azur. Kirjath Jearim was the place where the ark rested in the house of Obed-edom the Gittite, during the early part of the reign of King David. It is significant that one of

Obed-edom's sons was named Shemaiah, and that he in turn had a son Semachiah (1 Chron. xxvi. 4, 6, 7), both names which occur some centuries later in these Lachish Letters, and so support the identification of Kirjath Jearim.

The next Letter for our consideration shall be:

*Letter No. V* (tentative reconstruction).

1. May Jahweh let hear my (lord)
2. (tid)ings of good and (peace even)
3. now, even now.   Who is thy slave
4. a dog, that thou (hast s)ent to thy sla
5. ve, the le(tters of . . .) iah
6. (Now) has thy slave returned the let
7. ters of my lord.   May Jah-
8. weh let thee know what had happen
9. ed.   What has thy slave that he should
10. curse in (the name of) Jahweh seed to the king !

The letter, or letters, that Jaush appears to have sent Hoshaiah, which are referred to in the above, may have been letters from Uriah, or, as Professor Torczyner thinks, from Shemaiah.   Unfortunately the first syllable of the name in line 5 is missing, and the Divine suffix alone remains.   Lines 9 and 10 suggest Jaush had heard that Hoshaiah, in his indignation about the king's treatment of Uriah, had committed the grave offence of cursing the king's posterity.

*Letter No. IX* (tentative reconstruction).

1. May Jahweh let hear my lord
2. tidings of peace.   Who is thy slave
3. a dog that has sent the

4. letters of . . . . . . . . . . thy
5. slave has returned the
6. letters
7. May Jahweh let thee know (the thing)
8. that happened !
9. What it is.

It will be seen on examination that this Letter is an abbreviated repetition of the previous one quoted (Letter V). The charge of cursing the king has, however, been omitted from it.

*Letter No. XVI.* This is a small piece out of the middle of what was once a larger letter, written on both sides. On the reverse, allusions are made to—

'Pestilence and sword'

or pestilence and (noisome) beast, which may refer to threatened punishments for the murder of the prophet. A few years later Ezekiel, the prophet in Babylon, would be uttering his famous prophecy which includes the words:

"How much more when I send my four sore judgements upon Jerusalem, the sword, and the famine, and the noisome beasts, and the pestilence,"

(Ezek. xiv. 21.)

The following five Letters give no additional information:

*Letter No. X.* About thirteen lines are preserved. Here and there letters are distinct, but no words can be read with certainty.

*Letter No. XII.* It is clear that this Letter contains much the same statements as II and VI.

*Letter No. XIV* has traces of single letters, but the only words legible are:

> "May Jahweh . . . my lord.'

*Letter No. XV* is on the largest piece of pottery, but the writing is no longer legible.

*Letter No. XVII*, a fragment which only gives the words:

> "Slave . . . my lord"

and what was perhaps the name of Jeremiah spelt as on Letter I.

There remain three more Lachish Letters, which are associated here, because they mention the same name:

*Letter No. XI* carries traces of about thirteen lines. In line 5, the name "Semachiah" is certain.

*Letter No. XIII.* On one side of this potsherd, everything is illegible. But on the other side, or the reverse, occur the words—

1. "Stand up to do work
2. And Semachiah shall dig it out
3.                        quivers."

Professor Torczyner suggests that this may be the remains of a copy of an order, kept at Lachish, which was sent by its commander Jaush to Hoshaiah.

The next and last Letter is an important one:

*Letter No. IV.*

1. May Jahweh let hear my lord even now
2. tidings of good. According to whatever my lord has sent (written)
3. thus hath thy slave done. I have written on the page according to what

4. ever my lord has sent me. And when my lord has sent

5. about the sleeping house, there is nobo

6. -dy. And Semachiah him has taken Shemaiah and

7. Brought him up to the city, and thy slave, my lord,

8. shall write thither (asking) where he is;

9. because if in his turning he has inspected

10. he would know, that for the signal stations of Lachish we

11. are watching, according to all the signs which my

12. lord gives, because we do not see (the signals of) Aze-

13. -kah.

Reference has already been made to the fact that this Letter establishes the identity of Tell Duweir with Lachish (lines, 10, 11, 12).

The Letter raises anew the problem of where the Letters were written. Could it be possible that from the site which Professor Garstang has identified with Kirjath Jearim, fire signals of Lachish would be visible? It would be interesting to make an experiment. Why were Azekah's signals invisible? What was the nature of them? Was Hoshaiah's station, whether at Kirjath Jearim or elsewhere, a place where signals received from Lachish, and elsewhere, were transmitted to Jerusalem? The relative altitudes are as follows: Lachish, 876 feet; Azekah, 1066 feet; Kirjath Jearim, 1722 feet. So the latter place was 846 feet above Lachish. The Hebrew word used for signals is

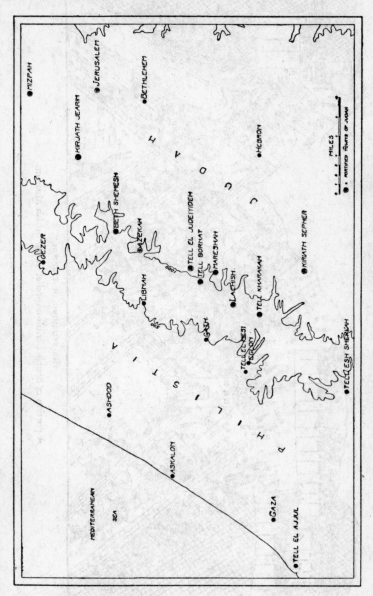

MAP SHOWING POSITION OF LACHISH, AZEKAH, KIRJATH JEARIM, ETC.

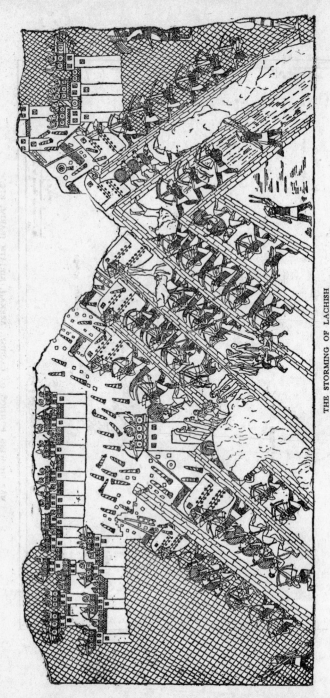

THE STORMING OF LACHISH.

A portion of Sennacherib's bas-relief in the British Museum.

"Maseth," which is said to only occur once in this sense in the Old Testament, thus:

"Flee for safety, ye children of Benjamin, out of the midst of Jerusalem, and blow the trumpet in Tekoa, and raise up a signal on Beth-haccherem: for evil looketh forth from the north, and a great destruction."

(Jer. vi. 1.)

It has already been pointed out that the words, "written on the page" in line 3 of this Letter, are a reference to writing on papyrus. The sleeping house would appear to be a khan, or lodging-house. Then come the names again of Semachiah and Shemaiah, the latter the same as Uriah's father, both names of men that centuries before resided at Kirjath Jearim. "The city" must again be Jerusalem. One or other of these men, probably Semachiah, was perhaps the signal officer. And the expression "in his turning" may be, "in his tour of inspection." If Shemaiah was the father of Uriah, then Semachiah may have taken him to Jerusalem to plead with the king for his son. But the general impression one gains from this Letter is that the end was approaching. Azekah might already have fallen to the enemy from the north—that is to say, the Babylonians. And Jehoiakim was about to meet his doom, as described by Josephus in the passage that has been quoted in this chapter. Perhaps the presence of Shemaiah and Semachiah, in Jerusalem at that time, influenced the course of events described by Josephus.

The Lachish Letters, taken as a whole, throw an interesting light upon the history of the period in which they were written. The denunciations of Jeremiah make it clear that, in the reign of Jehoiakim, the old abominable idolatries which had been abolished in the reign of his father Josiah, were revived in Jerusalem. And cruelty, oppression, and corruption accompanied them.

Yet outside Jerusalem, the reforms instituted by Josiah seem to have survived; at any rate, in western Judah. It would appear as though the governor of Lachish, and his subordinates, were God-fearing men, and represented the Puritans of their day. They lived in a generation which, under the leadership of their king, had all at once lapsed into corruption. They reverenced and respected inspired prophecy, and yet displayed a reluctant loyalty and allegiance to Jehoiakim. He, in the words of Josephus, was wicked and malignant, neither humble towards God nor merciful towards man (*Antiq.*, X, 5.2).

Taken in conjunction with Jeremiah's sayings, the reticence of both Kings and Chronicles concerning Jehoiakim's end, recall the familiar lines—

> " And doubly dying, shall go down
> To the vile dust from whence he sprung,
> Unwept, unhonoured, and unsung."

On the other hand, the influence of this strong undercurrent of religion at Lachish and elsewhere, is repeatedly manifested in the protection and preservation of the prophet Jeremiah.

The accusations made against Hoshaiah by Jaush,

seem to resolve themselves into the charge that he
made himself acquainted with the contents of confidential letters that passed between Lachish and Jerusalem by way of Kirjath Jearim; and that he divulged
some of their contents to third parties. Beside letting
Uriah know of Jehoiakim's threat to kill him, and
causing his flight to Egypt, he may have also inad-
vertently revealed the fact that Uriah had gone there,
to the officers of the king who were looking for the
prophet. In other words, Hoshaiah was accused of
having talked too much.

## XI

## SENNACHERIB'S ASSAULT ON LACHISH

### (701 B.C.)

IT rarely happens that excavators of a ruined city are provided with an illustration of the exterior as it stood more than two thousand six hundred years ago.

Since the site of Lachish has definitely been identified, the bas-reliefs of its siege, which once adorned the walls of Sennacherib's palace of Nineveh, can be studied with renewed interest. They were found as long ago as 1850 by Sir A. H. Layard, and brought to the British Museum.

The title of the whole series of pictures is written in cuneiform above the head of Sennacherib, seated on his throne, receiving the submission of the defenders of the city. It reads:

"Sennacherib, the mighty king, king of the country of Assyria, sitting on the throne of Judgement, before the city of Lachish.—I give permission for its slaughter."

The series of bas-reliefs are carved on thirteen slabs, and they record a succession of events. There is a siege, the assault, the capture, and the processions of prisoners and plunder passing on to Sennacherib.

The walls of Lachish are depicted on the summit of

a steep mound in two alignments. There are towers and projections, which are often pierced, on about the level of the parapet of the wall, with small barred windows. Wooden balustrading, and what look like round shields, project from the parapets of the towers. There are fortified outworks in the neighbourhood of the entrance, and a sally port, or water tower, below the fortifications about halfway down the mound. The country around is represented to be hilly and wooded. The walls and towers are alive with defenders, shooting arrows, and slinging stones, on the attacking forces. The latter have cast up no less than ten siege mounds against the stone glacis protecting the walls. These banks are built of bricks, stones, soil, and trunks of trees laid lengthways. There are seven battering-rams which have been rolled up these runways to the walls. These siege engines are each mounted on four wheels, and have bodies covered with leather, with hoods in front. They each give shelter to three men: one to work the battering-ram, or crowbar with a point, to pick out stones from the wall; another to shoot arrows from under cover of the hood; and a third to pour water from a ladle, with a long handle, upon the fire-brands which the defenders are raining down upon this primitive type of tank.

In the bas-reliefs everything seems to be happening at once: the investment, the siege, the assault, and the surrender. The Old Testament accounts lead us to believe that the siege of Lachish took some little time. The number, and the vigorous and lifelike attitudes of the Assyrian soldiers, making this final assault on the city, are vividly portrayed. Archers are kneeling in the front ranks, in the next they are bending forward, and in the third are standing upright, all portrayed discharging arrows up at the city's defenders. Shield-bearers, with wicker shields covered with hide, are there to protect the archers, who also take shelter behind the tanks. There are slingers and spearmen. Ladders that have been reared for escalading, are falling from the walls, and in a desperate effort to check the advance, the besieged are casting down their own chariots upon the assailants.

The general assault seems to finally sweep up the paved roadway to the city gates. There the work of the siege engines is causing towers, walls, and parapets to fall, and their defenders to be hurled headlong into the ranks of the advancing Assyrian infantry. Large bodies of horsemen and charioteers are shown in reserve.

While all this action is depicted around the city walls in the upper registers of the bas-reliefs, the lower ones are recording the after-effects of the struggle. Although a conflict rages round the water tower; although its turrets are lined with defenders, while a tank picks its masonry to pieces with a long pointed pike; yet from its gate below, there emerges a file of men and women with burdens on their backs. Immediately ahead of this peaceful group, captives are being impaled on stakes. The processions of prisoners and tribute then stream away to our right towards Sennacherib seated upon his throne. They are depicted in two main lines, one above the other. The upper one is headed by a high Assyrian officer and several soldiers. These are followed by half a dozen principal captives, three abjectly kneeling, and three with hands up in surrender. These in turn are guarded by two officers holding maces and wearing daggers. With their backs turned, behind this group, two scribes are questioning two more prisoners whose hands are raised. They are followed by three women, with head shawls which reach to the ankles; beside them is a little boy; they carry sacks, and other articles in their hands. There follows a wagon drawn by two oxen and led by a man. It is laden with sacks, on which sit two women; one nurses a baby, and beside her sits a small child. A man with a bundle on his back, a spearman, and two more male and female prisoners carrying skins of wine, and bundles, come next. Assyrian soldiers carrying plunder bring up the rear. The lower procession is headed by officers, or members of the royal guard, others, with their backs turned, appear to be beheading some prisoners. Then a bowman and spearman escort five prisoners with hands up; while behind, two more, stretched naked on the ground, are having their legs dislocated, perhaps because they had tried to run away. The line is continued by men carrying loads; women and girls, with various articles in their hands; followed by a two-wheel bullock cart led by a clean-shaven man with a turban, and holding a stick. A boy and a girl sit astride the contents of the cart, and behind it walks a very tall man, also wearing a turban and holding up a stick. A camel laden with sacks, led by another man with a turban, and followed by a man who urges on the beast, completes this procession. As already indicated, both these lines of people lead up to the figure of Sennacherib seated on a richly ornamented throne, placed on a mound, with hills in the background. The king's feet rest on a footstool, and behind him stand two attendants holding fans above his head. In the king's right hand are two arrows, and his left rests upon an upright bow. Behind is a royal pavilion, and richly caparisoned led horses. A chariot and horses are below, and a man carrying the royal parasol. Another chariot and more led horses bring up the rear.

At the back of all, there appears to be the ground plan of a fortified camp arranged in a broad oval enclosure. Inside there is an altar with two priests, a table with offerings on it, and various other devices, a sacred chariot, and what look like sections of the royal pavilion with external and internal views.

Such is a brief outline of the Lachish bas-reliefs. In places they are damaged, and some of the details appear to have become obscure. The picture presents us with some interesting characteristics. Most of the men depicted on them, both captors and captives, wear long hair and beards. The Assyrians are portrayed with long beards, and the Jews with short curled ones. The long hair of the Assyrians is curled at the ends and the Jews all over the head. Only the men with turbans appear to be clean-shaven; they may perhaps represent the Canaanite servants.

We have become rather accustomed to photographs and pictures of Egyptian monuments. As these depict clean-shaven men, so the representation of bearded warriors in sculptures of the same period from elsewhere, seems strange to us. Yet the Israelites may always have worn beards. Joseph, when he stood before Pharaoh at the age of thirty, had first to be shaved (Gen. xli. 14). There was a prohibition in the Mosaic Law against cutting off the corners of the beard (Lev. xix. 27), but it would seem to have fallen into disuse so far as the Lachish Jews were concerned, for they are depicted with rounded corners in contrast to the Assyrians, whose beards fall more towards a point. The beard was regarded as a mark of honour and distinction in the ancient East.

The Assyrians spoke a language similar to the Hebrews, and are thought to have been a mixed race with Semitic blood in their veins. On the bas-reliefs they resemble the full-featured Syrians, rather than the lean-faced Arabs.

It will be observed that the helmets of the Assyrian bowmen and slingers rise to a conical peak, while those of the shield-bearers and spearmen have a curious semi-circular projecting comb or crest, which remind us somewhat of our old-pattern firemen's helmets. One of these crests was found in the earlier excavations outside the walls.

The artist has depicted clusters of grapes, olives, figs,

and other trees growing in the surrounding country. The whole scene of the assault of Lachish by Sennacherib's army is somewhat reminiscent of Sir Walter Scott's account of the siege of the Castle of Torquilstone, in *Ivanhoe*. But the Assyrian archers are shooting from short bows instead of the long bows of our Saxon forefathers. Yet although siege operations against Sennacherib's Lachish, and Scott's Torquilstone, were much the same, they are separated by an interval of something like nineteen hundred years.

All that has now changed. Methods of waging war, after remaining constant for thousands of years, have, in our century, taken on a frightful aspect. Here is an excellent illustration of the result of cultivating the Sciences of Matter, and neglecting the Science of Man. Methods of Warfare have changed; but Human Nature remains much the same. Increased material knowledge, and less religious knowledge, are not bringing to civilization the blessings that were anticipated.

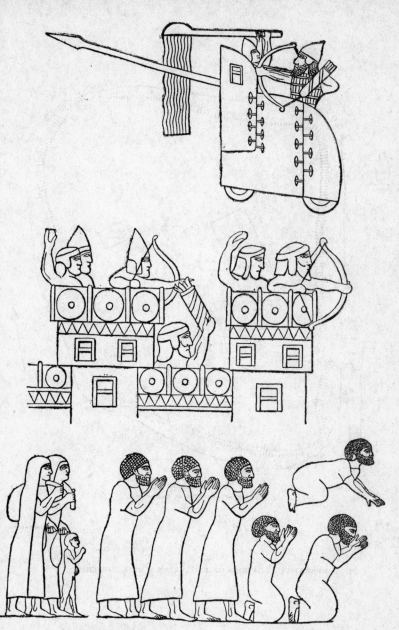

FROM SENNACHERIB'S BAS-RELIEF IN THE BRITISH MUSEUM

*Top :* Assyrian siege engine.   *Centre :* Inhabitant of Lachish hurling lighted
torch from a wall.   *Below :* Submission of the people of Lachish.

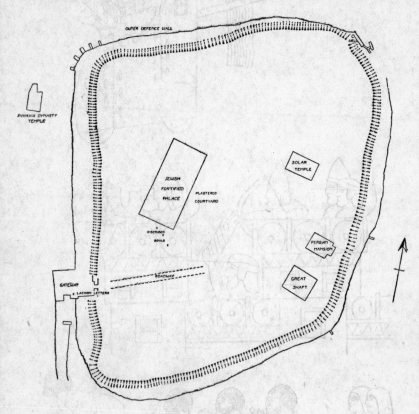

OUTER DEFENCE WALL

XVIII-XIX DYNASTY TEMPLE

SOLAR TEMPLE

JEWISH FORTIFIED PALACE — PLASTERED COURTYARD

INSCRIBED BOWLS

PERSIAN MANSION

ROADWAY

GREAT SHAFT

GATEWAY — LACHISH LETTERS

TELL EL DUWEIR
COMPARATIVE LOCATIONS OF EXCAVATIONS

SCALE = 1/1000

J.H.B.

COMPARATIVE LOCATIONS OF EXCAVATIONS, TELL DUWEIR

# XII

# 1936-37 EXCAVATIONS

T HE distinctive features of this season's excavations have been two important discoveries, both of which are surrounded by some mystery.

The first concerns what is known as the Great Shaft. In the south-east angle of the mound of Tell Duweir, the excavators had for some time noticed a depression shaped like a huge horseshoe. During the season 1934–1935, they dug down to bed-rock at the edge of this hollow, and found the corner of a great rectangular shaft descending vertically through the limestone. In the season 1935–36, they discovered that the surface area of this cutting exceeded eighty feet in one direction, and more than seventy feet in the other; and they reached a depth of forty-five feet, below the surface in one spot, without finding the bottom. The further examination of this rock-cut chasm, occupied a considerable amount of the attention and of the labour of the Expedition during this season. It revealed a very impressive piece of ancient work. Deep and extensive excavations, for foundations of public buildings, are a familiar sight in our large cities, and excite the curiosity of passers-by. People pause to obtain glimpses of the work, in spite of the screens erected to conceal the progress of such

operations. Deep excavations through solid rock, still
arouse pride in human achievement. And this despite
the fact that account is taken of the help of modern
mechanical labour-saving devices, such as power-
driven rock drills, steam navvies, and lifting cranes,
and such like. The great power of explosives is also
brought to bear to blast the mass of rock. And lastly,
the tools of the workers, the picks, the spades, the
chisels, the hammers, etc., are made of specially
toughened hardened steel; while the trucks, hoists,
and their accessories are also of steel or iron. But
suppose there had been none of these appliances; and
that the men engaged on the work had only primitive
tools, of flint, and copper, or at best of soft iron; and
neither labour-saving devices nor explosives to ease
the task of cutting away the solid rock. A huge pit,
that must have been cut with such primitive tools, is
surely a very remarkable piece of work? Such is the
shaft that has been found inside the city of Lachish.
Its surface area is eighty-four feet by seventy-four feet,
and it descends to a depth of eighty-five feet through
the limestone rock. Thus the ancient people of Lachish
quarried out, and removed, some five hundred thousand
cubic feet of solid rock from one place inside their city,
with the aid of tools which would to-day be regarded
as quite inadequate. Why did they do so? Here is
the mystery for which the Expedition is trying to find a
solution. In the meantime Mr. Starkey describes the
work, as representing one of the greatest engineering
feats achieved by the ancient craftsmen of Judah.

The task of digging out, and removing, the whole of the debris from this immense pit, is too great for the Expedition to accomplish in a single season. In order to discover the object for which the great shaft was cut, one corner only of it has been completely excavated. The remainder has been examined by well shafts; and tunnels have been driven through the partially water-laid debris filling the lower levels of the pit. Still the mystery remains unsolved. It is, however, evident that this chasm was clear and open to the weather when Nebuchadnezzar burnt the city; and the debris of that destruction was thrown into it to a depth of thirty-feet. But above that level, the filling abounds in the remains of the Persian occupation following the Exile, and even later. Thus a coin of Ptolemy II (285–246 B.C.) has been found at a depth of thirty feet from the surface. On the other hand, rain water had washed on to the exposed level, on the north side of the crater, a small steatite plaque of the Pharaoh of the Exodus—Amenhetep II (1447–23 B.C.).

The pick marks on the rock sides of the shaft are well preserved, and in some places look quite recent. The work on this excavation was hindered by frequent flooding from the heavy winter rains, and a Merry-weather pump was in constant use, in order to remove pools of water which were sometimes five feet in depth. The labour in the tunnels was hampered by the presence of big stones, that were solidly packed together with very little soil. These had to be broken under-ground before they could be removed. At the lowest levels were pottery fragments, mixed with lumps of charcoal and burnt stones, all remains of the Babylonian burnings of the city (600–587 B.C.); while the upper sides of the crater-like depression are lined by both large and small hewn stones which have cascaded down from the Persian city levels. Underneath these, were found a gold earring decorated with gold balls, an inscribed Rhodian jar handle, and some tall-necked flasks which belong to the Hellenistic period. These suggest that the wall of the Persian building above, fell as late as 150 B.C.

About the middle of February, the Expedition reached the base of this great shaft at the south-west corner. The approach to it was impeded by huge boulders of hard rock embedded in a deposit of mason's chips. The boulders may be part of a constructional arrangement; but where the rock drops away from them at a depth of eighty-eight feet, there proved to be an oval depression, formed by undercutting the rock floor of the shaft, which had been left as a double overhanging ledge.

The western extension of this excavation ended in a small low cave, on the floor of which lay a quantity of olive stones in a heap of burnt soil. This was a singular find to make so far below the surface of the soil. It may be that the little cave had housed some refugee when the Babylonians burnt the city.

The further work on the shaft proved that, while on the eastern side there had been a collapse of heavy stone walling, yet the water-laid soil against the south-west side was free from it. Another perplexing point has been the absence of any stairway down into the chasm, which rather suggests that the chasm may have contained a building.

At first the Expedition was disposed to fix a date of about 2000 B.C. for this important work. But the freshness of the tool marks round the lower part; the areas of chalk and limestone pavement on the surface level of the later city, which have apparently been quarried from the shaft; and the fact that a short-handled pick seems to have been used to quarry the sides, all suggest a date which would place the work in the period of the Jewish monarchy. It has also been found that the base of the roadway that runs into the city from the gate has been made up with small rock chips. These, both on account of their quantity as well as their quality, are thought to have come from the great shaft.

On the bas-reliefs of Lachish, carved by the artists of Sennacherib, a tower is depicted about halfway down the Tell, from which people are emerging with what look like skins of water on their backs. The suggestion is thus conveyed that this was the water gate, and it perhaps also served the purpose of a sally port. It is possible that this great chasm inside the city had some connection with this tower. The Jerusalem of the Jebusites contained a shaft, which ran down inside the city to the perennial spring in the Kedron valley, now known as the Virgin's Fountain. But the passage and the shaft which gave access to that spring, were of normal dimensions. Underground water tunnels have further been found at Megiddo and elsewhere; they are quite a characteristic of the fortified cities of Canaan. But the Lachish shaft is on a scale which surpasses anything previously discovered in Palestine. And perhaps, not without reason, it forcibly reminds us of the text:

"Look unto the rock whence ye were hewn, and to the hole of the pit whence ye were digged."

(Isa. li. 1.)

This prophet Isaiah lived in the reign of Hezekiah, and great rock cuttings were a feature of that time. Sennacherib, king of Assyria, made an aqueduct from the Gomel river to his capital city, Nineveh, a distance of thirty miles; in places it was cut through the hills. Again Hezekiah, king of Judah, had the Siloam tunnel cut through the hill below Jerusalem. The Lachish great shaft may be an enlargement, made in those days, of a far earlier work. Up to the end of the season, the Expedition were unable to reach the centre, on account of the quantities of loose stones. Mr. Starkey remains of the opinion that the purpose of the work was connected with the water supply of the city.

The second outstanding feature of the 1936–37 Excavations was the discovery of a large rock tomb, which differed from all the other rock tombs that have been examined in this area. Many of these others had been robbed, but the burials in this particular tomb had been destroyed by fire. This method of desecrating a tomb is unusual, and carries a good deal of significance. It has been enhanced by the fact that from the burnt ashes of this tomb, the children employed by the Expedition have sifted out no less than one hundred and ninety-two Egyptian scarabs, some gold-mounted. The tomb consisted of three separate chambers, and the contents of all three had been completely burnt out. The skeletons are in varying degrees of incineration, and some of the bronze, or copper articles, have been melted by the heat. Many of the scarabs have suffered from the burning.

There is no doubt that the tomb was the burying-place of important people; and the question arises whether it may be a royal one. This would account for the apparent wealth displayed in its contents, and for the gold-mounted scarabs. The scarabs include those of—

| | | | |
|---|---|---|---|
| Thotmes III | . | . | . 1501–1447 B.C. |
| Amenhetep II | . | . | . 1447–1423 B.C. |
| Thotmes IV | . | . | . 1423–1413 B.C. |
| Amenhetep III | . | . | . 1413–1377 B.C. |

Other objects found here were four alabaster toilet vases, a bronze razor, numerous arrowheads, toggle-pins, two cylinder seals of the Syro-Hittite type, fragments of glass vessels, and much bead-work. Beside the scarabs of the XVIII Dynasty of Egypt already mentioned, there are scarabs of King Shesha (or Apepa) of the XVI Dynasty. There were, further, a number of polished amethyst scarabs, one of which is very finely engraved, and displays a recumbent fawn surrounded by interlocking spirals. It is rare to find amethyst quartz scarabs that are engraved, even in Egypt. It will be seen that there exists considerable temptation to speculate concerning the history of this tomb. Judging from the scarabs and pottery found therein, its contents cover a long period of time. Its occupants had obviously been closely associated with Egypt, and, the many royal scarabs may even suggest, in an official capacity. The interments would seem to have come to an end in the reign of Amenhetep III, the Pharaoh who was ruling when Joshua conquered Egypt. And the last body placed in this mausoleum, must have been of a man who was so unpopular, that the people took the extreme step of desecrating his resting-place. The surrounding circumstances suggest the possibility that it is the family tomb of Zimrida, the Egyptian governor of Lachish who figures in the Tel el Amarna Letters. He played an important part in resisting the Habiru or Hebrew invasion. And he was made a prisoner in the gateway of the city. These little kings of Canaanite cities like Lachish, ostensibly ruled under the supreme authority of Egypt, at least from the time that Thotmes III conquered Palestine. And perhaps, even in earlier times, they were representatives of those Hyksos kings of the XVI Dynasty who governed both Palestine and Egypt: that would account for both the Hyksos and XVIII Dynasty scarabs. If the tomb belonged to one family, whether a royal one or not, we judge from the scarabs that its interments covered several centuries of time. It is interesting to notice that the contents of the tombs adjoining this desecrated one, proved to contain the scarabs of some of the succeeding Pharaohs, both of the XVIII and XIX Dynasties.

There may be significance in the fact that in the burnt tomb there are no scarabs of the Pharaohs who succeeded Amenhetep III, that is to say, of his son Amenhetep IV (Akhenaton), of Smenkhara, and of Tutankhamen. But the next tomb supplied the Expedition with a royal scarab of King Ay (1339–28 B.C.), the successor of Tutankhamen. Before he became Pharaoh, Ay was a priest, and is depicted on the walls of Tutankhamen's tomb, officiating at the funeral ceremonies. This is the first specimen of his scarab that has been found in Palestine. There were few interments in this tomb, but a third tomb immediately adjoining has supplied a scarab of the next Pharaoh, Horemheb. He was an old and faithful general to his predecessors; and, through marriage with a princess of royal blood, became the founder of the XIX Dynasty. Horemheb concluded an important treaty with the Hittites, which formed the basis of a later one made by Rameses II. The scarab of this celebrated and long-lived Pharaoh was also found in this same tomb. And, along with these two, one which appears to commemorate the reign of Aahmes I (1573–60 B.C.). He was the first Pharaoh of the eighteenth dynasty who originally drove out the Hyksos. So it may be said that the series of scarabs in these three tombs suggest that the people of Lachish were subject to Egyptian influence for a long time before, and after, the arrival of the Israelites. The break in the succession of Egyptian royal scarabs immediately following Amenhetep III, and the burning, may have some significance in connection with the Israelite occupation.

The excavations of this season also led to the uncovering of the Roman Road, which ran by Lachish in a south-westerly direction coming from Eleutheropolis (Beit Jebrin) further north. This is possibly the road mentioned by Eusebius in his *Onomasticon*, and increases the evidence for the identification for the site. Though we all of us know that the Romans were great road makers, and though the New Testament has made us familiar with the fact that they ruled over Palestine in the time of Christ, yet the sight of great Roman milestones lying on the ground not far from Tell Duweir comes as a surprise to visitors. These milestones probably once stood on the road that the Expedition has just uncovered. It must have been made on as substantial a scale as any of the Roman roads with which we are familiar in England and Wales. An aqueduct, or paved water channel, ran down one side, and there were boundary walls and a footpath. At the southwest summit of the western valley of Tell Duweir, there are the remains of a large dam and a reservoir, now silted up, called "The Pool of the Prophet." This source no doubt fed the channel that ran parallel with the road. The road itself had been buried deep in silt washed down from the surrounding hills. We reflect that this erosion might not have happened, if the trees on these hills had been preserved. It will be interesting to ascertain the further direction south of this important Roman causeway. It probably connected with the coast, and also formed one of the main routes to Egypt.

The remainder of the recent finds at Lachish include a dagger with an inscription down the centre of the blade. This inscription consists of four characters, two of which Mr. Starkey connects with the Sinai Hebrew script, and the others with the Minoan, Cypriote, or Hittite characters. The pottery found with this dagger in a tomb associates it with the Hyksos, and dates it not later than 1600 B.C. An important letter concerning this find, which has appeared in *The Times*, from the pen of Dr. Alan H. Gardiner, the principal authority on the Sinai Hebrew script, will be found in the Appendix on page 283.

In the neighbourhood of the tombs which have yielded the harvest of Egyptian scarabs, there has been found a beautifully polished carnelian quartz seal. Its under side is divided into three spaces. The upper displays the winged uraeus, before which is the "ankh" or life sign; the middle, has five Hebrew letters reading "To (*or* for) Shephatiah"; and the lower six letters signify "Asahiah." The inscription is peculiar in having the Hebrew letter "Tet" reproduced as it appears in the Lachish Letters.

There are ten Shephatiahs mentioned in the Old

Testament. It was the name of one of David's sons (2 Sam. iii. 4). In the time of Jeremiah the prophet there was Shephatiah, the son of Mattan, a principal man of Judah (Jer. xxxviii. 1). There was also an Asahiah who lived in this period.

Some eighteen feet below the surface, beneath the remains of Hyksos burials which date back to the days of Abraham, the Expedition have dug up the skeletons of a number of dogs and donkeys. The dogs belong to the "seluki" class, the ancestor of our modern greyhound.

The Lachish Expedition is fortunate, beyond all other Palestine Expeditions, in its finds of objects with writing upon them. Even as this book is going to press, the news comes of the discovery of the fragments of three inscribed bowls. The first found, designated as Lachish Bowl No. 3, had been broken into a number of fragments. Twenty-five of these have been recovered; they had been scattered broadcast on the earth ramp that had been thrown up against the south-east corner of the palace fort, below the upper burnt city levels. They were strewn over an area of about one hundred square feet. The bowl measures seven inches across, it is just over two inches deep, and the rim turns outwards. Inside are the faint traces of spiral writing in ink. The script has been identified as hieratic Egyptian, and is thought to date to about 1250 B.C.

So far as the writing on the bowl can be deciphered, it reads as follows:

*Interior of the Bowl.*

1. Year 4, 4th month of Akhet, day 26.

2. . . . chief (??) of (the land) . . . tisha I [ . . . ], wheat [measures] 1000+x hundred from the harvest of . . .

*Exterior of the Bowl.*

1. In the year 4, 2nd month of Inundation, day . . . wheat [measures] 420 . . . 1000 . . .

2. . . . year 4, 4th month of Inundation, day 1, wheat [measures] 300+x+3 . . . 900.

It is suggested that the bowl has been used to enumerate a tribute or offering which was formally presented with it to the civil authority. It is significant that the Egyptian calendar is employed, and that the system of enumeration is also Egyptian. The word "tisha" may be only part of a name which definitely stands for that of some tribe or nation. The bowl, and what it represented, may instead have been presented to a religious authority.

When the season's work came to an end, the excavators found that they had reached a large structure on the Tell which represents the remains of the late Jewish palace or citadel, and underneath and adjoining its ruins, the remains of still earlier palaces which go back to the time of David or Solomon.

The evidence of the two distinct destructions of Lachish at a brief interval from one another, both presumably in the days of Nebuchadnezzar, continues to increase. Inside the gate, the level of the road at the last destruction was found to be no less than seven feet higher than the previous one. The masonry that had fallen down, and blocked the earlier roadway, had been surmounted, but not cleared away. The fall had blocked the main drain of the city, and caused extensive inundation. Another, and a larger drain, had been constructed above this obstruction. This method of restoring a ruined city, according to present-day ideas, would seem to lack thoroughness, but it is of considerable assistance to archæological research work.

# XIII

## CONCLUSION

THIS present volume began by pointing out the importance of ascertaining whether the Bible still deserved the position assigned to it in the Coronation Service; or whether our national confidence in it, only belonged now to the order of conventional beliefs, and no longer carried any reality with it.

Or to put it another way: Had the book which Mr. Gladstone called "the Impregnable Rock of Holy Scripture," not only ceased to be impregnable, but ceased even to be a rock? It is evident that these searching questions are of supreme importance to our race, and indeed to the whole world at the present time. It is only fair to the rising generation that they should know where they stand. They are having a great deal more secular education thrust upon them by the educational authorities. Is it all true knowledge? Is it going to conflict with Bible knowledge? And if it does conflict, is it to supersede Bible knowledge? Is Holy Scripture to be put away on a back shelf, and that at the very time when the leaders of scientific thought are calling for the study and teaching of the Science of Man? Is there anything that can

245

supersede the Bible in the study of the Science of Man?

These are grave questions. It may be that the whole course of civilization is going to depend upon the attention we bestow upon them. If the Bible is untrustworthy, let us find some better text-book for the guidance of humanity. But if it reasonably satisfies the evidence of observed facts as we know them, and seriously conflicts only with conclusions that are, or may be, based on conjectures, and are consequently unreliable, then let the Bible be put once more in its proper position as the basis of Education.

These pages have briefly indicated how the trend of evidence of observed facts is confirming the Old Testament, and what is the nature of the outside testimony supplied by the Science of Archæology. After outlining some of the evidence that has come to light from various sources, and after discussing its bearing upon the Old Testament, the discoveries made at Lachish have been described in some detail. Many of our readers may agree that the latter have opened for us a new chapter in Bible history, and will remain famous for all time. It is true that much which has been found at Tell Duweir, resembles what has been found before, and requires classification, and grouping with objects dug up on other sites. Yet, compared with earlier excavations in Palestine, the way in which these discoveries fit into, and supplement, the Old Testament narrative, shows a growing significance. This is due partly to the system of pottery dating, and to other improved methods of excavation. For example, it will be noticed that a number of proper names of men who lived in Old Testament times have been brought to light. With scarcely more than two or three exceptions, these all figure in the Bible, and at the same periods of time. But what will make the Lachish discoveries so famous, is the fact that whole sentences of alphabetical writing, penned in Old Testament days, have been found for the first time. There are the white letters on the red bowl, reading "His righteousness is my hand (or support)," written little more than a century after the death of Moses. There are the Lachish Letters themselves, entirely unique documents of the time of Jeremiah. The contents of these writings testify to the authenticity of the Sacred Narrative at two periods of time seven centuries apart. They constitute outside contemporary evidence of its genuineness. But apart altogether from what their contents tell us, the mere finding of the Sinai Hebrew script, and of the Phœnician Hebrew script, are discoveries that perhaps surpass in importance, anything bearing upon the Old Testament which has been brought to light for centuries. And the value of these finds can be readily appreciated by others, beside the student and the scholar. They appeal to the widest circle, for they concern all peoples, nations, and languages; they affect every possessor of a copy of the Bible, in every language into which it has been translated, in every part of the globe. As education increases, those who read their translations of the Old Testament, naturally want to know more about its origin. When was it written? In what language? And through what medium has it been transmitted to this generation?

In the past, some have said one thing and some another, in answer to such questions. But now two Archæological Expeditions, working on two different sites, have supplied the definite answers. The Jericho Expeditions have fixed the time of Moses at 1520–1400 B.C.; the Lachish Expeditions have found the Sinai Hebrew and the Phœnician Hebrew alphabetical scripts; with evidence that certainly one, and perhaps both, were in use from these earliest days onwards. Together, these forms of writing cover the interval of time from Moses, right down to the introduction of the Assyrian Hebrew script, from which in turn our translations of the Old Testament have been made. And so the mediums employed for the transmission of Old Testament literature, from Moses to our British and Foreign Bible Society, have been identified and established; and the genealogy of the sacred writings has been traced. And it is to be further remarked, that the geographical ancestry of the Old Testament positively seems to be related to that of alphabetical writing; for the earlier books of the Bible take us to the region of Sinai, where the earliest of the alphabetical scripts has been found.

Anyone who in future suggests that the Israelites ever lacked facilities for literary expression, will be betraying his unacquaintance with modern discoveries of the first importance. All the theories of oral trans-

# CONCLUSION

mission, either of the whole, or of part, of the earlier books of the Old Testament, have of course ceased to be of any account. Reference has also been made to archæological evidence which suggests that events were recorded in writing about the time of their occurrence.

Again, the Mosaic Legislation and Ritual, fit so naturally into the age of Moses as it is now revealed to us by Archæology, that it has become ridiculous to date them to any other period than the one in which the Bible represents them to have been instituted.

The effect of these discoveries is to further discredit the whole process of destructive criticism. Archæology, a strictly objective Science, is disproving the subjective negations spun from the mentality of critics. Those who have shaken popular faith in the Bible, and undermined its authority, are in turn undermined themselves by the evidence that has been brought to light, and their authority destroyed. The spade is driving destructive criticism out of the field of questionable facts into that of recognized fiction. And it is pretty certain that the process will continue. Because the early Hebrew scripts had not been discovered in the past, was no evidence at all that they did not exist. Now the Lachish excavations have proved that they did. Because the background of the Mosaic legislation seemed to fit the end of the Jewish monarchy, was no evidence at all that the days of Moses did not fit it even better. The Ras Shamra tablets, the Semitic legislation of Hammurabi, the Egyptian moral code, the system of worship at Serabit in Sinai, all bear witness that they did. Such shattering discoveries must tend to disillusion those who have had confidence in the soundness of the critical system. They will begin to recognize the extravagance of its underlying assumption, that *what the critic did not know could not have been!* And how the apparatus of criticism put a premium on the critic's own ignorance.

This system of criticism of the Old Testament—this mother of unsound theories—took into its nest the theory of the evolution of Religion; and proceeded to identify the prophet Amos as the first exponent of Monotheism. The simultaneous discovery, by both the Sciences of Archæology and Anthropology, that Monotheism was the original Religion, seems to contradict the idea that the prophet Amos, or indeed any other prophet mentioned in the Old Testament, including Moses himself, was the first exponent of that Faith. It is surely time that distinguished scholars gave up the habit of representing exploded theories as historical facts. Even they cannot afford to treat the evidence advanced by the Sciences of Archæology and Anthropology as beneath their notice.

The study of all Religion, which has now been placed on a sound basis by these discoveries, is having further light thrown upon it by other Sciences, to which references have been made. The evidence of the Immanence of the Unseen, amply justifies St. Paul's statement, "In him we live, and move, and have our being" (Acts xvii. 28).

# CONCLUSION

In the pages of this volume attention has been repeatedly drawn to a fundamental error which is fatal to otherwise sound reasoning, and invalidates a good many modern beliefs. It is the error of unsound premises. It is an error indirectly illustrated in the New Testament through the parable of the man who built his house upon the sand. On the surface a school of learning may look an imposing edifice, as, for example, the walls of Jericho looked to the Israelites, but when tested, it may be as unreliable. The world is suffering to-day from the philosophy of men who were satisfied to base their conclusions on the surface of things, and to ignore the rest. Such superficial methods of approach to life led to the mechanical theory of the Universe. And absorption in the study of matter, caused materialism to be imposed upon education as a creed. Perhaps the worst consequence of these mistaken theories, accepted by the public in the belief that they represented conclusions of true Science, has been to cloud the conceptions of our civilization as to what constituted reality. And in spite of the evidence supplied to our senses by the radio, what men *do not see*, still remains vague and indefinite. This atmosphere of thought has had a stupefying effect upon the education of the world, and upon its intellectual and religious life. And the very men who should have been pioneers in preaching the Kingdom of God on Earth, have allowed their minds to be deflected into materialistic channels. Instead of adopting a constructive attitude towards Holy Scripture, they have attempted to destroy and even to supersede it. The Unseen has been conventionalized, and cold-shouldered, even in our very churches. Recent world happenings have shaken up our spiritual lethargy at the very time when past intellectual errors are also becoming evident. The more careful students of the book of Nature are drawing attention to much that has been unread or ignored altogether.

The recognition by modern Science of *the reality* of the Unseen has dealt a death-blow to materialism. The absence of complete uniformity discerned in nature has done the same to the mechanical theory of the Universe. Relativity has reduced even the more substantial theories of Physics to ruins. And, as it has just been pointed out, the Sciences of Archæology and Anthropology contradict the theory of the evolution of Religion; indeed they demand a drastic modification of the theory of the evolution of man, in order to bring it into line with the observed facts of ancient history.

It is now quite obvious that many conclusions, which we were led to believe sprung from Science, have no legitimate claim to such a distinction, because their premises have either been completely based on conjecture, or on an incomplete study of observed facts. Yet these erroneous conclusions are being used as foundations for further conclusions; which are often in turn taught as though they were ascertained truth, and broadcasted by the Press, and through the radio. So error is heaped on error. It will immensely simplify the present generation's outlook on life when people will take the trouble to trace back such fallacies to their source; and cease to accept the *ipse dixit* of wrongly educated pundits. We pride ourselves on living in an age of Science; why not therefore act up to our profession? Since there can be no true Science unless it is based on sound premises, nothing ought to be tolerated in future, much less taught, which has been discovered to lack this basis. Why proceed in the cultivation of intellectual weeds? The aim of Science is a splendid one, it is a search for Truth; and it arrives at Truth through independent study of the evidence of observed facts. Thus, in taking up the study of the Science of Man, account will have to be taken of both Man's qualities and defects, his strength and his weakness, and how his infirmities can be remedied. The Bible takes such account, its diagnosis was recognized by our forefathers as a sound one, and it points the way to a merciful cure for human nature's defects.

We are living now in an age that is moving so rapidly in the directions outlined in the first chapter of this work, that it does not seem as though we could afford to wait, while the recognition of the changing attitudes of Science and modern thought slowly percolate into and modify the contradictory, or the negative, or the sceptical teaching about the Bible, so often given in our colleges and schools.

The Archbishop of Canterbury's recall to Religion produced so many comments, and so much correspondence in the Press, that it was impossible to catalogue all the causes that were there advanced as responsible for the neglect. It will form a fitting conclusion to this book to point out that, strange as it may seem at first sight, the neglect of the Old Testament may be the main cause of the neglect of Religion. Because the Old Testament was believed to have been submerged by criticism, the latter half of the Bible has been treated as sufficient by itself.

So the clues that the Old Testament supplied concerning the origin and nature of Man, and concerning the need for the Gospel of the New Testament, have been neglected. It has, indeed, been worse than neglect. For in the place of the Old Testament account of the Creation and subsequent events, what have been justly described as "superficial ideas" about the theory of the evolution of Man, and the totally false hypothesis of the evolution of Religion, have been substituted. These have been grafted on to the New Testament, and the fruits are now evident. They show themselves either by indifference to Religion altogether, or by the substitution of Humanism for Christianity.

The teaching of Christ as applied to our fellow men is emphasized, but as applied to Himself it is neglected or even rejected. In effect, people are being told their duty towards their neighbour, and little is said of their duty towards God. Religion is being mistaken for philanthropy and social service, and nothing more. Surely we ought to know better than that? Any honest study of the nature of Man makes us profoundly aware of human frailties and imperfections, and the

# CONCLUSION

need for Divine Help to remedy them. This help, as revealed in the Bible, was offered under the old Covenant made through Moses, and is still offered under the new Covenant given through Jesus Christ. Humanism makes Christ but a great teacher. The Bible affirms Him to be the Supreme Power, and the Source of all Power. Is it not this Power that the world needs to-day to apply His teaching and to put matters right?

The Old Testament is concerned largely with the history of the children of Israel, who were ultimately merged into the Kingdoms of Israel and Judah. It represents their blessings and their misfortunes, to be associated with their adherence to, or their neglect of, the Deity. It is History, but it is viewed not from the side of their relationship with other nations, but from the side of their relationship with God. The British relationship with God, as a Nation, has recently been brought to our notice by the Coronation Service of King George VI. The course of events that preceded this Consecration, whether concerned with the affairs of the Crown, or of the Church, or of the State; or whether concerned with their relationship with each other, was of a highly dramatic character. The orientation of the Coronation may change the whole outlook on secular affairs, both national and international. Those of us who live under democratic rule have acquired the habit of expecting our governments to provide us with peace and prosperity. We seek for more secular education to bring happiness to our rising generation. We seek all manner of social reforms. We seek more leisure and more pleasure. But "*Should not a people seek unto their God?*"—God their Creator, their Redeemer, their Protector, the very Source of their Being. That is the message of the Old Testament; that is the message of the Coronation; and that is the question of first importance in these solemn times.

The present neglect of God must be associated with the non-observance of Sunday; with non-attendance at public worship; and with lack of contributions to His Service. Christ's statement that "the Sabbath was made for man," has been interpreted to mean that the day might be treated like Saturday afternoon; or its evening like any other evening in the week. But how if the Sabbath was made for man to enable him to tune in to the Power Station of the Infinite. No limitations can be placed on the possibilities that may flow from that Source. An eminent scientist is quoted in the first chapter of this work, as recognizing that even cases of cancer have been healed by prayer. Another authority—a great psychologist—writes that his wide experience has forced him to realize how the findings of psychology, in respect to personality and happiness, have been largely a rediscovery of old religious truths. And how if the Sabbath was made for man, as a time set apart, to enable him to express his gratitude to God for His Care and Love for His Creation. Can any one of us, looking back on our life, fail to realize that there is much for which we have to be thankful as individuals, and to discern the guidance of God along our path? Again, when we observe the present distress of foreign people, we realize for how much the English-speaking races have to be thankful. And we are moved to wonder whether the national blessings may be the fruit of the prayers for President and Country, offered by those simple folk who, Sunday by Sunday, still attend the places of worship in this Land.

The first and greatest Commandment tells us: "Thou shalt love the Lord thy God, with all thy heart, and with all thy mind, and with all thy soul, and with all thy strength."

What proportion of the population can be said to obey it? Let us realize that only perhaps a third of the people even display gratitude to God, or seek His Aid, by attending a place of worship. These are somewhat unpleasant, but salutary Truths. The recognition of them may perhaps save some from daring to blame the Deity for wars and rumours of wars.

The doubts cast upon the Old Testament, by what is now seen to be a worthless system of criticism, have been introduced, and installed, in the interpretation of the records and promises contained in the New Testament. Thus the records of the Incarnation and Resurrection are questioned, and explained away. Again, the Second Coming, as foreshadowed in the New Testament, is no longer anticipated at all. Prominent leaders of thought are content to call for the spirit of Christ among us, and to shut their eyes to the possibility of the Imminence of His Return in the

# CONCLUSION

Body. It is hard to understand how the emphatic statements of the Second Advent, both in the New Testament, and in the Creeds, can be ignored. The fulfilment of the prophecies concerning the Jews, is an ever-present reminder that the promises concerning His Coming will also be fulfilled. And when we take a comprehensive view of the world as it is at the present time, and compare it with the conditions foreshadowed in the Bible, we can hardly fail to recognize the resemblance. Those remaining prophecies, which announce the completion of this present Age, and the return of the Divine King of kings to set up His Promised Kingdom on Earth, may be rapidly ripening for fulfilment.

What have seemed most important issues of life, look trivial beside the weighty ones to which attention has been drawn.

The dawn of a true Science, the Science of Man and of his God, which we find set out in the Bible, may yet save our civilization from destruction, and rescue us from the further pursuit of vain substitutes. But have we any time to waste?

# APPENDIX I

## MONOTHEISM AS THE PREDECESSOR OF POLYTHEISM IN SUMERIAN RELIGION [1]

By The Late
STEPHEN LANGDON, M.A., B.D., Ph.D., F.B.A.
Professor of Assyriology at Oxford

I

THE Sumerians were probably the first people to emerge from barbarism some time before 4000 B.C. From them we obtain the earliest written information concerning the religion of mankind. Now it is obvious that a people so far advanced in culture as to live in organized society, to create good architecture, excellent pottery and to invent a written script, were far advanced beyond what the anthropologists call primitive and primary cultures. Australian, Tasmanian and American aborigines of to-day are still far more primitive than the races which founded civilizations in the valleys of the Euphrates and the Nile. Here we have a talented race emerging into a real culture about 4000 B.C. It may be argued that we cannot get at primitive religion with such advanced material. That may be true, but we have in the valley of the Euphrates an immensely ancient record of the progress of human religion; what is more, their concepts can be read in the most primi-

[1] This article appeared in the *Evangelical Quarterly* for April 1937. The grateful thanks of the Author of this book are accorded for permission to reprint it.

259

tive pictographic inscriptions. On the Map of Lower Mesopotamia you may see the locations of some of the great prehistoric cities of the Sumerians, latterly occupied by the Babylonian Semites. Ur, seat of the Moon-God in the South, north of it Erech, seat of the cult of Anu, the god of heaven and father of all the gods, above it, Nippur, seat of the cult of Enlil, the Earth-God, and near Babylon, Kish, seat of the cult of the Earth-mother goddess. Eridu, seat of the Water-God, lay twelve miles south-west of Ur. The cults of Erech, Nippur and Eridu, or sky, earth and water, formed the trinity of their pantheon.

Some of these sites have been excavated right down to virgin soil. Their last occupants were the Arabs of the Baghdad Caliphate. Consequently the excavator descends here through the ruins of states and empires, through the débris of many peoples over a period of at least 5000 years until he reaches palæolithic culture on virgin soil. In doing this with three hundred workmen at Kish, over a period of twelve years, I came to the conclusion that the vast Sumerian polytheistic system was preceded by monotheism. This conclusion was also made more clear to me by the excavations of the Germans at Erech and a city Shuruppak, between Nippur and Erech. To show you the line of evidence which led me to posit monotheism as the forerunner of the whole vast Sumerian pantheon, let me use our own results at Kish. There we found a table of stratifications from the age of Alexander the Great at the top right down through 10 metres to plain level. Then through 6 metres to modern water level. Then through 3 metres to virgin soil.[1] Sumerian civilization begins at virgin soil and ends considerably

[1] *Note by Author.*—Nineteen metres in all, represent a depth of about 63 feet.

above plain level. There are excavations down to water level among streets and buildings not later than 3500 B.C. These show the sand line deposit precipitated by a great flood which destroyed the city. At Kish pictographic tablets begin just above virgin soil, the oldest writings from the human hand, the earliest statements about the religious mind of man which will probably ever be recovered. This is real consecutive writing, and not long after the first rude pictographic period. At Erech a large number of inscriptions of this first stage of writing, which I date about 4000 B.C., were recovered. We have, therefore, considerable evidence about their economic conditions and religion. Kish produced only the one tablet (see Plate 31) from this first stage of writing. Now what do the Erech tablets tell us about the gods and the pantheon? We know from inscriptions of about 3000 B.C. that the Sumerian pantheon already contained about 750 deities. It is plain from my discovery of 300 tablets at Kish from a period a little later than the primitive pictographic period that the pantheon there consisted of only the Sky-God, the Earth-God, and the Sun-God.

Human pictographic writing cannot take us back to the primitive period of religion, to the primitive concept of deity or deities. But the following facts point unmistakably to monotheism, and a Sky-God as the first deity, from whom descended the vast Sumerian pantheon, attaining in the end to about 5000 gods.

And before we go into a serious anthropological and theological discussion you may wish to see how this ancient pictographic script was rapidly developed by the Sumerians, so that after 3000 B.C. they were able to produce a great literature. Plate 30 shows the famous

# APPENDIX I

Sumerian chronological record written by a scholar in 2100 B.C. I refer to this document of 400 lines, because it shows that the Sumerians at the end of their history believed in almost geological concepts for their early origins. He claims that the period before the Flood lasted 241,200 years, when there was already a polytheistic religion. He dates the Flood about 34,000 years B.C.

## II

We have 575 tablets in most primitive pictographs, mostly from Erech. Here only two deities appear. Anu the Sky-God and Innini "the Queen of Heaven." Obviously written documents from any city will always reveal a preference for the gods of the local cult. Erech was the centre of the worship of the Sky-God and the Queen of Heaven, Innini, latterly called Ishtar and Ashtoreth by the Semites. It is, however, certain that when we press back towards the beginning of religion on written documents the pantheon of 3000 B.C. dwindles down to four and then only two deities. If there really was a larger pantheon at the dawn of history these numerous tablets which are all temple records would have mentioned them. The Sumerologist knows that this must be true from temple records of later periods where dozens of deities occur on this class of documents.

There is a gradual diminution of the pantheon back through the stages represented by four periods of early writing before 3000 B.C., until at Erech only two deities are found. The Sumerian theologians themselves had two views about the oldest deity from which the whole vast pantheon sprang. The philosophically minded, basing their theory on the well-known

262

# APPENDIX I

Sumerian principle that the whole universe and all things in it were derived from the *logos* or word of the Water-God, regard the Water-God as the first deity. Another school which probably preserves the true tradition and true fact, always regards the Sky-God as primitive and founder of the pantheon.

I should add at once that in these primitive records there is no trace of magic or demons. Everything points to a primitive personal god with the name *An*, Heaven, Sky. That magic and so-called irrational or emotional elements did not exist then cannot be argued. Such evidence would not occur on temple records anyway.

I have not yet come to a discussion of the religions of far-flung Semitic races, who appear in history at much later periods, the Hebrews, Arabs, Phœnicians, Aramæans. Here again, nothing can be said about them until they began to produce written material. The Babylonians are of course far and away the oldest Semitic race so far as written history can be placed in evidence. They arrived in Mesopotamia as early as 3000 B.C. But here they lost about all evidence of their original Semitic religion ; in fact they simply accepted the entire Sumerian religion, pantheon, theology, liturgies, magic, in fact they lost their racial religion in the same way as European races lost theirs when they accepted Christianity.

In bringing my own conclusions into relation with modern anthropology I must confess at once that an Assyriologist and Sumerologist can make no pretensions to speak as an Anthropologist. His life is spent in deciphering inscriptions of advanced cultures.

I can lay claim to special knowledge of the history of only two great religions, Sumerian and Semitic, and I wish to apply the results of an enquiry into the history of these groups to the problems which confront the science of comparative religions. It is difficult for a student, originally trained to study the history of a given religion under the influence of Darwinism and trained in the days when nature and star myths were regarded as the origin of all religions, to reconstruct his method of investigation. I extracted myself from the lure of the totemistic theories of Jevons and Robertson Smith by my own study of Semitic religions, without the assistance of the devastating criticism of Foucart, Zepletal, Nöldeke, Sir James Frazer and W. Schmidt. To explain the origin of deities over the wide field of Semitic religion, in Arabia, Canaan, Phœnicia, Syria and Babylonia, as due to animals worshipped as ancestors of the various Semitic tribes, is obviously false. I am not passing any comment on totemism as found in other areas, but the whole argument has been hopelessly ruined for Semitic religions, and with it any attempt to defend polytheism as the original religion of the Semites by starting with animal totems. The great champion of totemism and consequently polytheism as the basis of Semitic religions, Robertson Smith, seems to elaborate this theory in order to explain sacrifice, one of the principal religious acts of communion with the deity. It seems to be an argument which begs the principle. Assuming that Kemosh, god of the Moabites, Melkart, a god of the Phœnicians, Yav, god of the Hebrews, were originally only totem animals and ancestors of the various tribes, to eat of such a sacrificial animal easily explained sacrifice, and that theory of sacrifice has been almost universally accepted by a school of Old Testament scholars. If that be so, then the Mosaic monotheism of the Hebrews is explained as an evolution from totemism.

# APPENDIX I

## III

The fundamental argument used by Robertson Smith and accepted by most of the Hebrew scholars after him was based upon linguistic evidence; most of Max Müller's nature myths as the origin of polytheism were based upon philological evidence. All our evidence for the history of Semitic religions must be linguistic and archæological. There are no longer any primitive Semitic tribes such as the anthropologists still have at their disposal in Australia, Africa and North America. But we possess immense written evidence for Arabia, Canaan, Phœnicia and Babylonia. Robertson Smith argued from the fact that in Arabic and Hebrew a large number of families, persons and cities are named after animals. For example, a town in north Israel was named *Layish*, lion, and a man has the same name, *Layish*. An Ammonite king has the name *Nahas*, serpent; a prince of Judah has the name *Nahas*, and a city in Judah is named *Nahas*. Now if animal names were given to tribes because these tribes descended from a totem animal, then animal names must be confined to the early stage of a religion. Several facts ruined this totemistic theory. When the earliest Arabic religion was discovered in the Yemen by the decipherment of Himyaritic inscriptions no animal names of cities or clans were found, and only three of men. Here there was an organized astral pantheon consisting of Moon, Sun and Venus. Arabian religion, therefore, in the first stage in which it can be studied belongs to the Polytheistic star myth, or nature myth type like most Indo-Germanic religions. We know them first in an advanced stage. It must be remembered by way of parenthesis that those scholars did not know the early South Arabic Himyaritic sources, and the vast field of Sumero-Babylonian religion was still closed to them.

Other facts destroyed the totem theory for Semitic religions even in the field which Robertson Smith and Jevons knew best, Hebrew, North Arabic, Phœnician and Aramaic.

Not one of the clans or families who bear animal names had a deity of its own. None of them were tribes, but only families in tribes; they are only clan names of ancestors who had animal names. For example, *Hezir*, one of the families of the tribe of Levi, means "swine," and there is a Hebrew named *Hezir*. The fact is that not one of the Semitic nations, tribes or cities which had a deity has an animal name. Moreover, the national or tribal deities of the far-flung Semitic races are now proved to be nature myths and every one of them star myths, except the national God of the Hebrews, Yav, Yahweh. Most of them are solar deities, a few in the Aramæan area are moon deities, and there is the corn deity Dagon; *dagon* in fact means "corn."

Another fact destroyed this theory. In the beginning of the history of Arabic religion animal names of men are rare, but the custom increases in the later stages until they become prolific in the age of Mohammed. That is also true of Babylonia. Animal names of men do occur in the earlier stages of Babylonian religion but rarely, and increase in number throughout the history of that culture. The Semitic religions of Babylonia appear first in an advanced stage of culture about 3000 B.C., and here the pantheon has been almost entirely borrowed from the Sumerians. Few traces of original Semitic religion can be traced in Babylonia, but such as are not wholly suppressed by the Sumerian pantheon prove that those Semites who intruded by conquest into the Sumerian kingdom before 3000 B.C. took with them the star myth pantheon of South Arabia.

No consecutive history of religion can compare in length of time, in richness of written sources, in evidence from all stages of its development, with the Sumero-Babylonian, not even the Indo-Germanic religions which have no written sources earlier than Hittite from the 15th century B.C. The Sanscrit sources may go back by tradition to 1500 B.C., but Sumerian can be traced in written record to 4000 B.C., and its continuous history traced to the Christian era.

It seems to be admitted that the nature myth gods of India, Greece and Italy and all Indo-Germanic religions started with a Sky-God, Zeus, Zeus-pater. Dyauspitar, Jupiter, "God the father," all derived from the root *div*, to "shine," whence the word *deus*, god. The history of the Sky-God has been elaborately studied by Leopold von Schroeder in his *Arische Religion* for Indo-Germanic in which he posits a monotheism based upon the Sky-God for all Indo-Germanic polytheism. Foucart, then, in a short article on *Sky and Sky-Gods* in Hastings' *E.R.E.* (six pages) on the basis of Egyptian and Indo-Germanic, came to this conclusion:—

"We may safely assume that the concept of Sky-God belongs to the most ancient period in the history of religious feeling and that it is at least as ancient as primitive naturalism and animistic fetishism. Whether it is even pre-animistic in its fundamental aspect is a question which must be reserved."

Foucart is an Egyptologist who interests himself secondarily in anthropology and comparative religion, and an Assyriologist is bound to suffer from the same limitations. It is obvious that when he suggests the primitive monotheistic concept of a Sky-God as possibly *pre-animistic* he is using language which anthropologists like Marett would condemn.

## IV

Animism or belief in souls, ghosts and ancestor worship connected with the great name of E. B. Tylor, is a perfectly comprehensible and clear definition of a stage of religion earlier than polytheistic nature gods. Tylor defined this stage of religion as "Belief in the existence of spiritual beings," and it is, I suppose, a stage which preceded all polytheistic religions. In this sense I can understand that the concept of primitive monotheistic and ethically pure Sky-God involves animism; in other words, is conceived of mentally as well as by volition as a creator spirit. But what Foucart means by defining this original monotheism of a Sky-God as pre-animistic I quite fail to understand. Marett writes on pre-animistic religion, "No anthropologist has ever supposed himself able fully and finally to explain the origin of belief in souls and spirits."

Andrew Lang and, more elaborately, W. Schmidt seem to have found races more primitive than animism and totemism in which there is a pure monotheism, a Supreme Being entirely free from magic and even without personality. This primitive monotheism widely distributed among races, still in existence and possible of being proved by Indo-Germanic and Sumerian philology, is elaborately defined by Schmidt in six huge volumes, *Der Ursprung der Gottesidee*. I do not pretend to have read all this, and I depend for an exposition of Schmidt's theory upon the English edition of his *résumé*, *Origin and Growth of Religion*.

# APPENDIX I

The various schools of thought, Max Müller's nature myths, Tylor's animism, Smith's totemism, Marett's magic, Lang's primitive monotheism, are all defined in this book. I know of only one criticism of Schmidt, that of the Regius Professor of Hebrew in Cambridge, who rejects Schmidt's arguments on the ground that this primitive monotheism found in Africa and North America is too nebulous and that it has no continuity of evidence; Marett has briefly noted Lang's theory of primitive monotheism or high gods with the remark, "I assume for working purposes that Mr. Lang's high gods must have had a psychological pre-history which would connect them with vaguer and even vaguer shapes," but "I have complete faith in Mr. Lang's high gods."

The Regius Professor also contends that Schmidt has paid no attention to higher culture religions, by which he means, of course, Indo-Germanic, Sumero-Babylonian and Egyptian. Unfortunately for his criticism, the specialists in Egyptian, Sumerian and Indo-Germanic have come to the conclusion that a Monotheism based on a Sky-God preceded polytheism. As to the history of the Sky-God in Semitic and Sumerian, Schmidt bewails the fact that there is no study of this subject, and I supplied it in my *Semitic Mythology*, 1931, the date of the appearance of Rose's English edition of *Origin and Growth of Religion*.

Volume 4 of Schmidt's great German work appeared in 1933; Volume 5 in 1934; Volume 6 in 1935; altogether over 3000 octavo pages. In the last volume he analyses fifteen reviews, mostly favourable; but of Cook's review, seventeen closely printed pages, no mention ; of Junker's history of Egyptian religion, 1931, in which the same thesis for Egypt is defended, not a syllable; of my own book, 1931, parts of which were expressly written in response to his demand for an investigation of the Sky-God in Babylonia, no mention. Does Professor Schmidt confine himself entirely to the sphere of lower anthropology?

Now Lang and Schmidt on the basis of lower cultures, and especially on the basis of the pygmies in Africa, the Indians of North America, define the original monotheism in these words. "The really monotheistic character of the Supreme Being is clear even to a cursory examination. This is true of the Supreme Being of most Pygmy tribes, of the Tierra del Fuegians, the primitive Bushmen, the Kurnai and Yuin of South-East Australia, the peoples of the Arctic culture, the primitives of North America. Among other races the fact of their original monotheistic belief has been obscured." This Supreme Being is defined in some areas as First Father, corresponding to Greek Zeus-pater, Latin Jupiter, and Schmidt might have added the widespread Semitic custom of calling any deity "father, my father." There is everywhere in this great work evidence that the author cares nothing at all for the witness of the great culture religions even though he complains that specialists give him no material. He emphasizes the pure and moral character of this Supreme Being who in most areas is a Sky-God in the sense that he resides in the sky. For him this pure and highly moral original monotheism was degraded all over the world into polytheism. He uses the word "degradation," and Cook's criticism of this view is unanswerable. To compare the pygmy religion with its undoubted concept of a Supreme Being, with Greek, Sumerian and Egyptian religion on grounds of religious and cultural values is downright absurd. Polytheism may be a *degradation* of primitive monotheism in a scientific sense, but it is obviously untrue that monotheism of this primitive type is associated with a higher culture than the derived polytheism. The greatest culture ever produced in the ancient Semitic world arose under the most polytheistic religion ever known in Babylonia.

Now, as I have said, it is possible to trace Sumerian religion back through its long periods of intense Polytheism based on nature, star and theological myths to a period of pictographic writing; this vast polytheism of the Sumerians became the religion of Babylonia and Assyria ; it was largely adopted in the Western and Northern Semitic lands. It was impregnated with magic which gave rise to the physical sciences of which they were the founders in the ancient world. They became under their system of theologically organized polytheism the founders of astronomy and mathematics of a high order. I came to the conclusion that the whole intricate polytheism of Sumer and Babylonia originated in a monotheistic concept for the following reasons. In the first place the Sumerian word for god, *digir*, means both "high" and "to be bright," and the sign used to write this word also means "sky." This is precisely parallel to the history of the Indo-Germanic word for the Sky-God from the root *div*, to be bright, *deus*. The pantheon in full bloom contained more than 5000 deities great and small. The early history of this pantheon can be traced back through the inscriptions to the most primitive pictographs. A large body of early texts from about 3300 B.C. shows a pantheon of only 500 gods. In all theological treatises of the pantheon right back to 3300 the Babylonians and Sumerians always place the Sky-God at the beginning and regard him as father of all the gods, whether personifications of nature, the stars and planets, or of abstract ideas, War, Industry,

Justice, etc. The Sky-God has the name *An*, which is the ordinary word for sky, heaven. The early Sumerian texts and the conclusion deduced from them were published in 1928, or three years before Schmidt's *Origin and Growth of Religion* in which he clamoured for such evidence.

The evidence all points to the same conclusion as the Anthropologists Lang and Schmidt maintain; it agrees with Schroeder's great investigation of Indo-Germanic religions and of recent historians of Egyptian religion.

This Sky-God *An* or *Anu* of the Sumerians is known to have been personified and anthropomorphic, for there is a drawing of him on a seal where he is characterized as a rain god, and the texts relate the myth that in high heaven were kept the bread and water of eternal life.

## V

As to the defence of this same thesis in the pure Semitic religions of Arabia, Canaan, Phœnicia and Syria. It is impossible to get behind the nature and star worship stage of Semitic polytheism here on the basis of the written sources; the word for god common to every Semitic language, *ilu, el, elah, eloah*, is of unknown origin and its root inexplicable. It is argued by Brockelmann that the development of the Islamic god *Allah* into a monotheistic god is really a revival of a prehistoric monotheistic Semitic deity. The fact is that in pre-Islamic polytheism the term "god" meant the Moon-God and in north Semitic or Phœnician and Canaanite "god" came to mean Sun-God. That is due to obvious facts. In Arabian Polytheism the *Moon-God* is the principal deity; in north Semitic the

Sun-God overshadows all other deities. Consequently "god" in Arabian Polytheism took the place of the proper name of the Moon-God "Wadd," and in Canaan and Phœnicia "god" took the place of "Shemesh," the proper name of the Sun-God.

The literary remains of the oldest culture religions of Western Asia therefore substantially support the conclusions of Andrew Lang and Wilhelm Schmidt. The earliest conception of deity is really monotheistic; in the primitive races of the world to-day, this conception is vague, almost impersonal. Such a primitive stage is anterior to our Sumerian and Semitic sources. When we first catch a glimpse of the religious mind of man at the dawn of history in Egypt and Babylonia, this primitive Supreme Being has become a very definite personal Sky-God, creator of the Universe and of Man. But one thing seems very clear to me. When man first found himself in the presence of the vast problems of life and death, of the forces of nature and the inexplicable universe, he placed his faith in the Supreme Spiritual Being. This for me was surely a rational process. It has no primary emotional basis, no mere irrational instinct, but the decision of a real *homo sapiens*. Religion was necessary to make anything rational out of the meaning of human existence, and without it there could be no cultural progress. We are dealing here with *man* and not with *monkeys*, with a mind and soul which, in my opinion, has no more to do with evolution from animal life than the progress of religion has to do with evolution.

These conclusions have a very vital importance in Christian Theology as well as in Anthropology. Atheism and Communism in our time are based very considerably on the conclusions of Anthropologists who posit an irrational and emotional origin for the religion of man. Applied to the origin of the great Mosaic ethical monotheism of the Old Testament and taught even in theological colleges, how could it have anything but a disastrous effect upon the power and enthusiasm of Christianity? Darwinian evolution applied to the origin and progress of religion can only have one result: it must destroy the faith of mankind that there is any reality in religion at all. That is the conclusion which a very large part of mankind has now drawn from this Anthropological movement, a conclusion for which even Christian theologians are not blameless. Do anthropologists and theologians really know the history of man down the ages from the dawn of culture? Does the atheism of modern times really understand that religion was the basis of all human culture, and that it began in the rational nature of man?

S. LANGDON.

UNIVERSITY OF OXFORD.

NOTE.—It should be stated that when I wrote my *Semitic Mythology*, in which the conclusions stated in this paper were first published, I was unaware of W. Schmidt's similar conclusions on other grounds, nor had I yet seen Leopold von Schroeder's *Arische Religion*.

S. L.

# APPENDIX II

## THE MOSAIC AGE [1]

### ALPHABETIC INSCRIPTIONS

#### To The Editor of *The Times*

Sir,—In your issue of 24th June, under the title
"Antiquities from Lachish," Mr. Starkey published an
inscription on a bowl written in archaic Canaanite
letters, similar to the Sinaitic script, now recognized
to be the oldest known form of the West Semitic alphabet, the so-called Phœnician alphabet. Specimens of
writing in this early script have been found previously
by Starkey at Lachish and by Grant at Beth Shemesh.
Those previously recovered could not be translated,
although some of the letters were identified. But even
the presence of an alphabetic script of the Mosaic
period in Canaan was a great discovery, proving the
existence of alphabetic writing then and in a script
from which the ordinary Hebrew letters were derived.
There can be then no doubt but that the Hebrews
were writing documents in this period.

Mr. Starkey dates the new inscription between 1295
and 1262 B.C. The inscription as published in *The
Times* should be inverted and read from left to right;
for this was the original direction of writing the
Sinaitic script. In the copy and on a photograph
supplied to me by Sir Charles Marston the inscription

[1] *The Times*, October 5, 1935.

# APPENDIX II

seems to be complete, but the last four letters are
uncertain. The value of this new discovery lies in the
fact that at least the first seven letters can be construed
and prove that the language is identical with the
Canaanite glosses in the Amarna Letters, but the

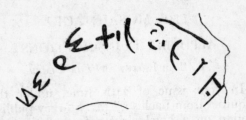

phraseology, "His righteousness is my support," is
strikingly similar to that of the Hebrew monotheistic
writers.

My identification of the letters is: Z—D—Q—W
Q—T—.—Y  W—(?)—Y—(?)—H. This I read as
*zidqo qati we . . .* , "His righteousness is my hand
and . . ."

The Canaanites and Hebrews, who wrote at that
time, were under Babylonian influence linguistically,
as were all the Palestinian and Phœnician writers of
the Amarna period. The Phonetics of this inscription
reveal the same tendency to employ *zayin* (Z) for *Tsādê*,
as do the writers of the Amarna cuneiform letters.
The use of the word *qat*, "hand," for "support, help,"
is found also in the Amarna Letters where Canaanite
glosses explain the Babylonian word *qat*, "hand," by
the Canaanite word *zuruh*, the Hebrew *zerōa'*, "hand,"
"arm."

The inscription on the Lachish bowl employs the
Babylonian word for "hand" in precisely the same

# APPENDIX II

manner as Isaiah xxxiii. 2 employs the Hebrew word for hand in "Be thou their arm." The existence of a passage of this kind in Canaan at that time suggests a religious literature closely resembling the earliest Hebrew documents, and it proves that the Hebrews were able to write such documents in the Mosaic age. Moreover, in my opinion the Canaanites and Hebrews had already invented the method of pointing the semi-vowel *y* with a dot (here before the *y*) to denote the long vowel *ī*. The same method of pointing to denote the long vowel *ē* by three dots one above the other occurs on the Lachish ewer, previously found by Starkey, in the word *matanê*, "gifts of," a fact which was not clear to me when I saw the ewer last year.

I can do nothing with the last word on the Lachish bowl; the letters are, in fact, not entirely certain. But the discovery of alphabetic inscriptions of the Mosaic age and of a type in which accuracy in pointing long vowels has already appeared makes it entirely believable that the pre-Mosaic literature also existed in alphabetic script. These are not traditions handed down the ages by memory only. They were actually incorporated into written documents as early as the thirteenth century. Obviously we have here the most important discovery of modern times in respect to Biblical criticism.—Yours sincerely,

S. LANGDON.

OXFORD.

*P.S.*—I have given Starkey's dates for this bowl, but on the basis of epigraphy alone I should give an earlier date, *circa* 1500 B.C., on the evidence of the forms of the letters of the fourteenth century at Gebal (Byblus).

# APPENDIX III

## THE DATE OF JOSHUA'S DESTRUCTION OF JERICHO [1]

### From the Quarterly Statement of THE PALESTINE EXPLORATION FUND, July 1936

THE conclusion of six seasons' researches among the ruins of Jericho seems to call for a definite pronouncement about the date of the Bronze Age city's fall, if only to put an end to needless controversy. A review of the evidence leaves no reasonable doubt upon this question.

Results obtained successively in city and necropolis have all pointed steadily towards a date about 1400 B.C., during the reign of the Pharaoh Amenhetep III, whose scarabs mark the end of a long series of official and private seals. At the same time the tomb deposits, which represent the continuous burial practice of chiefs and people for more than 800 years, come abruptly to an end; while within the city the signs of a general catastrophe accompanied by the falling of its massive walls are found wherever the Late Bronze Age levels are preserved.

The sparse deposits of the next five centuries, amounting to $\frac{1}{2}$ per cent. of the whole, represent a partial and discontinuous occupation of portions of the site by later settlers. About the age of Solomon a strong block-house occupied the old palace site, but

[1] This letter also appeared in *The Times* of 21st April 1936.

the city walls show no signs of restoration until the general reoccupation of the area in the second Iron Age, known to have been effected in the time of Ahab.

This season, in response to Sir Charles Marston's desire, we have made a final search in the vicinity of the ancient palace and located a small undisturbed area immediately below the Iron Age débris. As elsewhere at this level, its buildings were found to have been completely burned out, but among the ashes were found some distinctive deposits, including painted pottery, Cypriote importations, lamps, and cooking pots. The whole group is characteristic of the early part of the Late Bronze Age, while the painted wares in particular find ready parallel in the Tuthmosis III and pre-Amenhetep III levels at Beisan. On the other hand, the peculiar art products of the Tel-el-Amarna period were entirely wanting, as also were Mycenæan wares.

Allowing for the possibility that the finding of two scarab-seals of Amenhetep III in a royal tomb suggests the appointment of two local dynasts within that reign, with a third still in office, we may logically conclude that the fall of Jericho took place between 1400 B.C. and the accession of Akhenaton. No other conclusion will satisfy the archæological evidence as a whole.

It will be realized that this result is independent of any literary indications, and it is not affected by computation or theory as to the date of the Exodus.

ALAN ROWE
(*Ex-Director, Beisan Expedition*).

JOHN GARSTANG
(*Ex-Director, Jericho Expedition*).

ACRE.

# APPENDIX IV

## THE DATE OF THE EXODUS

THE date of the Exodus from Egypt of the Israelites under the leadership of Moses has been a problem of long standing. Indeed, the problem may be so old that it perhaps already existed at the time of our Lord. The works of Josephus, the Jewish historian (A.D. 70), contain a number of references to Old Testament dates; but it has already been pointed out that, as recorded in our translations of his writings, these contradict themselves. This contradiction may be due to interpolations, or alterations in the text; but it may also have been caused by the existence of conflicting theories in the days of Josephus as to when the Exodus actually occurred.

With our present knowledge of Egyptian chronology, and altogether apart from the Jericho dating, the Old Testament statements, *as they stand*, seem entirely to fit into their proper places. The essential one runs as follows:—

"And it came to pass in the four hundred and eightieth year after the children of Israel were come out of the land of Egypt, in the fourth year of Solomon's reign over Israel . . . that he began to build the house of the Lord."       (1 Kings vi. 1.)

It is obvious that in order to obtain a date for the Exodus from this passage, it is necessary to know the

280

date of Solomon's accession. The Cambridge *Ancient History* places it at 970 B.C.: Sir Flinders Petrie fixes it at 960 B.C.: and figures supplied by Josephus work out at 964 B.C. These dates enable us to say that the founding of Solomon's temple occurred between 967 and 957 B.C. If the 480 years mentioned in the text are added to them, the possible years for the Exodus range between 1447 and 1437 B.C. This margin of dates is of peculiar significance. It has already been pointed out in Chapter III, that the event which led up to the return of Moses from Midian was the death of the Pharaoh from whose wrath he had fled. Thus we read:—

"And it came to pass in the course of those many days, that the king of Egypt died." (Exodus ii. 23.)

Now the Egyptian chronology of Sir Flinders Petrie, and of most recent authorities, place the death of Thotmes III in 1447 B.C., that is to say in the very first year of this margin of dates. So the entire range of dates, based on the founding of Solomon's temple, point to the years immediately succeeding the death of Thotmes III. And it is significant that the long reign (54 years) of this Pharaoh, allowed of his being the same Pharaoh from whom Moses had fled some forty years before. The Septuagint version of 1 Kings vi. 1, instead of making the interval of time four hundred and eighty years, makes it four hundred and forty. This can be accounted for by the fact that the Israelites were forty years in the wilderness; and that therefore the Septuagint dates from the entry into Canaan, and not from the actual Exodus. Attempts have also been made to measure the interval of four hundred and eighty years from the entry into Canaan. In that case the Exodus took place between 1487 and 1477 B.C. But if the Egyptian chronology of Thotmes III is correct, it sternly negatives the proposal. If it could be shown that this Pharaoh died in 1487 B.C., that would remove this vital objection; but the earlier chronology back to Abraham, verified by the astronomical date for Hammurabi (Amraphel), would then be out of gear. And that the date of Hammurabi is correct, can be proved from archæological discoveries other than those used in the astronomical calculations. The archæological date of 1400 B.C. for the destruction of Jericho, of course suits the margin of dates 1447–1437 B.C. for the Exodus. As the Israelites were wandering forty years in the wilderness, Jericho would be destroyed between 1407–1397 B.C. The pottery dating certificate of Garstang and Rowe, reproduced in Appendix III, admits a possible date of the destruction of Jericho as late as the accession of Akhenaton (1377 B.C.). But the Bible figures, based on the date of the founding of Solomon's temple, make 1397 B.C. the latest year. There is therefore a converging testimony which suggests that Jericho must have been destroyed between 1400–1397 B.C. Authorities have long decided that the Tel-el-Amarna Letters were written between 1400–1360 B.C. As they record the Hebrew invasion of Canaan, they also point very definitely to this date.

The whole chronology from Abraham to Rehoboam is at the end of this appendix. It will be seen to be consistent with the Old Testament, and to coincide with Egyptian, and Israelite, history and chronology.

CHARLES MARSTON.

# APPENDIX V

## ORIGIN OF OUR ALPHABET [1]

### AN INSCRIPTION ON A DAGGER

#### To the Editor of *The Times*

Sir,—On a number of different occasions you have opened your columns to new information in connexion with the origin of our alphabet. In this respect the important excavations conducted at Tell el-Duweir by Mr. J. L. Starkey for the Wellcome-Marston Archæological Research Expedition have been particularly prolific. On 9th June 1934, you reproduced the inscription on a ewer dating from about the time of Rameses II (thirteenth century B.C.), and this, as I pointed out in a letter published in *The Times* a few days later, drew special significance from the fact that the characters obviously stood midway between the much-discussed semi-hieroglyphic Sinai script and the later Phœnician alphabet, just as Tell el-Duweir itself, the ancient Lachish on the borders of Philistia, lies geographically midway between the peninsula of Sinai and the coast towns of Phœnicia. On 24th June 1936 you depicted a similar inscription of about the same date, and on 17th October of the same year the late Professor Langdon attempted the decipherment of yet a third bowl inscription of like character. In spite of

---

[1] Letter in *The Times*, 16th July 1937, from Dr. Alan H. Gardiner, D.Litt., M.A., F.B.A., F.S.A.

all difficulties of interpretation—and it must be frankly admitted that no certain meanings have been derived from these brief texts—Mr. Starkey's inscriptions all tell the same clear tale. They exhibit what is probably the oldest indigenous Palestinian script shorn of its purely pictorial elements, and thus well on the way to becoming the non-pictorial writing familiar from

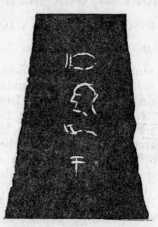

the early Phœnician and Aramaic alphabets, as well as the oldest forms of Greek.

A further discovery from the same site, made public by Sir Charles Marston in January, goes far towards corroborating this conclusion, while, as seems inevitable in archæological discoveries, raising new problems of its own. The cleaning of a bronze dagger of undoubted Hyksos date (about 1700–1555 B.C.) brought to light a vertical inscription of four signs (see the annexed cut), of which the second, a clear man's head, evidently corresponds to the same sign in the Sinai script, where on the strength (1) of the letter-name *rēsh*, signifying "head," and (2) of the rough resemblance of the Phœnician letter, it had been identified by me as the prototype of our own R. The third sign appears to be the snake common in the Sinai texts and possessing a fairly clear descendant on the abovementioned ewer; this had been identified on similar grounds as the original N. The first and last signs on the dagger are much more obscure. A desperate conjecture might equate the former with the "door" D or with the "noose" that some (*e.g.* Professor Butin) take to be S, the Hebrew *ṣādē*; for the latter the only conceivable identification would be the "cross" or "mark" T, although both the earlier and the later forms of this have elsewhere one bar, not two. What the word DRNT or SRNT might mean I cannot guess; an uncompounded proper name in Semitic would probably consist of three radicals only.

The importance of the new find lies partly in its providing a link between the Sinai inscriptions and those previously found at Tell el-Duweir, and partly in the inference to be drawn from the finding of unmistakably pictorial letter-shapes as late as the Hyksos period. Mr. Starkey has shown me that there can be no doubt as to the date; the dagger was found in an untouched tomb-group with two characteristically Hyksos scarabs, good pottery of the same period, as well as other objects. Now if the generally accepted theory be right, we cannot here be far removed from the actual invention of the alphabet; for the whole of the history points to a rapid degradation from pictorial to linear and non-pictorial forms. Hence the late Professor Sethe's hypothesis that the Sinai inscriptions belong to the Hyksos period may perhaps become preferable to my own view assuming them to the end of the Twelfth Dynasty.

# APPENDIX V

It has to be admitted that the appearance on the dagger of two signs that cannot readily be identified with equivalents in the Sinai script presents a new obstacle in the way of accepting the latter as the prototype of the Phœnician alphabet; on the other hand, the two signs that can be so identified are no less strong confirmation of that theory, to which an increasing number of scholars are now leaning. I am personally convinced that, though much remains to be explained, the inscriptions from Sinai and Tell el-Duweir do really contain the key to the origin of our alphabet, and that no equally plausible case can be made out for its origin from the cryptic and very ancient hieroglyphic writings that have of recent years been discovered at Byblos.—I am, Sir, your obedient servant,

ALAN H. GARDINER.

9 LANSDOWNE ROAD, W. 11.

# COMPARATIVE CHRONOLOGY
# OF EARLY BIBLE HISTORY

# COMPARATIVE CHRONOLOGY OF EARLY BIBLE HISTORY

## AS ESTABLISHED BY EXCAVATIONS, AND VERIFIED BY ASTRONOMY AND HISTORY

| EGYPT | | OLD TESTAMENT | | BABYLON | |
|---|---|---|---|---|---|
| | B.C. | | B.C. | | B.C. |
| Xth Dynasty | 2812–2627 | | | SARGON | 2751 |
| XIth Dynasty | 2627–2584 | | | NARAM-SIN | 2671 |
| XIIth Dynasty | 2584–2371 | | | SUMU-ABUM | 2169 |
| XIIIth, XIVth and XVIIth, contemporary with Hyksos Dynasties | | | | | |
| XVth Dynasty | 2377–2111 | Abraham born | 2160 | SUMULAILUM | 2155 |
| XVIth Dynasty | 2111–1583 | | | ZABUM | 2119 |
| | | | | APILSIN | 2105 |
| | | Abraham entered Canaan | 2085 | SINMUBALLIT | 2087 |
| | | Destruction of cities of the Plain | 2061 | HAMMURABI | 2067 |
| | | | | (Amraphel) | |
| | | Isaac born | 2060 | SAMSUILUNA | 2024 |
| | | Jacob born | 2000 | ABIESUH | 1986 |
| | | Jacob went to Egypt | 1870 | AMMIDITANA | 1958 |
| | | Israel in Egypt | 1870–1440 | AMMIZADUGA | 1921 |
| | | Israel in Egypt | 1870–1440 | SAMSIDITANA | 1900 |
| | | Moses born | 1520 | | |
| XVIIIth Dynasty— | | | | | |
| Aohmes | 1573 | | | | |
| Amenhetep I | 1560 | | | | |
| Thotmes I | 1539 | | | | |
| Thotmes II | 1514 | (Period of Hatshepsut) | | | |
| Thotmes III | 1501 | Moses fled to Midian | | | |
| Amenhetep II | 1447 | Exodus from Egypt | 1480 | | |
| Thotmes IV | 1423 | Wandering in Wilderness | 1440 | | |

288

| | | | |
|---|---|---|---|
| | | the Elders to . . . | 1360 |
| Semenkha . . | 1361 | } Israel oppressed by Hittites for 8 years to | 1352 |
| Tutankhamen . | 1351 | | |
| Ay . . | 1339 | | |
| Setymeramen . | 1328 | | |
| Horemheb . . | 1322 | Israel at rest for 40 years until . . | 1312 |
| XIXth Dynasty— | | | |
| Rameses I . | 1318 | | |
| Sety I . | 1317 | Israel oppressed by Moab 18 years to . | 1294 |
| Rameses II . | 1295 | Shamgar ben Anath, and 80 years' rest to | 1214 |
| Mernephthah . | 1229 | (Mernephthah's raid) | |
| Sety II . . | 1210 | | |
| XXth Dynasty— | | | |
| Amenmesu . | 1205 | | |
| Tausert . . | 1204 | Oppression of Sisera 20 years to . . | 1194 |
| Arisu . . | 1197 | | |
| Sepnekht . | 1196 | | |
| Rameses III . | 1195 | | |
| Rameses IV . | 1163 | | |
| Rameses V . | 1157 | 40 years' rest to . . | 1154 |
| Rameses VI . | 1153 | Midianite oppression 7 years to . . | 1147 |
| Rameses VII . | 1145 | | |
| Rameses VIII . | 1138 | | |
| Rameses IX . | 1137 | Gideon 40 years to . . . | 1107 |
| Rameses X . | 1137 | | |
| Rameses XI . | 1118 | | |
| Rameses XII . | 1112 | | |
| XXIst Dynasty— | | | |
| Smendes . . | 1083 | Abimelech 3 years to . . . | 1104 |
| | | Ammonite oppression 1 year . . | 1103 |
| | | Jephthah 6 years to . . . | 1098 |

## COMPARATIVE CHRONOLOGY OF EARLY BIBLE HISTORY—continued

| EGYPT | | OLD TESTAMENT | | BABYLON |
|---|---|---|---|---|
| | B.C. | | B.C. | B.C. |
| Psusenes . . . | 1057 | Samson, and Philistine oppression 40 years to | 1058 | |
| | | Eli, and Philistines 20 years . . | 1038 | |
| | | Samuel 20 years to . . . | 1018 | |
| Neferkheres . . | 1011 | Saul 15 years to . . . | 1003 | |
| Amenofthis . . | 1007 | | | |
| Osochor . . . | 992 | } David 40 years to . . . | 963 | |
| Psinaches . . | 975 | Solomon's 4th year (founding of temple) | 959 | |
| Psousennes . . | | | | |
| XXIInd Dynasty— | | | | |
| Shishak . . . | 940 | Rehoboam . . . . | 923 | |
| Usarken I . . | 919 | Fifth year . . . . | 919 | |

290

The Babylonian dates are based on the Venus Tablets of Ammizaduga.

The Egyptian chronology is from Sir Flinders Petrie's "Revision of History" (*Ancient Egypt*, March 1931). This chronology was made on a basis entirely independent of that of the Jericho dating, which Sir Flinders did not even accept. Nevertheless, these Egyptian dates fit into the Old Testament chronology based on the Jericho dating. In particular, attention is drawn to the eighty years' rest commencing in the second year of Rameses II, and to the forty years' rest commencing in the second year of Rameses III : while the fifth year of Rehoboam, when he paid tribute to Shishak (1 Kings xiv. 25, 26) coincides with the last year of that conqueror's reign.

Jephthah's statement that the Israelite occupation of Transjordania extended to three hundred years (Judges xi. 26) furnishes a further check on the date of 1400 B.C. for the destruction of Jericho, as does, of course, the 480 years for the date of the Exodus (1 Kings vi. 1) from the fourth year of

# INDEX

## A

# INDEX

Arrowheads, 237

Arrows, 225, 226

Asahiah, 241

Ashdod, city of, 76, 77, 122

Ashmolean Museum, 34, 262

Assumptions that are invalid, 20

Assyrian-Hebrew script, 8, 16, 183, 248

Assyrians, 34, 226 to 230

Astarte or Ashtaroth, 148, 159, 161

Astronomical reckoning for Abraham, 48, 49, 55

Aura-Mazda or Ormuzd, 132

Ay, king, 239

Azekah, 125, 127, 196, 220

## B

Baalat, 170

Baalil, 173, 174

Babylon, 25, 124, 125

Babylonia, 25, 29, 266

Babylonian Dynasty, fall of, 127

Babylonians, 34, 196, 263

Badarian civilization of Egypt, 37

Baghdad Caliphate, 260

Baku, mentioned in Book of the Dead, 36, 37

Balaam, 205

Barley, 143

Baruch, the scribe, 186, 190, 203

Bas-Reliefs, Sennacherib's, 118, 120, 126, 224 to 227

Beads and bead work, 148, 149, 237

Beer, Canaanite, 140

Beetle, on seals and scarabs, 137

Beit Jibrin, 109, 240

Belief, intellectual, 24

Belshazzar, 127, 128

Berosus, the historian, 33, 34

Beth Shan (Beisan), 164

Beth Shemesh, 171

Bible and the coronation, v
,, archaic words, meaning lost, 17
,, background, 1
,, chart of history, 11
,, civilization and the, 1, 20

Bible, discredited or doubted, v, 2, 13
,, disregarded, 21
*Bible is True*, vi, vii, 5
Bible, manuscripts of, 16, 181
,, progressive study of, 15, 16, 17, 245
,, Textbook of Science of Man, 1, 11, 15, 21, 246
,, textual errors in transcription, 17
Bowl, Lachish No. 3, 242
,, red pottery, inscribed, 172, 247
Brass, mention of, 129, 147, 148
Bread of Life, 28, 272
Breasted, Professor, 59
British Museum, x, 118
Brockelmann, exponent of Totemism, 272
Burning Bush, vision of, 64
Burton, Sir Richard, on Midian, 62
Butin Father, and Serabit, 171

## C

Caiger, Rev. S. L., 66

Calendar, ivory, 145

Canaanite glosses, 276

Carchemish, 193

Carmel, Mount, 157

Carrell, Dr. Alexis, 3, 10, 11

Caucasus, civilization traced to, 36 to 39

Cauldron for meat offerings, 154, 174

Censer, decorated pottery, 154, 174

Chaldeans, 125

Chaldees, Land of the, 25

Chedorlaomer, king of Elam, 47, 48, 51

Children of Israel (*see* Israelites)

Children's toys, 148

Christian worship, need of Bible, 12

Chronicles, references to Books of, 77, 116, 120, 125, 130, 137, 193, 212

Chronology, 49 to 51, 88, 89

292

# INDEX

# INDEX

# INDEX

Hamutal, 203

Hatshepsut, Princess and Queen of Egypt, 57, 58, 61, 63, 65, 169

Hazael, the Syrian, 206

Healing by prayer, 3

Hebrew language, archaic form of, 16, 31, 43, 73, 74
,, religion, 26

Hebrews, 8, 42, 72, 90, 91
,, Epistle to the, 53, 58
,, land of, 43
,, laws before Moses, 72

Hebron, 137

Helladic period vase, 160

Herodotus, date of Tyre, 40

Hezekiah, 119, 120 to 123, 138, 194, 214, 236

Hieroglyphics, 167 to 171

Hilkiah, 139, 202

Hiram, king of Tyre, 179

Hissiliah, 201

History, 21, 22

Hittites, 239

Hodaviah, 209, 210, 211

Holy of Holies, 5

Honey, 143

Horemheb, 239

Hornet, the, 91, 92

Horses, use of, 114 to 118

Hoshaiah, 188, 189, 206 to 211, 216, 222

Hoshama, 212

Human nature, 6, 230

Hyksos, arrival of, 41, 42
,, expelled from Egypt, 56
,, dynasties, length of, 41, 136
,, fortifications, 41, 42, 113
,, meaning of word, 42, 43
,, length of rule over Egypt, 41
,, where driven to, 63, 64
,, who were they, 42 to 44

## I

" Iah," divine suffix, 192

Immanence of the Unseen, 250

Incarnation, wonder of the, 81

Indo-Germanic religions, 27, 265, 267

Inn or Khan at Lachish, 115, 145

Innini, Queen of Heaven, 262

Inscriptions (pictographic), 26, 174, 260, 285

Inspiration in the Old Testament, 79, 80, 187

Irak, kingdom of, 25

Iran, kingdom of, 39

Ireland and Irish, 53, 148, 160

Iron, use of, 129, 147, 232

Isaac, 53, 80, 144

Isaiah, references to Book of, 75, 120, 129, 236
,, the prophet, 119, 120, 128, 236

Ishtar (Ashtaroth), 262

Israel, priests of, 75

Israelites assumed to be illiterate, 7, 176, 248

Israelites, or children of Israel, in Egypt, 56, 58, 62 to 68
,, Exodus of, 68, 69, 280
,, in the Wilderness, 49, 69, 70, 76
,, Mosaic Ritual for, 60, 67, 70, 71, 77 to 81, 115
,, under Joshua in Canaan, 66, 70, 82, 88, 91, 92, 96 to 101
,, under Judges, 162

Italy, nature myth gods of, 27

## J

J, E, P, supposed sources of Pentateuch, 9

Jaazaniah, 201 to 203

Jacob, patriarch, 54, 55, 72, 80, 114, 115, 129, 144

Jaddua, 209, 211

Jah, original name for Jehovah, 63, 192

Jahweh, correct name for Jehovah, 63, 192, 205 to 208, 216 to 219

Japhet or Japhetic, 38, 39

Jaush, 189, 205 to 211, 216 to 219, 222

# INDEX

# INDEX

Lachish, destruction of, by Nebuchadnezzar, 126, 127, 194 to 199

  „   defences of, 113, 116, 117, 225, 226

  „   Expedition Members, xi

*Lachish Letters*, 183

Lachish Letters, 16, 181, 182, 184, 187 to 189, 195, 221, 247

Lachish Letter No. I, 198, 201

  „   „   No. II, 198, 205

  „   „   No. III, 198, 208, 211, 212

  „   „   No. IV, 213, 219

  „   „   No. V, 217

  „   „   No. VI, 198, 206

  „   „   No. VII 198, 207

  „   „   No. VIII, 198, 201, 208

  „   „   No. IX, 217

  „   „   No. X, 218

  „   „   No. XI, 219

  „   „   No. XII, 198, 218

  „   „   No. XIII, 219

  „   „   No. XIV, 219

  „   „   No. XV, 219

  „   „   No. XVI, 198, 218

  „   „   No. XVII, 203, 219

  „   „   No. XVIII, 198, 202, 204, 207

Langdon, Dr. S. H., ix, 25 to 29, 172, 173, 283

Langdon, Dr., Article in *Evangelical Quarterly*, 259 to 274

Langdon, Dr., Letter in *The Times*, 275 to 277

Latin Monotheism, 27

Law from Mt. Sinai, 60, 71, 77

Layard, Sir A. H., 224

Leather as material for writing, 185

Ledge handled pots for beer, 140

Lentils, 143

Leviathan, 75, 76

Leviticus, Book of, 72, 75, 79

Libnah, 121, 203

Life, phenomena of, 15

Linen garments, 143

Llanmaes in South Wales, 54, 55

Logos, or word, 262

Longevity, 54

Loom weights, 143

Lord Chamberlain, title of official, 138

## M

Maachathite, 202

Maas, 139

Maat feather, 146

Maccabees, family of, 183

Machpelah, cave and mosque of, 54

Madyan, place in Midian, 61

Maghara, district in Peninsula of Sinai, 167

Magna Charta, 181

Maiden Castle, excavations at, 113

*Man the Unknown*, 10

Manganese in Sinai, 167

Manifestations from Unseen, 79

"Maseth," Hebrew word for "signal," 221

"Matan," Hebrew word for "gift," 172

Mattaniah, 201, 203

Matter, the phenomena of, 15

Matthew, St., references to Gospel, 212

Megiddo, 64, 114, 115, 157, 193, 194, 236

Meinertzhagen, Colonel, 54

Melchizedek, 53, 75, 81

Memsheph, pottery town, 137

Meroe on the Nile, 57

Mesopotamia, 25

Mibtahiah, 201, 203

Micah, reference to Lachish, 118

Midian, Land of, 61, 62, 168, 176

Midianites, 70, 76, 167, 177

Military outpost near Lachish, 149

Milk, boiling kid in mother's, 74

Milk bowl from Cyprus, 160

# INDEX

Palestine, vi, viii, x, 18, 19, 43, 114, 115, 135, 136, 141, 142, 151, 158, 171, 238
   ,,   Exploration Fund, x, 52, 89, 111
   ,,   Oriental Society, 200
Pantheon, the, 261, 262, 266, 271
Papyrus, use of, 151, 185
Paradise, 28
Passover, the, 67
Patriarchs before the Flood, 33
Pedaiah, son of Jeconiah, 212
Pella, city of, 90, 91, 92
Pentateuch, Books of Moses, 75, 183
Perfume flask, 155
Persian Art, Antiquity of, 39
   ,,   Gulf, 25, 37
   ,,   remains at Lachish, 130, 131
Personal God, 10, 12, 29, 256
   ,,   ,,   (primitive), 263
Pharaoh Necho, 124, 193, 194, 213
Pharaoh's daughter, 57, 58
Philistine garrison at Lachish, 124
Philistines, 77, 149
Phœnician-Hebrew script, 8, 16, 183 to 187, 248
Phœnicians, 142. 165
Physics (see Science of)
Playing pieces, 145
Poe, Edgar Alan, stories of, 73
Polytheism, 7, 26, 29, 35, 78, 260, 262, 264, 271
Pool of the Prophet, 240
Potsherds, 182, 184, 189, 205
Potters, reference to, 137
Pottery dating, 19, 134, 135, 246
Power from the Unseen, 23, 256
Preconceived ideas, obstacle to truth, 4
Prediction, reality of, 3, 12, 128
Priests' fork, 145, 154
Primeval monotheism, 60
   ,,   morality, 60
   ,,   revelation, 34, 35
Primitive people, 28
   ,,   races, 27

Prophecies, 7, 12, 17, 79, 258
Prophet, in Lachish Letters, 204, 205
Prophetic books, inspiration of, 79
Prophets, Old Testament, 59
Proverbs, anticipated in Egypt, 60
Psalms, anticipated in Egypt, 59, 60
   ,,   references to, 53, 75, 157, 185
Psychic phenomena recognized, 3
Ptah-hotep, proverbs of, 185
Ptolemy II, 233
Puritans of Lachish, 222

# R

Rabsaris, Sennacherib's official, 119
Rabshakeh, Sennacherib's official, 119, 120, 121, 138
Rahab, woman of Jericho, 84, 86, 87
Rameses II, 156, 158, 163, 239
Ramoth Gilead, 194
Ras Shamra, x, 46, 53, 63, 72 to 78, 175
   ,,   ,,   date of tablets, 77
   ,,   ,,   offerings resemble Mosaic ones, 74, 249
Razor, bronze, 237
Rebekah, 144
Rechabites, 202
Red Sea, 61, 115
Rehoboam, 51, 88, 116
Relativity, 30, 252
Religion before the Flood, 34, 262
   ,,   man's most important asset, 33
Religions, mystery, 34
   ,,   primitive ones discussed, 259 to 274
Renaissance decoration, 156
Reshef, Syrian war god, 160
Revelation, 24, 31, 32, 35, 79
Rhodian jar handle, 234
Rituals, 34

# INDEX

# INDEX

Shuruppak, city before Flood, 34, 260

Signet ring, 136

Sihon and Og, Amorite kings east of Jordan, 92

Silk, use of, 144

Silli-bel, king of Gaza, 122

Siloam inscriptions, 184

Siloam, tunnel and pool of, 52, 236

Sinai-Hebrew script, 8, 77, 156, 171, 172 to 175, 180, 185, 241, 247, 275

Sinai, Mount, 70

   ,, Peninsula of, 58, 166, 175

Sisera's army, 157

Skins, as material for writing, 185

Skulls, 144

Sky-god, 27, 261, 267 to 272

Smenkhara, 239

Smith, George, account of Flood, 35

Smith, Robertson, exponent of Totemism, 264, 265, 266

Socoh, 137

Sodom and Gomorrah, 43, 49, 50, 51

Sojourn of Israelites in Egypt, 67 to 69

Solomon, 114, 179, 187, 243, 278

   ,, date of, 280, 281, 290

Solomon's horses, 114

Speculation, unsound basis for Sciences, 33

Sphinx, 66, 67

Stabling, 114, 115

Starkey, viii, 109, 152, 232, 275, 283

Suburb of city of Lachish, 139, 152

Sudan, 140

Suez Canal, 61, 166

Sumerian records, 34, 259, etc.

   ,, religion, 25, 26, 259, 261, 263, 271

   ,, religion, antiquity of, 266, 267

Sunday, non-observance of, 256

Sun-god, 261

Sun shrine at Lachish, 131

Superstitions, modern ones about Time, 30

Syria, 90, 122, 162

Syrian deities, 160

Syrians, 125, 229

## T

Tabernacle, resemblances at Ras Shamra, 74, 75

Tables of the Law, 185

Tartan, Sennacherib's official, 119

Taylor Prism, 121

Tel el Amarna Letters, 41, 89 to 108, 111, 112, 113, 121

Tell Asmar, 147

Tell el Duweir, viii, 110, 111, 133, 220, 231, 283

   ,,    ,,    ,, size of, 110

Tell el Hesy, former identification with Lachish, 111

Temple, ruins of, at Lachish, 151 to 163

Temples, dating of, 160, 162

Temptation, story of, 32, 136

Ten Commandments, before Moses' time, 60

   ,, Plagues, 68

Thermuthis, Josephus' name for Moses' protectress, 57

Thotmes I, 57

Thotmes II, 57

Thotmes III, the great conqueror, 57, 58, 63, 64, 114, 115, 237, 281

Thotmes IV, 66, 67, 145, 237

Thyi, Queen of Amenhetep III, 92, 153

Tigris, River, 25

*The Times* references to, 89, 275, 278, 283

*Time and its Mysteries*, 33

Time before the Flood, 33, 34

   ,, extravagant speculations concerning, 30, 31

   ,, introduction of, 148

# INDEX

Printed in Great Britain
by T. and A. Constable Ltd.
at the University Press
Edinburgh

PLATE I.—THE LACHISH RED BOWL WITH SINAI-HEBREW INSCRIPTION (B.C. 1295-1262)

See pages 172 and 275, etc.

PLATE 2.—JAMES LESLIE STARKEY, F.S.A.

Field Director of the Lachish Expeditions, 1932–1938.

Murdered by Arab brigands since this book was first published
—aged 43. Mr. Starkey's memory will live in History as the
discoverer at Lachish of the alphabetical scripts, used by
Israelites and Jews from the days of Moses down to the
Babylonian Captivity.

PLATE 3.—SOME OF THE RUINS OF HATSHEPSUT'S TEMPLE AT SERABIT

PLATE 4.—SUMMIT OF JEBAL MUSA FROM WADY SEBAIYEH—THE TRADITIONAL MOUNT SINAI

*(Photo from Ordnance Survey, 1869.)*

PLATE 6.—AN OLD ENGRAVING FROM GERMANY REPRESENTING THE FALL OF THE WALLS OF JERICHO

PLATE 7.—PHOTOGRAPH OF A BEAUTIFUL SMALL BUST OF QUEEN THYI, WIFE OF AMENHETEP III—THE PHARAOH WHO WAS REIGNING WHEN JERICHO WAS DESTROYED

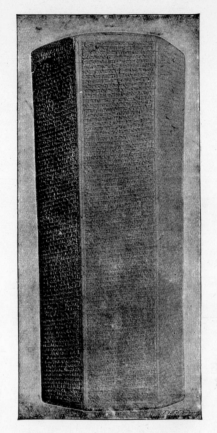

PLATE 8.—THE TAYLOR PRISM CONTAINING
SENNACHERIB'S ACCOUNT OF HIS
CONQUEST OF JUDAH

(A portion quoted in the text on page 123.)

PLATE 9.—MISCELLANEOUS

*Top* : An impression of a hæmatite cylinder seal—a religious scene with details indicating a connection with North Syrian art. Found in middle temple level, Lachish.

*Centre : Left*—An Assyrian seal, supposed to portray the Temptation. *Right*—Gold pendant of features of bearded man surrounded by circle of dots ; from the middle temple level, Lachish.

*Below* : Bronze Maat feather overlaid in gold. Egyptian emblem of Truth and Justice. Found under wall of Ramesside period house, XIX Dynasty.

PLATE 10.—RUINS OF LACHISH ON TELL DUWEIR

Looking north from above city gate across western terrace, showing area excavated 1935-36. Beyond open area are the remains of the burnt city level, dipping down southwards from south-west corner of Palace-Fort, part of the commercial quarter of the city. Low area in foreground of excavations marks line of main road, passing westwards to outer gate, extreme left.

PLATE 11.—RUINS OF LACHISH TEMPLE

Showing stone altar bench of Middle Temple and pottery deposit on the floor of earlier temple below. Four-handled

PLATE 12.—THE LOWEST TEMPLE AT LACHISH

Looking south-west across corner of sanctuary showing earliest mud bench with triple altar. One of the two stone bases for wooden roofing support, bottom right. Centre right: priests' chamber to west. Note circular rubbish pits for

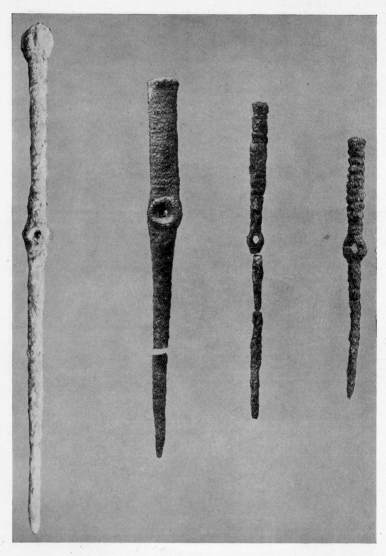

PLATE 13.—COPPER TOGGLE PINS FOUND AT LACHISH—PERIOD OF 2000 B.C.
These pins were used for fastening the cloak.   See page 148.

PLATE 14.—LACHISH : RELICS FROM THE TEMPLE

*Left*: Large commemorative scarab of Amenhetep III and his wife, Queen Thyi, recording the killing of "lions terrible 102" by the tenth year of his reign, 1403 B.C.: found in shrine of upper temple level.

*Right*: Carved ivory circular box from shrine in XVIII–XIX Dynasty temple: bulls and a bird in low relief.

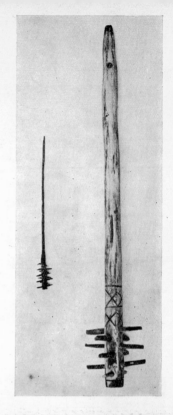

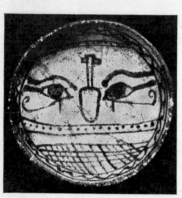

PLATE 15.—FOUND IN THE TEMPLE AT LACHISH

*Top : Left*—Lid of toilet spoon, engraved design similar to one in use on the
dagger found on Tutankhamen's mummy in Egypt. *Right*—Bronze
culinary whisk (left); compare wooden example (right) still in use in
neighbouring village of Qubeibeh.

*Bottom : Left*—Blue faience bowl, with black decoration showing the two eyes
of Horus either side of a "nefer" sign, XIX Dynasty. From cache
of toilet objects found in shrine. *Right*—Faience censer. The heads are
pierced vertically for suspension by cords.

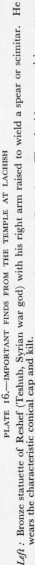

PLATE 16.—IMPORTANT FINDS FROM THE TEMPLE AT LACHISH

*Left*: Bronze statuette of Reshef (Teshub, Syrian war god) with his right arm raised to wield a spear or scimitar. He wears the characteristic conical cap and kilt.

*Centre*: The first complete form of late Helladic II ware to be found in Palestine. The double-stemmed ivy pattern, changing from black to red, is characteristic of the period in Greece, 1500–1400 B.C.

*Right*: Perfume flask, carved from ivory tusk, representing a lady wearing long skirt. Loop handles suggest shoulders and arms. The head, terminating in a hand, forms a stopper through which a hole is drilled for the passage of fluid.

PLATE 17.—FOUND IN TOMBS AT LACHISH

*Top :* Pottery vase in the form of a bull—from a tomb of about 1400 B.C.
*Bottom :* Censer and decorated cover, of similar ware to the " Duweir Ewer."
The pierced lug handles took strings for suspension. On the underside
of the cover are painted three signs in the early Sinai-Hebrew script.

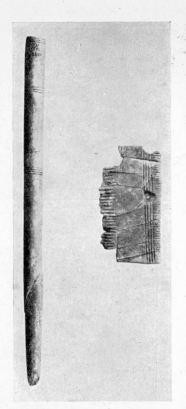

PLATE 18.—LACHISH FINDS

*Above : Left*—Ivory comb and rod, possibly a hair curler: found in XVIII
Dynasty tomb of period Amenhetep III, 1400 B.C. *Right*—Iron fork,
forged from one piece of metal: found in chamber tomb of about 900 B.C.
The occupant of the tomb may have been an assistant ṛriest in the Temple
(see 1 Samuel ii. 13, 14).

*Below :* Rectangular strip of metal with raised central rib pierced with holes at
either end—probably piece of iron scale armour of an Assyrian soldier.
Found at the base of outer defence wall.

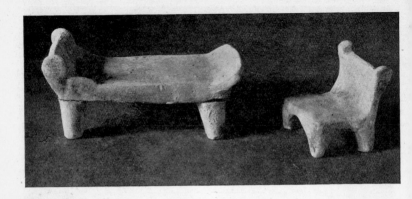

PLATE 19.—LACHISH FINDS

*Top :* Model bed and chair made in pottery. Found in a tomb of the Jewish
kingdom period, 700 B.C.

*Bottom : Left*—Clay sealing with inscription "For (or belonging to) Hilkiah
the son of Maas." On reverse side is the impress of papyrus, to which it was
attached. *Right*—Jar handle with seal impression "For Shaphan the
son of Seraiah."

PLATE 20.—FINDS FROM LACHISH

*Top :* Handles and finials of toilet objects from the cache discovered beneath the ashes burying the shrine of the XVIII–XIX Dynasty temple. All of ivory, including mask from rubbish pit east of temple, reminiscent of the Tel-el-Amarna style.

*Bottom :* Goblets, offering bowls, a censer and lamp, from the mass of offering bowls found in the upper level temple sanctuary.

PLATE 21

*Top: Left to right*—1. The contemplative ape. 2. Amulet in the form of a sow. 3. The homely cat, always symbolic of the divine one Bast. All from a group of Egyptian blue-glaze amulets.

*Bottom: Left to right*—1. The dwarf Bes, god of children, dance and games, most popular of deities, wearing ostrich plumes; an Egyptian amulet. 2. A sphinx, with a curiously expressive face; one of a group of six blue-glaze Egyptian amulets. 3. The sacred ram of Khnum, creator of mankind, fashioned on the potter's wheel, one of a

PLATE 22.—BRONZE DAGGER FROM TOMB 1502

After cleaning in the laboratories of the Palestine Museum, Jerusalem, showing on the rib of the blade an incised inscription of four pictographic signs, which cannot be later than 1600 B.C. on the evidence of associated objects. See pages 174, 241, 284.

(*Photo by kind permission of the Director of Antiquities, Jerusalem.*)

PLATE 23.—INTERIOR OF A TURQUOISE MINE AT SERABIT, PERHAPS MADE
IN THE DAYS OF MOSES

*(Courtesy of Egypt Exploration Society.)*

PLATE 24.—LACHISH LETTER NO. III IN THE PHŒNICIAN HEBREW SCRIPT

Obverse and reverse—translation on page 208.

PLATE 25.—LACHISH LETTER NO. IV

Obverse is the upper fragment—reverse, the lower.
(Translation on pages 219, 220.)

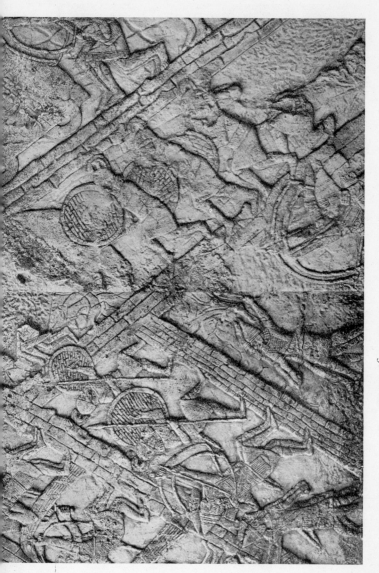

PLATE 26.—ASSYRIAN SOLDIERS ATTACKING LACHISH

As depicted on the Sennacherib bas-relief in the British Museum.

PLATE 27.—VIEW LOOKING SOUTH ALONG WEST SIDE OF CRATER SURROUNDING TOP OF GREAT SHAFT

Workers digging down through water-laid deposit on to scree of stones running down from Persian city levels ; scaffolding (*right*) erected over south-west corner of shaft. Workman taking discharge from subterranean excavations

PLATE 28.—THE GREAT SHAFT AT LACHISH

Showing western end of examination tunnel with workman descending ladder against western face of rock cutting.

PLATE 29.—BURNT TOMB AT LACHISH

Tomb No. 4004. View from entrance of southern chamber across main chamber
to north, showing sill below destroyed entrance, with secondary entrance cut to
the right.

PLATE 30.—THE WELD-BLUNDELL PRISM

Sumerian dynastic list giving the capitals and kings before and
after the Flood down to 2100 B.C.

(*Ashmolean Museum.*)

PLATE 31.—SPECIMEN OF EARLIEST PERIOD OF SUMERIAN PICTOGRAPHIC WRITING
FOUND AT KISH

This tablet does not contain the name of a deity, but others of the same period
from Erech contain the names of two deities, the Sky-god and the Queen of
Heaven.